Teach Them ALL to Read

SECOND EDITION

OTHER BOOKS BY ELAINE K. McEWAN
FROM CORWIN

Ten Traits of Highly Effective Schools: Raising the Achievement Bar for All Students (2008)

40 Ways to Support Struggling Readers in Content Classrooms, Grades 6–12 (2007)

Raising Reading Achievement in Middle and High Schools: Five Simple-to-Follow Strategies, Second Edition (2006)

How to Survive and Thrive in the First Three Weeks of School (2006)

How to Deal With Teachers Who Are Angry, Troubled, Exhausted, or Just Plain Confused (2005)

How to Deal With Parents Who Are Angry, Troubled, Afraid, or Just Plain Crazy, Second Edition (2004)

Seven Strategies of Highly Effective Readers: Using Cognitive Research to Boost K–8 Achievement (2004)

Ten Traits of Highly Effective Principals: From Good to Great Performance (2003)

Making Sense of Research: What's Good, What's Not, and How to Tell the Difference (with Patrick J. McEwan) (2003)

Seven Steps to Effective Instructional Leadership, Second Edition (2002)

Ten Traits of Highly Effective Teachers: How to Hire, Coach, and Mentor Successful Teachers (2001)

The Principal's Guide to Raising Math Achievement (2000)

Managing Unmanageable Students: Practical Solutions for Administrators (with Mary Damar) (1999)

Counseling Tips for Elementary School Principals (with Jeffrey Kottler) (1998)

The Principal's Guide to Raising Reading Achievement (1998)

The Principal's Guide to Attention Deficit Hyperactivity Disorder (1997)

Leading Your Team to Excellence: How to Make Quality Decisions (1996)

FROM CORWIN CLASSROOM

The Reading Puzzle: Comprehension, Grades K–3 (2008)

The Reading Puzzle: Fluency, Grades K–3 (2008)

The Reading Puzzle: Phonemic Awareness, Grades K–3 (2008)

The Reading Puzzle: Phonics, Grades K–3 (2008)

The Reading Puzzle: Vocabulary, Grades K–3 (2008)

The Reading Puzzle: Comprehension, Grades 4–8 (2008)

The Reading Puzzle: Fluency, Grades 4–8 (2008)

The Reading Puzzle: Spelling, Grades 4–8 (2008)

The Reading Puzzle: Vocabulary, Grades 4–8 (2008)

The Reading Puzzle: Word Analysis, Grades 4–8 (2008)

ELAINE K. MCEWAN

Teach Them ALL to Read

SECOND EDITION

Catching Kids Before They Fall Through the Cracks

CORWIN
A SAGE Company

For information:

Corwin
A SAGE Company
2455 Teller Road
Thousand Oaks, California 91320
(800) 233-9936
Fax: (800) 417-2466
www.corwinpress.com

SAGE India Pvt. Ltd.
B 1/I 1 Mohan Cooperative Industrial Area
Mathura Road, New Delhi 110 044
India

SAGE Ltd.
1 Oliver's Yard
55 City Road
London EC1Y 1SP
United Kingdom

SAGE Asia-Pacific Pte. Ltd.
33 Pekin Street #02-01
Far East Square
Singapore 048763

Printed in the United States of America

Library of Congress Cataloging-in-Publication Data

McEwan, Elaine K., 1941-
Teach them all to read: Catching kids before they fall through the cracks / Elaine K. McEwan. —2nd ed.
    p. cm.
Includes bibliographical references and index.
ISBN 978-1-4129-6497-5 (cloth)
ISBN 978-1-4129-6498-2 (pbk.)
    1. Reading (Elementary) 2. Language arts (Elementary) I. Title.

LB1573.M3915 2009
372.4—dc22   2009011783

This book is printed on acid-free paper.

09 10 11 12 13 10 9 8 7 6 5 4 3 2 1

Acquisitions Editor:	Cathy Hernandez
Editorial Assistant:	Sarah Bartlett
Production Editor:	Melanie Birdsall
Copy Editor:	Marilyn Power Scott
Typesetter:	C&M Digitals (P) Ltd.
Proofreader:	Christina West
Cover Designer:	Anthony Paular

Contents

List of Figures

About the Author

Elaine K. McEwan is a partner and educational consultant with The McEwan-Adkins Group, offering workshops in leadership and raising student achievement, K–12. A former teacher, librarian, principal, and assistant superintendent for instruction in a suburban Chicago school district, she is the author of more than 35 books for parents and educators. Her Corwin titles include *Leading Your Team to Excellence: Making Quality Decisions* (1996), *The Principal's Guide to Attention Deficit Hyperactivity Disorder* (1997), *How to Deal With Parents Who Are Angry, Troubled, Afraid, or Just Plain Crazy* (1998), *The Principal's Guide to Raising Reading Achievement* (1998), *Counseling Tips for Elementary School Principals* (1998) with Jeffrey A. Kottler, *Managing Unmanageable Students: Practical Solutions for Educators* (1999) with Mary Damer, *The Principal's Guide to Raising Math Achievement* (2000), *Raising Reading Achievement in Middle and High Schools: Five Simple-to-Follow Strategies for Principals* (2001), *Ten Traits of Highly Effective Teachers: How to Hire, Mentor, and Coach Successful Teachers* (2001), *Teach Them ALL to Read: Catching the Kids Who Fall through the Cracks* (2002), *Seven Steps to Effective Instructional Leadership, Second Edition* (2002), *Making Sense of Research: What's Good, What's Not, and How to Tell the Difference* (2003) with Patrick J. McEwan, *Ten Traits of Highly Effective Principals: From Good to Great Performance* (2003), *Seven Strategies of Highly Effective Readers: Using Cognitive Research to Boost K–8 Achievement* (2004), *How to Deal with Parents Who Are Angry, Troubled, Afraid or Just Plain Crazy, Second Edition* (2004), *How to Deal with Teachers Who Are Angry, Troubled, Exhausted, or Just Plain Confused* (2005), *How to Survive and Thrive in the First Three Weeks of School* (2006), *Raising Reading Achievement in Middle and High Schools, Second Edition* (2006), *40 Ways to Support Struggling Readers, Grades 6–12* (2007), *The Reading Puzzle Classroom Books*, a series of 10 grade-leveled resources (2008) based on the bestseller *Teach Them ALL to Read: Catching the Kids Who Fall Through the Cracks*; and *10 Traits of Highly Effective Schools: Raising the Achievement Bar for All Students* (2008).

Elaine was honored by the Illinois Principals Association as an outstanding instructional leader, by the Illinois State Board of Education with an Award of Excellence in the Those Who Excel Program, and by the National Association of Elementary School Principals as the National Distinguished Principal from Illinois for 1991. She received her undergraduate degree in education from Wheaton College and advanced degrees in library science (MA) and educational administration (EdD) from Northern Illinois University. She lives with her husband and business partner E. Raymond Adkins in Oro Valley, Arizona. Visit Elaine's Web site at www.elainemcewan.com where you can learn more about her writing and workshops or contact her directly at emcewan@elainemcewan.com.

Preface

When the first edition of *Teach Them ALL to Read* was published in 2002, many educators were skeptical about the likelihood of teaching all, or even the majority, of their students to read on grade level, particularly if those students were at risk of reading failure. However, the grade-level achievement of students at risk in hundreds of schools around the country is dramatic evidence that it can be done. Educators in these schools have shifted their paradigm from waiting for students to bloom, like Leo, the winsome Leo Lionni (1971) character, to preventing reading failure—catching students *before* they fall through the cracks.

Dawn DeTurk, a Reading First coach, describes the change in her school:

As we look back, we realize that we did not have the knowledge we have today regarding what works for kids. We were doing a hodgepodge of things. We've become more scientific about using our data. Our expectations for students have changed dramatically. We never pushed them before. Now we know that they can and should be reading, often even in preschool. We've immersed teachers in professional development, teaching them how to teach all students to read. And we've followed up with mentoring, coaching, and instructional support. We've become students of time management in our classrooms. We did a lot of fluff before, and now we realize how precious time is. We used to give every student the same amount of instructional time and refer those students who didn't make it to remedial reading or special education programs. Now we tailor the time and the interventions to students' needs. We are constantly monitoring students' progress and we do everything we can to prevent reading failure.

More than 25 years ago, effective schools guru Ron Edmonds (1981) said,

We can, whenever and wherever we choose, successfully teach all students whose schooling is of interest to us. We already know more than we need to do that. Whether or not we do it must finally depend on how we feel about the fact that we haven't done it so far. (p. 53)

Although Edmonds (1981) was writing in a broad sense about student achievement, his statement could well be paraphrased to describe the current status of reading instruction: *We can, whenever and wherever we choose, successfully teach all children to read. We already know more than we need to do that. Whether or not we do it must finally depend on how we feel about the fact that we haven't so far.*

Today, more educators than ever before are feeling empowered to teach all children to read. They are working collaboratively to build collective efficacy and instructional capacity in their schools. They have moved beyond personal feelings of doubt to become energized by the success of their students.

■ THE STORY BEHIND THIS BOOK

This edition of *Teach Them ALL to Read* is informed by my personal experiences as a parent, grandparent, teacher, media specialist, principal, assistant superintendent for curriculum and instruction, and more than 10 years of consulting and writing. When I wrote *The Principal's Guide to Raising Reading Achievement* (1998) based on raising reading achievement in my formerly low-performing school, I also developed a workshop for the National Association of Elementary School Principals. There were always several middle and high school principals in the workshops looking for ways to increase literacy levels in their schools. To respond to their unique needs, I developed a training program for secondary educators and wrote *Raising Reading Achievement in Middle and High Schools: Five Simple-to-Follow Strategies* (2001), now in its second edition (2007).

Although my workshops were primarily intended for principals, many administrators brought teams of teachers or invited me to present to their staff members. I discovered that educators knew very little about scientifically based reading research instruction and realized that a book was needed to communicate that information in an accessible way. The first edition of *Teach Them ALL to Read: Catching the Kids Who Fall Through the Cracks* (2002) was written to meet that need.

As I continued to work with educators, I discovered that even when K–3 teachers taught their students how to read, there were frequently declines in comprehension scores beginning in fourth grade. My review of the cognitive research resulted in a book about how to teach comprehension: *The Seven Strategies of Highly Effective Readers: Using Cognitive Research to Boost K–8 Achievement* (2004). I then became aware of the huge numbers of struggling readers in secondary content classes who were unable to read their textbooks. To help teachers make content standards more accessible to students, I wrote *40 Ways to Support Struggling Readers in Content Classrooms, Grades 6–12* (2007).

During 2006–2007, I worked with a group of creative educators whose practical experiences in the classroom are featured in a 10-book series of K–8 classroom books: *The Reading Puzzle Series* (2008). This experience motivated me to take a fresh look at the reading puzzle and resulted in the puzzle changes I will shortly describe.

Last, I undertook a two-year study of the effective schools research and examined schools that were beating their demographic odds in terms of student achievement. My efforts culminated in the writing of *Ten Traits of Highly Effective Schools: Raising the Achievement Bar for All Students* (2008). This endeavor revealed several critical attributes of effective schools that are particularly germane to the topic of building a school culture in which literacy can flourish. This new edition of *Teach Them ALL to Read* summarizes the most up-to-date research on reading, instructional practices, and leadership to help educators teach them all to read.

■ HOW THE READING PUZZLE HAS CHANGED

In the first edition, I constructed the jigsaw puzzle shown in Figure P.1. Many teachers and principals have attested to its power in keeping them focused on the essentials as they designed and executed their reading programs.

Figure P.1   The Original Reading Puzzle

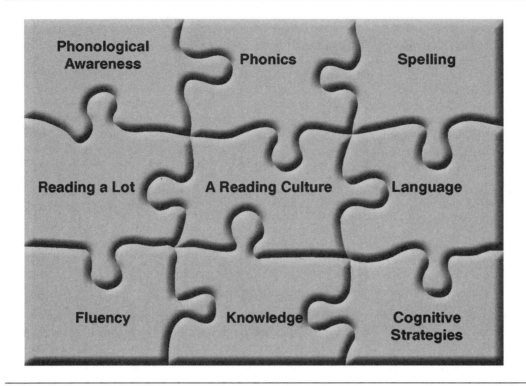

Source: McEwan (2002a).

Based on the input of practitioners and a review of the current research, I have made some changes to the original puzzle to make it more relevant. The revised puzzle is shown in Figure P.2.

- *Phonological Awareness* has been changed to *Phonemic Awareness* since it is the term most commonly used by educators. Phonological awareness is an umbrella term that encompasses a broader range of abilities, of which phonemic awareness is the most critical.
- The *Language* and *Knowledge* pieces have been combined to become *Word and World Knowledge.*
- *Cognitive Strategies* has been renamed *Comprehension.* Although cognitive strategies are essential to comprehension and are the focus of that chapter, the term *comprehension* is more familiar to educators.
- A brand-new piece, *Writing,* has been added to the Reading Puzzle. There is a growing body of research describing the power of writing before, during, and after reading as an essential aid to comprehension and retention. Furthermore, most state assessments require that students write in response to a passage they have read as a part of the reading test.

Figure P.2   The New Reading Puzzle

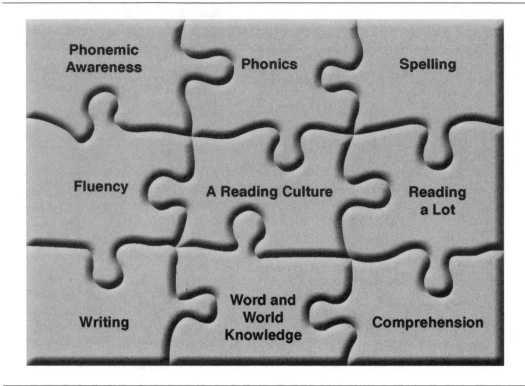

■ THE MEANING OF *ALL*

In this edition of *Teach Them ALL to Read,* the meaning of the word *all* in the title requires clarification. Some practitioners are so overwhelmed by the goal of getting all students on grade level in reading by a particular point in time, they are reluctant to even commit to what is arguably a more achievable goal, getting *95%* of their students on grade level (Fielding, Kerr, & Rosier, 2007). A solid body of experimental intervention research over the past 20 years has shown that while "intensive preventive instruction can bring the average word-reading skills of children at risk for reading disabilities solidly into the average range, even under the best-known instructional conditions, a substantial proportion of children (6%) will remain relatively impaired in word-level reading skills at the conclusion of the intervention" (Torgesen, 2002, p. 96). Since educators cannot know with certainty which students will have serious reading difficulties until they actually intervene, they have a moral imperative to teach all children using research-based instructional materials and methods while firmly believing that they all will learn to read. That is what "teaching them all to read" means in the context of this book. It means believing that all children will learn to read, until there are solid data documenting an individual child's failure to respond to well-conceived and research-based intensive interventions delivered in the general education classroom. This approach to teaching reading is similar to the measures taken by the best physicians when they are confronted with seriously ill patients. Dedicated doctors do not give up until they have exhausted all of their treatment options. We can do no less with our students at risk.

THE GOALS OF THIS BOOK ■

The goals of this revised edition are as follows:

- To update educators on the most current reading research so they can make informed decisions regarding curriculum and instruction
- To illustrate with vignettes and examples precisely how educators in successful schools are teaching them all to read
- To reiterate with more fervor than ever that learning to read is only the first step; students must also develop fluency, acquire cognitive strategies, and continue to read a lot to deepen their word and world knowledge
- To focus attention on the variables at work in classrooms, schools, and districts that can be altered to create a reading culture and raise the achievement bar for all students
- To close the gap that exists between what is known about the most effective ways to teach all students to read and what educators are currently doing in their classrooms and schools
- To motivate educators to accept the leadership challenge and teach them all to read

WHO THIS BOOK IS FOR ■

This book has been written for a broad audience. There are few, if any, educators today who are not deeply concerned with literacy levels in their schools. From superintendents to the most recently hired teachers, everyone is feeling the relentless pressure of high-stakes tests. This book is intended for the following groups:

- Teachers of all kinds and levels—regular classroom, special education, bilingual education, and remedial reading—who are looking for ways to teach all students to read
- Literacy coaches, interventionists, speech pathologists, and other educational specialists who are designing interventions and teaching individual students and intervention groups in the regular classroom
- Special education, bilingual, and Title I administrators who need assistance in evaluating current programs and providing a district framework for response to intervention (RTI) and early intervening services (EIS)
- Superintendents and principals who need up-to-date and research-based information about how to raise reading achievement in their districts and schools
- Central office administrators (e.g., those responsible for school improvement, grant writing, professional development, and curriculum selection) who need a quick-reading and practical compendium of the best practices in reading instruction
- College and university professors who are looking for a beginning-level, comprehensive book on reading instruction

■ OVERVIEW OF THE CONTENTS

The Introduction enumerates and describes in detail three simple-to-follow steps for teaching them all to read: (1) Consider the various paradigms that impact reading achievement and be prepared to challenge and ultimately change any beliefs that are interfering with all students learning to read, (2) become knowledgeable about the research supporting the role that each piece of the reading puzzle plays in facilitating high literacy levels, and (3) tap into all available leadership and instructional expertise to raise literacy levels in your classroom, school, or district.

Chapters 1 through 8 provide in-depth discussions of each of the curricular puzzle pieces organized in the following format:

- A brief definition and description of the puzzle piece and how students acquire it
- The role the piece plays in skilled reading
- The scientific evidence related to the piece
- Effective instructional practices and strategies
- Sample instructional activities
- Suggestions for structuring classroom interventions

Knowledge about how to teach all students to read is essential, but only to a point. The goal of this book is to help readers make the transition from knowing to doing—implementing research-based instruction and curricula in their classrooms, schools, and districts. Chapter 9 is the "doing" chapter. It features the story of how one district has created a reading culture. You hear the story from teachers, coaches, principals, central office administrators, and parents.

■ PROGRAM RECOMMENDATIONS

In the first edition of *Teach Them ALL to Read*, I reviewed a number of reading programs. The task at that time was simple: there were few programs and interventions that met the stringent research-based criteria. Today, there are dozens of programs and interventions designed for a variety of purposes and students. Specific reading programs are only cited as they occur in the various examples and case studies throughout the book.

■ SPECIAL FEATURES OF THE SECOND EDITION

The following special features can be found throughout the book:

- Brief vignettes that illustrate important ideas and concepts
- Links in the form of visual sticky notes that connect to other discussions in the book, relevant Web sites, or bits of information to help you understand and remember the text
- Graphic organizers that summarize key concepts and vocabulary
- The most up-to-date research on what works in reading instruction

Acknowledgments

I am indebted to the many talented teachers, principals, and central office administrators who shared their opinions, reflections, ideas, and experiences regarding their life's work with me. During the period between June 2006 and December 2008, they kept my inbox filled with e-mail, my post office box filled with snail mail, and my phone messaging system filled with voice mail. Their voices are heard throughout this book. Individuals are quoted by name except where anonymity has been requested. In that case, an asterisk is placed after the individual's pseudonym. To save the busy reader time, I have omitted dated citations for these quotations unless they have appeared in a published work.

There is one individual who deserves special recognition: Lynette Block, director of Reading First in Nebraska from 2003–2009. This book is dedicated to Lynette, her assistant Alice Fournell, and Nebraska's Calibration Team: Jeanette Jackson, Alice Epstein, Terry Fusco, and Kathy Senior. Lynette and her staff represent all of the committed educators across the country who have sacrificially given of themselves to the cause of Reading First and the goal of teaching them all to read, often in the face of tremendous political opposition and harsh criticism. Lynette is a tireless advocate for students at risk in Nebraska. Thousands of them have learned to read because of Lynette's courageous leadership in the cause of research-based reading instruction. She has empowered and energized hundreds of educators in Nebraska who have discovered the thrill of teaching them all to read. She and her staff have also touched my life with their dogged determination and humble spirits.

Writing this book would not have been possible without the help of others. I gratefully acknowledge the contributions and suggestions of the dozens of educators who have read all or portions of this manuscript, made substantive comments and suggestions for improvement, answered specific questions I had about various pieces of the reading puzzle, or shared their experiences down in the trenches.

I am, as always, grateful and lovingly indebted to my husband and business partner, E. Raymond Adkins. He plays a variety of roles during the writing of all of my books—copy editor, sounding board, encourager, supporter, and even nursemaid. He anticipates my every need, he is always there when I need him, and his advice is unfailingly sound. He is the unsung coauthor of this book.

■ **PUBLISHER'S ACKNOWLEDGMENTS**

Corwin gratefully acknowledges the contributions of the following reviewers:

Darlene Carino, First-Grade Teacher
Barringer Road Elementary School
Ilion, NY

Candace Darling, First-Grade Teacher
Barringer Road Elementary School
Ilion, NY

Barb Friesth, Professional Services Coordinator
Educational Service Unit 7
Columbus, NE

Michelle Judware, First-Grade Teacher
Barringer Road Elementary School
Ilion, NY

Crystal Loose, Literacy Coach
Highland Elementary
Ephrata, PA

Joni Runge, Staff Development & Curriculum Services
Educational Service Unit 5
Beatrice, NE

Tara Tuck, District Inclusion Specialist
Seminole County Public Schools
Sanford, FL

Introduction

We will never teach all of our students to read if we do not teach our students who have the greatest difficulties to read. Another way to say this is: Getting to 100% requires going through the bottom 20%.

—Torgesen (2006, p. 1)

Teaching all students to read is both easier *and* more difficult now than it was when the first edition of *Teach Them ALL to Read* was published in 2002. First—the good news. The goal of literacy for all students as spelled out in the No Child Left Behind Act of 2001 (NCLB, 2002) is more readily attainable for two reasons. First, there is a growing body of experimental research to show educators what works. Second, there are large numbers of successful schools against which to benchmark leadership behaviors, curricula, instructional approaches, grouping practices, and assessments (American Institutes for Research, 2008; Chenoweth, 2007; Denton, Foorman, & Mathes, 2003; Fielding et al., 2007; Foorman & Moats, 2004; Luce & Thompson, 2005; McEwan, 2009; Waits et al., 2006).

However, there is also discouraging news—the achievement target keeps moving. Bringing students to reading and writing proficiency today is more challenging than it was even one or two years ago as expectations continue to rise on high-stakes tests. If you and your colleagues want to bring all of your students to grade-level reading proficiency, *regardless of their readiness to read* when they enroll in your school, take these steps: (1) Consider the paradigms that impact reading achievement and be prepared to challenge and ultimately change the prevailing beliefs that are interfering with all students learning to read; (2) become knowledgeable about research regarding the role that each of the reading puzzle pieces play in facilitating high literacy levels; and (3) utilize your unique leadership and instructional expertise to raise literacy levels in your classroom, school, or district.

We begin with Step 1 by examining how certain assumptions, beliefs, and values (paradigms) affect your success in teaching all of your students to read.

SHIFT YOUR PARADIGMS ■

The solution to the problem [of teaching them all to read] is like most significant breakthroughs in human history—it comes from a fundamental break with old ways of thinking.

—Covey (2004, p. 10)

Philosopher Thomas Kuhn (1962/1996) coined the phrase *paradigm shift* to describe a fundamental change in approach or underlying assumptions that govern the behavior of an individual, group, organization, or society. Teaching all students to read requires that everyone involved in the process (teachers, administrators, support personnel, school board members, students, and parents) share a basic set of assumptions and then act in accordance with those assumptions. For some educators, that means making a break with the past and starting over with a new set of beliefs and behaviors. Figure I.1 enumerates the eight paradigms that impact reading achievement, and just ahead we'll examine each one in detail.

Figure I.1 Paradigms That Impact Reading Achievement

Problem or Issue	Former Way of Thinking	New Way of Thinking
1. Determinant of students' academic destiny	Demographics	Opportunities to learn
2. Solutions for struggling readers	Wait and see	Intervention and prevention
3. How students learn to read	Reading is natural	Reading is rocket science
4. The best way to teach reading	Whole-group instruction	Whole group instruction *and* differentiation
5. Basis for selection of materials and instructional methods	Teacher autonomy	Scientifically based reading research (SBRR)
6. Accountability	Unaccountable	Accountable
7. Causes of student failure	Inalterable variables	Alterable variables
8. School culture	Competitive	Collaborative

Paradigm 1: *Demographics* Versus *Opportunities to Learn*

Reading failure is not, as once believed, the product of poor mothering, low IQ, or lack of motivation. Most scientists agree that reading is an unnatural acquired language skill that requires mastery of a written cipher or code through which speech and language are accessed. Spelling and writing require the inverse of that process and are even more demanding than reading. . . . Thus, the teacher's challenge is to defy the predictions based on incoming levels of reading ability.

—Moats (2006, p. 31)

The question of whether schools as institutions have the power to make a positive impact upon the academic achievement and future success of their students, irrespective of their demographic characteristics—such as socioeconomic levels, family characteristics, language and culture, or minority status—has been debated for more than 40 years. In one of the first school effects studies, James Coleman and his colleagues (1966) concluded that students' demographics largely determine their academic destinies: "The inequalities imposed on children by their home, neighborhood, and peer environment are carried along to become the inequalities with which they confront adult life" (p. 325).

Although we cannot change the demographic variables of our students, we do have the power to teach them all to read by providing research-based and differentiated opportunities to learn. Only a small percentage of students (6%, according to Torgesen, 2002) will have bona fide reading difficulties when the paradigm shifts from offering excuses and placing blame to providing sufficient opportunities for all students to learn to read (Fielding et al., 2007; McEwan, 2009). The next paradigm describes the nature of these new opportunities in more detail.

Paradigm 2: *Wait and See* Versus *Intervention and Prevention*

The difficulty of playing catch up may develop into one of the most powerful arguments for investment in preventive instruction with children who are at risk for the development of reading disabilities.

—Torgesen (2002, p. 102)

The second paradigm relates to how educators respond to students who come to school at risk of reading failure. Experienced kindergarten teachers are skilled at identifying these students. The question is, Do they wait and see or intervene? The wait-and-see paradigm believes that many children are not developmentally ready for the rigors of reading and therefore need time to mature or "bloom," like *Leo, the Late Bloomer* (Lionni, 1971). The wait-and-see paradigm hypothesizes that a lack of readiness for reading instruction will eventually be remediated by maturity. The fallback position when advancing age fails to result in readiness is usually a remedial program like Reading Recovery or Title I. The fallback to the failure of remedial programs is special education, a solution that inevitably comes too late to teach them all to read (Klinger, Vaughn, Hughes, Schumm, & Elbaum, 1998; Zigmond & Baker, 1996). One anonymous contributor suggested that our efforts over the years have been akin to letting students fall off a cliff and then sending ambulances to pick them up, rather than preventing their precipitous descent in the first place.

I was a principal in the 1980s, and I still remember the kindergarten students who failed to bloom in my school. Their teacher reassured me on many occasions, "They're not ready yet." At the time, I believed her. I didn't know any better. Historically, after years of special education or remedial reading, we sent these so-called late bloomers on to middle school severely limited in what they could accomplish academically. Often there were students who seemed certain to be candidates for special education services at some later date but for whom we could offer no systematic help immediately. As each child fell through the proverbial cracks, we stood helplessly by, waiting for the school psychologist to document a discrepancy between their achievement and ability.

The prevention paradigm focuses on the early identification of reading difficulties that are immediately and prescriptively treated by intensive interventions (Scammacca, Vaughn, Roberts, Wanzek, & Torgesen, 2007; Torgesen, 2006). Ideally, if we envision a kindergarten class beginning school together and enrolling no new students, we can safely say that 94% or possibly more of those students can achieve grade-level literacy by the end of third grade (Torgesen, 2002).

Paradigm 3: *Reading Is Natural* Versus *Reading Is Rocket Science*

Programmatic research over the past 35 years has not supported the view that reading development reflects a natural process—that children learn to read as they learn to speak, through natural exposure to a literate environment.

—Lyon (1998, p. 3)

The third paradigm is related to what educators believe about the kind of instruction most children need in order to acquire grade-level literacy skills. The former version of the paradigm assumes that children learn to read naturally, the same way they learn to talk, and that teachers are meant to function as guides and facilitators to the world of reading rather than as explicit and systematic teachers of the alphabetic principle, fluency, and cognitive strategies.

The ease with which a very few children acquire reading proficiency and the effortless way in which skilled readers construct meaning and gain understanding from what they read have led some to theorize that learning to read and the teaching of reading are relatively easy things to do (Goodman, 1986, 1996; Smith, 1971). This seductive notion has been an appealing one to educators and for obvious reasons. Facilitating the development of literacy by immersing children in outstanding literature is both a loftier sounding goal and a far less demanding task than to directly and systematically teach the skills and knowledge at-risk students need in order to succeed academically. Although some children do learn to read effortlessly, the majority of students need a highly skilled and knowledgeable reading teacher.

The "reading is natural" paradigm was once widely known as *whole language.* Its chief theorists are Ken Goodman (1986, 1996) and Frank Smith (1994), while its major apologists are Fountas and Pinnell (1996), Routman (1988), and Weaver (1994). The whole-language approach to teaching reading may work in communities like Lake Wobegon where all of the children are above average.[1] Above-average students flourish in settings that are meaning focused, with less teacher-directed instruction and more opportunities for students to manage their own learning (Connor, Morrison, & Katch, 2004). However, there is a problem in many Lake Wobegon districts that is only discussed by parents of students who are reading disabled and who attend their schools: whole language doesn't work for students with serious reading disabilities. These students need explicit, systematic, scientifically based reading instruction. Stanovich (1994) summarizes it: "That direct instruction in alphabetic coding facilitates early reading acquisition is one of the most well established conclusions in all of behavioral science. . . . The idea that learning to read is just like learning to speak is accepted by no responsible linguist, psychologist, or cognitive scientist in the research community" (pp. 285–286).

Louisa Moats (1999) has said that "teaching reading is rocket science," and I submit that for many beginning readers, assembling the pieces of the reading puzzle is also akin to rocket science. Figure I.2 contrasts the instructional beliefs and practices of the *reading is natural* paradigm with the *reading is rocket science* paradigm.

Paradigm 4: *Whole-Group Instruction* Versus *Whole-Group Instruction and Differentiation*

Life on many levels would be simpler if one flavor, size, or approach worked for everyone. In the real world, however, whether it's coffee, shoes, or learning to

Figure I.2 *Reading Is Natural* Versus *Reading Is Rocket Science*

Reading Is Natural	Reading Is Rocket Science
Reading is thought to be a natural process that is acquired through a child's immersion in literature guided by an enthusiastic teacher who is sensitive to the developmental needs and readiness of each child.	Reading is a complex multilinguistic process. Reading is challenging to teach, requiring a vast repertoire of knowledge and skills and for all but a few students is a challenging skill to acquire.
Word identification is taught through memorization, picture cues, and contextual guessing using an approach called the *three cueing system*, which has no research to substantiate its effectiveness.	Word identification is taught using five different linguistic systems: phonological, orthographic, morphological, semantic, and mental orthographic images.
Phonemic awareness and phonics are taught implicitly in the context of reading literature.	Phonemic awareness and phonics are taught in an explicit, systematic, and supportive way.
Reading materials for beginning readers include predictable books, which are generally memorized and leveled trade books with uncontrolled text that is often too difficult for students to read independently. Colorful illustrations give too many picture cues and often distract struggling readers.	Reading materials for beginning readers include decodable text in which at least 95% of the words can be independently decoded based on prior instruction.
Students are encouraged to memorize whole words.	Students are taught to pay close attention to individual letters, word parts, and word patterns and to reread words multiple times until they have established mental orthographic images that can be automatically retrieved during the reading process.
Teachers frequently read aloud to students as they follow along in their own books before students have any opportunity to use their independent reading skills.	Students orally read independently so teachers can closely monitor their developing abilities to identify words automatically and accurately.
Teachers rarely teach skills to mastery, believing that students will eventually catch on to reading.	Teachers, especially those teaching intervention groups for struggling readers, teach phonemic awareness and phonics to mastery.
Most of the reading materials for students have colorful illustrations, removing the need for students to visualize as they read, an important skill to develop in anticipation of moving to chapter books.	Pictures are sometimes included in small, decodable books, but they are simple line drawings. Students are encouraged to focus on identifying the words and making mental pictures to illustrate what they are reading.

read—no one flavor, size, or approach meets everyone's needs. The notion that one teacher can teach all students to read in a whole group without also providing differentiated opportunities to learn is a paradigm that does not work. Individual students or small groups need different amounts of time, kinds of teaching, and curricula. Teaching to the whole class is undeniably an important part of every school day, but there are periods of the reading block where instruction must be skillfully differentiated to meet the needs of all students, whether at risk or gifted.

Skillfully managing a differentiation model in the classroom requires close attention to the following variables: (a) the amount of time spent, (b) the content of the lesson, and (c) who manages the instruction (teacher or student). Differentiation takes structure, organization, and exceptional time management, but the results are worth the effort. Classrooms in which teachers differentiate instruction based on students' documented needs produce higher overall reading growth for both the students who need more explicit teacher-managed instruction as well as for those who can work more independently and manage their own learning (Connor, Schatschneider, Fishman, & Morrison, 2008).

Paradigm 5: *Teacher Autonomy* Versus *Scientifically Based Reading Research*

Paradigm 5 speaks to the issue of teacher autonomy with regard to what is taught and how instruction is delivered. I call the kind of teacher autonomy that thrives in many schools and districts the Julie Andrews syndrome. Remember her sweetly singing, "These are a few of my favorite things," in *The Sound of Music*. At issue is the reality that teachers may or may not get results with their favorite things. The former paradigm based on the positive emotional feelings of teachers for their materials and methods is dramatically shifting to using materials, methods, and assessments that are grounded in scientifically based reading research (SBRR).

One elementary school principal explained the problem this way: "We tend to move from one fad to another in order to demonstrate that we are 'state of the art' even though most of the activities have little impact. There is big money in selling education programs, and consultants use 'research says' to sell programs that purportedly can fix just about anything. Most . . . teachers and administrators can't differentiate viable research from poor research" (Walker, 1996, p. 41).

There are two reasons for taking the time to understand and use the research: (1) "Research is the most powerful instrument to improve student achievement—if only we would try it in a serious and sustained manner" (National Educational Research and Priorities Board, 2000, p. 1) and (2) it's the law (NCLB, 2002).[2]

Those teachers who are willing to give research a chance are thrilled with the results. Charlotte,* a kindergarten teacher, believed that implementing phonemic awareness instruction along with tiered interventions in her classroom would take the fun out of teaching. Her favorite things were units, play time, creative writing, and centers; she excelled at generating fun for her students. Charlotte was an excellent teacher and in high demand by parents in the community, so it wasn't pretty when the principal told her the letter people had to be put away in the store room and she could no longer read predictable stories, such as *Brown Bear, Brown Bear* (Martin, 1967) during the reading block. They were not research based.[3]

Charlotte's paradigm shifted seismically midyear. Her reading coach reported, "Charlotte came to me with tears in her eyes and said, 'I am so sorry that I have been so difficult. I am eating crow. Will you forgive me? All of my students are reading. Not as a group, but individually. I was so afraid that I was going to be robbing them of their childhood. Then I realized that I had been robbing them of being able to read.'" Charlotte was so proud of her students and their accomplishments that she spread the word throughout the community about the power of scientifically based reading instruction and materials.

---

* Pseudonym

Paradigm 6: *Unaccountable* Versus *Accountable*

Paradigm 6 is about accountability. Teaching them all to read requires a shift from feeling no responsibility for student mastery of content standards to suddenly feeling *and being* accountable for what students ultimately know and can do. It is a heavy responsibility and requires that educators have a high degree of efficacy, a belief that they can teach all students to read.

In workshops, I use an activity called Agree or Disagree. I put a slide up on the screen with the title, Agree or Disagree? Underneath the title is this statement: *Student performance is a measure of teacher performance.* Before the workshop I put up signs in each of the corners of the room: Agree, Strongly Agree, Disagree, and Strongly Disagree. I ask the participants to read the statement and then go to the corner that aligns most closely with their belief. Some individuals stand up and quickly walk to a corner. There's no doubt in their minds what they believe. Then there are the individuals who want to put a foot in a couple of corners, leaving some wiggle room for excuses or special cases. When everyone has made a decision, I ask each group to talk about why they chose the corner they did and then to select a reporter who can make the group's case to the rest of the participants. I have never been disappointed by the discussion that follows. But I have been disappointed on occasions when a crowd gathered in the Strongly Disagree corner, indicating the necessity for some major paradigm shifting.

Paradigm 7: *Inalterable Variables* Versus *Alterable Variables*

This paradigm relates to what educators believe are the causes of student failure. When I assumed the principalship of a suburban Chicago elementary school in the early 1980s, reading achievement was at an all-time low—the 20th percentile for Grades 2 through 6 on the Iowa Test of Basic Skills. I was brand new to administration and knew nothing about raising test scores. All of my teaching experience had been in communities similar to humorist Garrison Keillor's (1985) imaginary Lake Wobegon, Minnesota, where all of the students are above average. At the first faculty meeting, I asked teachers why *they* thought achievement was so low. They had plenty of reasons for the dismal state of affairs: the students, the parents, and the school board, to name just a few. Too many students were on free lunch, too many parents didn't speak English, and the school board didn't particularly care. The teachers didn't mention any role they might have personally played in the test results, but their reactions were not unlike those of most teachers faced with failing students. In retrospect, my staff fit the following description to a T: "We say we believe that all children can learn, but few of us really believe it" (Delpit, 1995, p. 172). Faced with what may appear to be insurmountable obstacles, teachers often feel powerless to make a difference, and unfortunately, they frequently communicate their low expectations to each other and their students.

I decided that what my staff needed was a good dose of Benjamin Bloom. At the time, Bloom (1980) identified what he called "alterable variables" and scolded his readers for whining about things over which they had no control (e.g., characteristics of students and their parents). He urged them to focus their energies and creativity on the alterable context and environmental variables that affect student learning (Weinstein & Hume, 1998, p. 101). As we brainstormed what those variables might be at Lincoln School, the list began to grow and so did our excitement and motivation to change the way we conducted the business of schooling. During the eight years we worked together as a team, reading achievement climbed to between the 70th and 80th percentiles. There were few individuals on the staff, in the student body, or among our parent community who were not profoundly changed by the process. We discovered that we were all capable of achieving far more than we imagined. We stopped making excuses and started changing what we had the power to change. We stopped acting defensive, argumentative, and hopeless. Instead, we became focused, optimistic, and empowered. And together, as educators, parents, and students, we celebrated our successes. Figure I.3 describes 9 categories of variables that when changed in research-based ways, have the power to increase literacy levels in your school or district.

Figure I.3   How to Alter Contextual, Instructional, and Environmental Variables to Increase Literacy Levels

Alterable Variables	How to Change the Variables
Paradigms	
Change your beliefs and behaviors.	In order to teach them all to read, educators need to change their beliefs and behaviors. In the real world where students are failing and accountability is upon us, behaviors must change in advance of beliefs. Usually, however, when teachers achieve results, their beliefs begin to change. Using research-based programs where results are likely to occur is critical to maintain credibility and facilitate paradigm change.
Goals and Focus	
Change your focus.	Rather than trying to do everything, determine the one or two most important things that must be accomplished (all students learning to read and write on grade level by third grade) and zoom in on those specific goals with a laserlike focus, refusing to become distracted by the next new thing. *"The litmus test for a good school is not its innovations but rather the solid, purposeful, enduring results it . . . obtain[s] for its students"* (Glickman, 1993, p. 50).
Change how goals are set, stated, and evaluated.	Write goals that are concise, meaningful, and measurable. Daily, weekly, and monthly progress (no matter how small) for every child will lead to solid schoolwide achievement gains (Schmoker, 1999). Beware of mistaking activity for achievement (Wooden, 1997).
Content, Curriculum, Instruction, and Assessment	
Change what is taught.	Align content standards with curriculum and instruction. Teach the content standards mandated by your district, state, or both.
Change the program or curriculum.	Choose materials that are research based and have been shown to get results, particularly with students at risk of reading failure. Don't make decisions based on glitzy sales presentations, the recommendation of a consultant, or the fact that a neighboring district is doing it. Find out if the program actually works with students like yours.
Change how teachers teach.	Ensure that teachers have focused lessons, outstanding classroom management, use time wisely, keep students on task, and can differentiate their instruction to meet the needs of varied students.
Change how teachers assess.	Use daily formative assessment to determine lesson effectiveness and plan for the next lesson. Use regular benchmark assessments to form instructional groups and set short-term goals.

Alterable Variables	How to Change the Variables
Implementation	
Change how implementation is monitored and supervised.	In order for goals to be reached, one or more administrators with evaluative power must be monitoring (doing classroom walk-throughs daily to determine if teachers and students are focused on the goal). In cases where individuals have lost their focus, the individuals with e-power (administrators) must supervise, provide resources and assistance to teachers who can't, and conduct assertive interventions with teachers who won't (McEwan, 2004a).
Change to data-based progress monitoring.	Collect data to track the effectiveness of the implementation. Give tests according to an assessment schedule that helps teachers to make midcourse corrections and develop interventions for students who are struggling.
Time	
Change the amount of time allocated for reading instruction.	If most students are failing to succeed, consider changing the amount of time allocated for reading instruction. "The primary and immediate strategy for catch-up growth is proportional increases in direct instruction time" (Fielding, Kerr, & Rosier, 2004, pp. 52–53).
Change the amount of time students practice.	When individual students are struggling or have not yet achieved mastery, they may need more practice. Practice beyond mastery is essential for students to achieve the kind of automaticity that is needed to leave the working memory free for problem solving and creative endeavors. Practice is essential for three types of learning: (1) the core skills and knowledge that will be used again and again, (2) the type of knowledge that students need to know well in the short term to enable long-term retention of key concepts, and (3) the type of knowledge we believe is important enough that students should remember it later in life (Willingham, 2004).
Change the amount of interactive teacher time.	For struggling students, there is no substitute for teacher-directed instruction focused on skills and strategies needed to become fluent readers.
Change the amount of time that is wasted.	Reduce wasted time by teaching routines, rubrics, and rules to students during the first three weeks of the school year, thereby reclaiming thousands of minutes of previously wasted time for interactive instruction with a trained teacher (McEwan, 2006).
Change the amount of time spent on actual reading in classrooms.	Audit the amount of oral reading at a student's independent reading level in Grades K–2 until fluency is established, and monitor silent reading in Grades 2–6 with accountability requirements, such as writing in response to reading.
Grouping	
Change how students are grouped for instruction.	If students are struggling in whole-group instruction, place them in small intervention groups. In contrast, when working on comprehension strategies or engaging in critical discussion of text, it is essential that students who are struggling observe as the teacher and more advanced students model comprehension strategies.

(Continued)

Figure I.3   (Continued)

Alterable Variables	How to Change the Variables
Professional Development and Planning	
Change how professional development is delivered.	Professional development is most effective when it is embedded in the specific goals of the school. Build instructional capacity by identifying teachers who can become teacher leaders and tap their expertise to become professional developers in the school. Recommended practices include (a) giving teachers a chance to observe a model in action, (b) offering ample opportunities to practice the new behavior in a safe context, and (c) trying out the behavior with peer support in the classroom (Learning First Alliance, 2000, p. 8).
Change how planning time is used.	Use planning time for collaborative (not individual) planning. Collaborative planning is essential to teaching them all to read.
Alignment	
Change the vertical alignment.	Ensure that assessment, curriculum, content standards, and instruction are closely aligned as students move from kindergarten through the upper grades. Without a tight linkage, students will fall through the cracks. Children who come to school poorly prepared to learn to read are totally dependent on their teachers to gradually build their knowledge and skills in a systematic and sequential fashion. This requires K–3 teachers in particular to share a vision of the strategies and knowledge they expect their students to master.
Change the horizontal alignment.	When all of the teachers of one grade level are planning collaboratively, using similar pacing guides, assessing on the same time line, and forming intervention groups to meet the needs of struggling or fast-paced readers, achievement will move steadily upward. When teachers are acting as independent contractors, students will fall through the cracks.
Expectations	
Change expectations for teachers.	Expect all teachers to be growing and improving through personal professional growth plans. Expect all teachers to work collaboratively, implement programs with fidelity, and teach all students to read.
Change expectations for students.	Expect all students to set personal goals, work hard at school, ask questions when they are confused, and learn cooperatively with their classmates.
Change expectations for parents.	Expect all parents to do everything they can, to the extent they are able, and to ask for help in supporting their children in learning to read when it is needed.

Source: McEwan (1998, 2002a, 2002b, 2006, 2007, 2009).

Paradigm 8: *Competitive* Versus *Collaborative*

Paradigm 8 is focused on the degree to which educators in a school collaborate to improve instruction and achievement. When I began my teaching career, my colleagues and I were like independent contractors with complete curricular and instructional autonomy. We were collegial and friendly, but we rarely worked together.

There was even a measure of competition that existed between teachers for the most elaborate bulletin boards or the best end-of-the-year parent program. The only thing the other fifth-grade teacher and I shared was a set of ancient *World Book* encyclopedias on a rolling cart.

A lone teacher, even a highly effective one, cannot achieve the goal of on-grade-level reading single-handedly. Reaching this goal requires a collaborative school culture in which educators have a collective sense of accountability for all students. Collaboration is the only way a diverse faculty with diverse students can hope to achieve the alignment of content standards, curriculum, instruction, and assessment that is needed to raise the achievement bar for all students.

The beliefs that you and your colleagues share regarding these eight paradigms will impact the degree to which you can collectively teach them all to read. When fewer than 80% of staff members, including administrators, do not believe that teaching them all to read is possible, the goal will be difficult, if not impossible, to attain.

PUT TOGETHER THE READING PUZZLE ■

The second step to teaching them all to read is learning all you can about reading instruction. There are a variety of perspectives, theories, stages, and models advanced by theorists and researchers that describe how individuals learn to read (Chall, 1983; Perfetti, 1989; Pressley, 1998). I have chosen a simple nine-piece jigsaw puzzle to illustrate the critical components of teaching all students to read.

Everyone has assembled a jigsaw puzzle at least once and knows that if even one piece of the puzzle is missing or out of place, the final product will be incomplete. Those who are putting the puzzle together get frustrated by the missing piece or pieces, much like students get upset when they sense they are missing key pieces of the reading puzzle. Figure I.4 displays the nine reading puzzle pieces paired with their definitions, and Figure I.5 shows the grade levels at which the various pieces are taught. We will assemble the puzzle one piece at a time in Chapters 1–9, but in classrooms and schools where literacy is a priority, many of the pieces are so tightly woven into the fabric of the school day, they are scarcely indistinguishable from each other. According to Mehta, Foorman, Branum-Martin, and Taylor (2005), literacy is "a multifaceted phenomenon that includes numerous dynamically evolving components including phonological [phonemic] awareness, word recognition [phonics], spelling, reading comprehension, and writing" (p. 88).

BECOME AN INSTRUCTIONAL LEADER ■

The final step in teaching all students to read is to embrace a leadership role in your school or district. Whether you are a teacher or an administrator, your contribution to building leadership capacity in your school or district is essential to the goal of literacy for all. Principals are powerless to make a difference without the support and collaborative energy of teacher leaders. Conversely, teachers need highly effective principals to provide resources; protect their time for teaching; and facilitate problem solving, decision making, and collaborative planning and teaching. Teachers and principals need central office administrators and support professionals—like speech pathologists, psychologists, and behavior management specialists, to name a few— who bring courageous leadership skills to their job roles. A leader is a "person who is in a position to influence others to act and who has, as well, the moral, intellectual,

Figure I.4   Reading Puzzle Definitions

Puzzle Piece	Definition
Phonemic awareness	The ability to identify and manipulate the sounds letters represent, including blending sounds to make words, creating rhyming patterns, and counting phonemes (individual sounds)
Phonics	An understanding of the alphabetic principle (that letters either singly or in combination represent various sounds) and the ability to apply this knowledge in the decoding of unfamiliar words
Spelling	Recognizing, recalling, reproducing, or obtaining orally or in written form the correct sequence of letters in words
Fluency	The ability to read so effortlessly and automatically that working memory is available for the ultimate purpose of reading—extracting and constructing meaning from the text. Fluency can be observed in accurate, automatic, and expressive oral reading and makes silent reading comprehension possible (Adapted from Harris & Hodges, 1995, p. 85, and Pikulski & Chard, 2005, p. 510)
Word and world knowledge	Knowing the meanings of words, knowing about the relationships between words (word schema), and having linguistic knowledge about words; world knowledge is having an understanding (background knowledge) of many different subjects and disciplines (domains) and how they relate to one another
Comprehension	The extraction and construction of meaning from text using the seven cognitive strategies of highly skilled readers, as appropriate
Reading a lot	The mindful and engaged reading of a large volume of text both in and out of school, at increasing levels of difficulty, with personalized accountability
Writing	The ability to communicate through various written formats, such as graphic organizers, short answers, essays, and reports; writing employs the skills of handwriting or keyboarding, spelling, and punctuation; it draws on knowledge of vocabulary, syntax, and textual conventions and requires an understanding of the audience and purpose for writing
A reading culture	The collective attitudes, beliefs, and behaviors of all of the stakeholders in a school regarding any and all of the activities associated with enabling all students to read at the highest level of attainment possible for both their academic and personal gain

and social skills required to take advantage of that position" (Schlechty, 1990, p. xix). Schools, especially traditionally low- and under-performing ones, need strong leaders who perceive the moral imperative of teaching all students to read, regardless of their demographics or lack of readiness. Effective teacher leaders have an important role to play.

Effective Teacher Leaders

Traditionally, educators think of principals as leaders and teachers as teachers. However, "in good schools the image is one of teachers with voice and vision. Teachers [leaders] are knowledgeable and discerning school actors who are the

Figure I.5 The Reading Puzzle Across the Grades

Grade	Phonemic Awareness	Phonics	Spelling	Fluency	Word and World Knowledge	Comprehension	Writing About Reading	Reading a Lot
PreK	×				×	×		×
K	×	×	×		×	×	×	×
1	×	×	×	×	×	×	×	×
2		×	×	×	×	×	×	×
3			×	×	×	×	×	×
4			×	×	×	×	×	×
5			×	×	×	×	×	×

primary shapers of the educational community" (Lightfoot, 1983, p. 24). If you want to be part of a school or district where demographics don't determine the destiny of your students, where colleagues collaborate to find solutions for the most challenging academic problems, and where people are focused on results, not excuses, I urge you to become a part of the leadership team. Use and enhance your instructional and leadership expertise to raise literacy levels in your district, school, or classroom. Take what you learn from reading this book and put it into practice. Here are some ways that you can lead your colleagues in the creation of a reading culture in your school:

- Mentor and coach novice teachers.
- Collaborate with all staff members, regardless of personal affiliation or preference.
- Learn and grow with a view to bringing scientifically based reading instruction to your classroom and school.
- Polish your writing and presentation skills to share knowledge with others.
- Lead a book study to build common vocabulary and values among faculty.
- Engage in creative problem solving and decision making with increased student learning as a goal.
- Create a buzz about something new and exciting that is going on in the classrooms of your school.
- Be willing to take risks by inviting colleagues into your classroom to observe and talk about your lessons.
- Be willing to share ideas, opinions, and evaluative judgments confidently with the principal. (Adapted from McEwan, 2003)

Strong Instructional Leaders

Strong principal leaders execute essential management functions through skilled delegation while at the same time focusing intently on teaching and learning. Strong instructional leaders have high expectations for themselves and inspire the same kind of work ethic in their staff and students. They refuse to blame students for their inability to learn and hold themselves and teachers accountable for student achievement. They realize the importance of using every minute of every day and are dedicated to protecting classroom time for teaching and learning. Strong instructional leaders always have their doors open, but in reality, they are seldom sitting behind their desks. They seem to be everywhere at once—hallways, auditorium, bus stop, cafeteria—but they spend most of their time in classrooms and meeting with teachers in small groups or individually. They go to bat for their staff at central office, running interference for them so they can concentrate on teaching. They are somehow able to find the money to release teachers for collaborative work or to hire an instructional specialist for a team that needs assistance with developing supplementary materials. Although other schools in town have fewer challenging students with whom to work, the test scores at schools with strong instructional leaders are comparable and in some grade levels higher—a strong indicator that this is a highly effective school led by a strong instructional leader.

The following seven steps to effective instructional leadership are drawn from a qualitative study of strong instructional leaders as identified by their staff members and peers (McEwan, 2003). These leaders

1. Establish, implement, and achieve academic standards.

2 Are instructional resources for staff members.

3. Create school cultures and climates conducive to learning.

4. Communicate the vision and mission of their schools.

5. Set high expectations for staff as well as for themselves.

6. Develop teacher leaders.

7. Develop and maintain positive attitudes with students, staff, and parents.

■ SUMMARIZING THE INTRODUCTION

The best way to summarize this Introduction is to ask yourself these four questions before reading Chapter 1:

1. Do I have any beliefs that may be standing in the way of my students achieving literacy? Are there any paradigms that I need to shift?

2. Am I doing all that I can in my classroom, school, or district to ensure that all students reach expected or higher levels of literacy?

3. Am I conversant with the critical components of the reading puzzle that need to be in place to achieve the goal of teaching them all to read?

4. In what ways can I enhance my leadership skills to advance the goal of teaching them all to read?

■ NOTES

1. I use the term *Lake Wobegon,* the mythical Minnesota community featured in Garrison Keillor's (1985) work, as a metaphor for affluent districts and communities where test scores

are high but where many students are falling through the cracks because teachers are doing no regular reading assessments and there are no interventions to support struggling readers.

2. *Scientifically based research,* as defined in NCLB (2002),

> (a) Means research that involves the application of rigorous, systematic, and objective procedures to obtain reliable and valid knowledge relevant to education activities and programs; and (b) Includes research that (1) Employs systematic, empirical methods that draw on observation or experiment; (2) Involves rigorous data analyses that are adequate to test the stated hypotheses and justify the general conclusions drawn; (3) Relies on measurements or observational methods that provide reliable and valid data across evaluators and observers, across multiple measurements and observations, and across studies by the same or different investigators; (4) Is evaluated using experimental or quasi-experimental designs in which individuals, entities, programs, or activities are assigned to different conditions and with appropriate controls to evaluate the effects of the condition of interest, with a preference for random-assignment experiments, or other designs to the extent that those designs contain within-condition or across-condition controls; (5) Ensures that experimental studies are presented in sufficient detail and clarity to allow for replication or, at a minimum, offer the opportunity to build systematically on their findings; and (6) Has been accepted by a peer-reviewed journal or approved by a panel of independent experts through a comparably rigorous, objective, and scientific review. (NCLB, 2002, Section 9101 [37])

3. Research shows that teaching the letters in alphabetical order without a phonemic component that stresses the ability to identify and manipulate sounds is not effective. In addition, predictable text can easily be memorized, which is an entirely different cognitive process than independently decoding text (Adams, 1990, 1998).

1

Phonemic Awareness

> *Phonemic awareness* is the ability to identify and manipulate the sounds letters represent, including blending sounds to make words, creating rhyming patterns, and counting phonemes (individual sounds).

In my early reading workshops for principals shortly after the publication of *The Principal's Guide to Raising Reading Achievement* (McEwan, 1998), I routinely asked participants if they had heard of phonemic awareness (PA). There were seldom more than one or two individuals in a group of 50 to 100 principals who knew the term. It was exciting to share the power of PA instruction with practitioners, to help struggling readers learn to read. Years later, one of the earliest

Phonemic Awareness

attendees contacted me to report that she had dubbed PA "the magic words." As she and her staff implemented explicit, systematic PA instruction in kindergarten and first grade, their student achievement started climbing and never stopped. Their previously low-achieving school went on to become a National Title I Distinguished School (Dobberteen, 2000) and a Chase Change Award winner (Dobberteen, 2001).

WHAT IS PHONEMIC AWARENESS AND HOW DO STUDENTS ACQUIRE IT?

The most important insight of modern reading research has been the recognition that phonics instruction may not "take" with young readers unless they are aware of the segments of speech represented by the graphemes used to spell words in an alphabetic writing system.

—Moats (2006, p. 3)

Although PA has only become an essential aspect of reading instruction during the past 10 years, research investigating the role of this constellation of skills in learning to read has been ongoing for over two decades (Liberman & Shankweiler, 1985; Wagner & Torgesen, 1987). The terms *phonemic* and *phonological* are often used interchangeably, but technically, phonological awareness is a more encompassing concept that includes all levels of the speech sound system, including words, syllables, rimes,[1] and phonemes (Moats, 2000, p. 234). Think of phonological awareness as an umbrella and the various levels of the speech system as its spokes.

Examples of PA abilities include blending sounds together to build words, generating a list of rhyming words, or counting the number of individual sounds (phonemes) that are heard in a given word. Following are the PA skills that are most commonly assessed and taught:

- *Phoneme Isolation.* Recognizing individual sounds in words; for example, "Tell me the first sound in *paste*" (/p/).
- *Phoneme Identity.* Recognizing the common sound in different words; for example, "Tell me the sound that is the same in *bike, boy,* and *bell*" (/b/).
- *Phoneme Categorization.* Recognizing the word with the odd sound in a sequence of three or four words; for example, "Which word does not belong: *bus, bun, rug?*" (rug).
- *Phoneme Blending.* Listening to a sequence of separately spoken sounds and combining them to form a recognizable word; for example, "What word is /s/ /k/ /u/ /l/?" (school).
- *Phoneme Segmentation.* Breaking down a word into its sounds by tapping out or counting the sounds or by pronouncing and positioning a marker for each sound; for example, "How many phonemes in *ship?*" (three).
- *Phoneme Deletion.* Recognizing what word remains when a specified phoneme is removed; for example, "What is *smile* without the /s/?" (mile).

Many children acquire PA effortlessly, but there are many more, irrespective of their IQs, for whom PA tasks are extraordinarily difficult. Without PA, a child will have difficulty with seemingly simple tasks, such as generating some words that rhyme with *cat* or substituting the /h/ sound for the /k/ sound in *cat* and figuring out what the new word is. Before children can accomplish those tasks, they must be able to identify and manipulate the individual phonemes in words. This skill is a critical prerequisite to acquiring the alphabetic principle: *the concept that there is a systematic relationship between the sounds of our language and the written letters.* Students who enter kindergarten with low PA skills are at high risk of reading failure and need immediate and intensive interventions. Children do not tend to outgrow phonemic deficits or develop PA skills with physical maturation (Liberman & Shankweiler, 1985).

There are four ways students can acquire PA. They can be genetically endowed so as to acquire PA skills in a seemingly effortless way. They can be environmentally blessed with parents and other caregivers who have talked to them constantly, played word games incessantly, and read aloud nursery rhymes and poetry every night at bedtime. Students can even be doubly blessed with great genes *and* a fabulous environment. Or, failing the advantages of nature, nurture, or both, they can acquire PA skills from highly effective teachers using research-based curricula taught explicitly, systematically, supportively, and intensively.

WHEN SHOULD PHONEMIC ■ AWARENESS BE TAUGHT?

Students who have difficulty acquiring PA may lack the experiences with language necessary to foster it, and/or may not be "wired" or biologically predisposed to figure out the structure of speech and connect that with print.

—Moats (2006, p. 3)

In a meta-analysis of early literacy studies, the National Early Literacy Panel (2008a) found that conventional reading and writing skills that are developed between birth and five years (preschool and kindergarten) are strongly related to later conventional literacy skills. Among the variables was PA and the ability to detect, manipulate, or analyze the auditory aspects of spoken language (including the ability to distinguish or segment words, syllables, or phonemes), independent of meaning.

Teaching children about the alphabet (e.g., letter names or letter sounds) or simple phonics tasks (e.g., blending letter sounds to make words) seemed to enhance the effects of PA training. The National Early Literacy Panel (2008b) found the following in their synthesis of scientific research on the development of early literacy skills in children from birth to five years of age:

> The code-focused instructional efforts reported statistically significant and moderate to large effects across a broad spectrum of early literacy outcomes. Code-focused interventions consistently demonstrated positive effects directly on children's conventional literacy skills. (p. 3)

This report confirms and builds on the findings of the Report of the National Reading Panel (National Institute of Child Health and Human Development [NICHD], 2000), finding that children's PA skills (their ability to distinguish sounds within auditory language) are an important predictor of later literacy achievements and suggesting that preschool is not too early to begin PA instruction.

In a comparison of studies conducted with kindergarten through second-grade students severely at risk, those programs with a literacy focus [i.e., explicit instruction in phonemic awareness and decoding] yielded an estimated mean effect size between approximately three and a half to four times larger than those for studies that did not use a literacy-focused curriculum (National Early Literacy Panel, 2008a, p. 196).

For students who are deficient in PA skills as determined by an assessment or students who exhibit other signs of disability or delay in kindergarten, the time to begin PA training is immediately, *before* formal reading instruction is initiated (O'Connor, Jenkins, & Slocum, 1993). If students begin formal reading instruction and fail, which they are almost certain to do without the ability to identify and manipulate the phonemes of the English language, both teacher and students will be frustrated. As students learn to read, PA diminishes in importance (Mehta et al., 2005), but at the preschool and kindergarten level, it should be the central focus of instruction for those students who do not have it.

■ THE ROLE OF PHONEMIC AWARENESS IN SKILLED READING

Effective preschool and kindergarten teachers have always included word play and rhyming games in their lesson plans. Perhaps they have instinctively known that children need these language skills to be successful readers. However, the difference between that kind of incidental instruction and the way we now know PA must be taught in order to catch students at risk of reading failure is huge. Our earlier conception of language skills as developmental in nature permitted us to explain away those students who didn't get it as not ready (Francis, Shaywitz, Stuebing, Shaywitz, & Fletcher, 1996). We believed that students who didn't readily catch on to natural and informal language activities just needed more time to mature. We retained them in kindergarten to give them another year to mature or placed them in a developmental first-grade or an ungraded primary class. Marilyn Adams (1990) reminds us that

> The key to phonemic awareness seems to lie more in training than in age or maturation. If these children have not received the proper exposure to print and sound in either their homes or their kindergarten classrooms by age five and a half, what is there to suggest that they will by the time they are six and a half? (p. 331)

The big idea of learning to read is known as the *alphabetic principle.* This principle has nothing to do with knowing the alphabet song or being able to identify isolated letters by name. It is *"the understanding that there are systematic and predictable relationships between written letters and spoken sounds"* (Armbruster, Lehr, & Osborn, 2001, p. 12). When students understand that spoken sounds correspond to letters of the alphabet, they are on their way to becoming skilled readers and writers. As students acquire PA skills, they are gradually led to an understanding of the alphabetic principle (Liberman, Shankweiler, & Liberman, 1989). Absent PA skills, students come to a dead-end on the learning to read road.[2] Students without PA can be found in affluent suburban schools as well as in high-poverty inner-city schools. One cannot assume that any given child has PA skills; that is why early assessment is critical. When eager kindergarten teachers launch immediately into their favorite food phonics activities or begin to teach the letter names along with the sounds, they are literally closing the door to literacy for students at risk.[3]

Most published phonics programs assume that students already have phonemic abilities, and some students do. However, those students who do not have PA will struggle to make sense of phonics instruction and exhibit difficulties with sounding and blending new words, retaining words from one day to the next, and learning to spell (Snow, Burns, & Griffin, 1998, p. 55). These students will muddle through kindergarten, hit a brick wall in first grade, and shortly thereafter begin to exhibit behavior problems, emotional distress, or even symptoms of physical illness.

If you have ever tried to teach a very bright student who had reading difficulties and you were unable to solve the riddle of why nothing seemed to work, lack of PA may well have been the reason. Because phonological abilities are relatively independent of overall intelligence (Vellutino & Scanlon, 1987; Wagner & Torgesen, 1987), a teacher can fairly assume that if a student with a normal or even high IQ and satisfactory listening comprehension is floundering in reading, one highly probable explanation for the problem is lack of PA skills. The student who cannot hear the individual phonemes in spoken words is unable to take the next step in acquiring the ability to read: learning how these sounds correspond to the letters of the alphabet.

When I asked one researcher about the importance of PA, he called it the "500-pound gorilla." The description is not terribly scientific, but it succinctly summarizes the major role that PA plays in reading success. If a 500-pound gorilla doesn't get your attention with regard to the importance of PA instruction, consider the scientific evidence found in the next section.

SCIENTIFIC EVIDENCE FOR PHONEMIC AWARENESS INSTRUCTION

The Report of the National Reading Panel (NICHD, 2000) reviewed multiple experimental and quasi-experimental studies of PA instruction and reported positive effects on reading, spelling, and phonological development, not only for students at risk but also for normal achievers (Ball & Blachman, 1991; Byrne & Fielding-Barnsley, 1989; Cunningham, 1990; Lie, 1991; Lundberg, Frost, & Peterson, 1988; O'Connor et al., 1993; Torgesen, Wagner, & Rashotte, 1997; Vellutino & Scanlon, 1987). In a comprehensive review of the following most time-intensive intervention studies (Brown & Felton, 1990; Foorman, Fletcher, Francis, Schatschneider, & Mehta, 1998; Iversen & Tunmer, 1993; Torgesen, Alexander, et al., 2001; Torgesen, Wagner, Rashotte, & Herron, 2003; Torgesen, Wagner, Rashotte, Rose, et al., 1999), Torgesen (2002) concluded, "Intensive preventive instruction can bring the average word-reading skills of children at risk for reading disabilities solidly into the average range" (p. 94). There are several prerequisites to implementing the kind of PA instruction that Torgesen describes:

- Knowledgeable, skilled, and committed teachers
- Strong instructional support from administrators, specialists, and coaches
- Adequate amounts of time to bring students to mastery

EFFECTIVE INSTRUCTIONAL PRACTICES FOR TEACHING PHONEMIC AWARENESS

In order to teach them all to read in kindergarten, instruction must be *differentiated, explicit, systematic, supportive, intensive,* and *specialized.* These six attributes of instruction are applicable and important at every grade level and in every content area, but they are especially critical in beginning reading instruction where early failure and discouragement can lead to a downward spiral of academic defeat. Figure 1.1 defines these six attributes, and I discuss them more fully just ahead.

Differentiated Instruction

To fully appreciate the importance of differentiating PA instruction in kindergarten, consider the range of PA skills or abilities that an average class of students brings to school on the first day. As we describe the various levels of PA among the students in this class, consider how you might differentiate instruction for them according to the definitions in Figure 1.1. Figure 1.2 illustrates our average classroom of 24 students graphically. The percentages given in this description apply to the total population of kindergarten students across the nation and are seldom found in exactly this configuration in your district, school, or classroom.

The single student in the Row 1 comes to school knowing how to read. He will be reading independently and often widely from the first day. You may have no students who

Figure 1.1   The Attributes of Effective Instruction for Students at Risk

Differentiated	
Specifically designed to match the differing instructional needs of students with differing instructional approaches and programs	Differentiated instruction, in the context of providing reading instruction, especially to students at risk, is based on and evaluated by various assessments. Although there are models of differentiation that describe varying instructional approaches based on pathways to the brain (Sprenger, 1999), multiple intelligences (Gardner, 1983), or various learning styles (Sternberg, 1996; Gregorc, 1985; McCarthy, 1997), they do not meet the stringent research-based requirements of response to intervention (RTI) and the Individuals with Disabilities Education Improvement Act (IDEA; 2004). When differentiating in the context of teaching the core program, establishing student centers based on task difficulty or reading level is advisable (see the Case Study in Chapter 2). However, differentiated instruction as related to RTI and IDEA focuses on particular weaknesses of students who have failed to respond to whole-group instruction and need more explicit, systematic, and supportive instruction in a small group, or failing progress in the classroom, more intensive and specialized instruction outside of the classroom.
Explicit	
Plain in language, distinctly expressed, clearly stated, not merely implied	The sequences of teaching and teacher actions during intervention instruction must be conspicuous (Dixon, Carnine, & Kame'enui, 1992). For example, during phonemic awareness and phonics instruction, there must be adequate teacher modeling (I do it) in order for students to see, hear, and understand the task or the skill and ample opportunities for students to concretely represent sounds with manipulatives or say the sounds with teacher support (we do it), before moving to the final phase of the instructional sequence when students are able to demonstrate the task or skill on their own (you do it).
Systematic	
Characterized by the use of a method of plan	The skills that are needed to acquire the alphabetic principle cannot be learned sporadically or planned on the spur of the moment. To be effective, instruction must be organized and sequential, particularly for phonemic awareness and phonics.
Supportive	
To uphold by aid, encouragement, or countenance; to keep from failing or declining	Instruction must be scaffolded (i.e., the tasks that students are asked to do must be graduated in difficulty, with each one being only slightly more difficult than the last). Scaffolded instruction ensures success and keeps students feeling confident and motivated to learn.
Intensive	
Concentrated, extensive, and thorough	For the students most at risk, instruction must be intensive in one of three ways: (a) time intensive, sometimes providing two or three times as much instruction as required for other students, (b) teacher intensive, sometimes requiring teachers with more specialized training, and (c) content intensive, requiring a more extensive and thorough exposure to the skills and knowledge that are needed.
Specialized	
Designed for a specific purpose, more expert	For the students most at risk, instruction must be designed with their learning difficulties and profiles in mind. The instructional scripts, scope and sequence, and examples and nonexamples must be chosen to meet their unique learning needs.

Figure 1.2   Average Kindergarten Class

Row 1: 5% of students will come to school already reading.

Row 2: 20%–30% of students will learn to read regardless of the instructional approach that is used.

Row 3: 20%–30% of students will require systematic, explicit, and supportive instruction, as well as additional opportunities to learn.

Row 4: 20%–30% of students will require systematic, explicit, and supportive instruction with intensive opportunities to learn.

Row 5: 5% of students will have a reading disability and will require special education services.

Source: Eldo Bergman, MD (personal communication, July 2000), McEwan (2004b), and J. K. Torgesen (personal communication, July 2002).

are reading at this level, or you may have enough for an instructional group. The students in Row 2 arrive at school on the cusp of learning to read. They will learn to read regardless of the instructional approach or materials being used. When presented with lessons from the core reading program, they readily acquire the alphabetic principle. They are motivated,

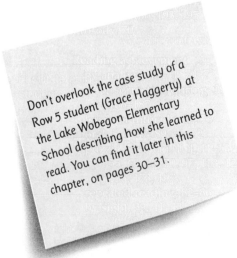

See page 48 for a description of how to provide differentiated instruction using centers in heterogeneously grouped first-grade classrooms. To explore the research regarding skill-based instructional groups, see pages 48–49. For a way to group students for reading that targets instruction to students' precise instructional levels and gets astounding results, see pages 189–192.

enthusiastic, and successful in their reading and likely will be strong students throughout their school careers. In some schools, there may be more students sitting in the first two rows than you find in this figure. Conversely, in other schools there may be few, if any, students in the first two rows. Students in Rows 1–2 readily learn all you have to teach and are often even ready to independently manage their own instructional activities, or if encouraged and instructed, to help other students. Ideally, these students will have an enrichment booster session with appropriate instruction while students more at risk are receiving intensive interventions.

The 20%–30% of students in Row 3 requires explicit, systematic, supportive PA instruction and may even need enhanced opportunities to learn in addition to the top-notch core program instruction they receive during the regular reading block. These opportunities could include small group instruction to supplement the core reading program, instructional enhancements designed by the teacher as part of the reading block instruction, buddy readers at school, and whenever possible, strong parental support at home. Row 3 students are particularly vulnerable to inconsistent instruction and classroom management. They will only be able to maintain the gains they realize in Grades K–3 and achieve grade-level reading scores in the upper grades if they have highly effective teachers with high expectations, excellent classroom management skills, and warm, caring relationships with students throughout their elementary school careers.

The Row 4 students in our imaginary classroom are at high risk for reading failure. They not only require *explicit, systematic,* and *supportive* instruction, but they also will likely need *intensive* and *specialized* intervention instruction. The intervention program might be taught by a specialist like a special education teacher, speech pathologist, or trained interventionist who has extensive experience in bringing the most challenging readers to grade level. It will focus on the precise and immediate needs of the student. The intervention may be taught during one or even two periods of the school day in addition to the regular reading class.

The single student in Row 5 is the only student from this average class who has a documented reading disability and thus is eligible for special education services. The primary difference between the Row 5 student in our imaginary class and similar students in schools without intensive and specialized PA instruction is that our student will begin learning to read on the first day of preschool or kindergarten.

Don't overlook the case study of a Row 5 student (Grace Haggerty) at the Lake Wobegon Elementary School describing how she learned to read. You can find it later in this chapter, on pages 30–31.

The models selected by schools to structure how differentiated instruction is delivered depend on the number of students at risk, the size of the school, and the availability of support personnel to deploy at certain periods of the school day. In a study investigating practices in high-poverty Reading First schools with strong interventions programs as measured by the percentage of students who began a school year at risk for reading difficulties but who met grade-level expectations by the end of the school year, reading instruction was scheduled in two ways (Crawford & Torgesen, 2007, p. 7):

- A 90-minute reading block and 30–45 minutes of time scheduled outside of that block to deliver intervention instruction. In this format, the intervention instruction was provided by teachers other than the classroom teacher.
- A reading block of 105–120 minutes in which intensive intervention was included and the instruction was provided by the classroom teacher or other support personnel in the classroom.

Each highly successful school in the study brought its own unique problems and solutions to the challenge of finding the time and people to teach them all to read. In some instances, in large schools with a majority of students needing intensive instruction, students were homogeneously grouped for a "walk to reading" period in which every available teacher was deployed to work with one group of three to five students, usually a smaller group than in the average classroom. Here is an important ratio: The greater the number of students at risk of reading failure in the school overall, the greater the number of smaller groups required. Some schools used special area teachers (art, music, and PE) who were especially trained in the use of a structured and scripted intervention, to reduce group sizes, and provide targeted instruction (Crawford & Torgesen, 2007, pp. 8–10).

Decisions about how to differentiate the content or program, the amount of time needed, and the level of teacher expertise are based on formative assessment data using instruments that are normative and research-based as well as programs that are known to get results.

Case Study

Explicitly Teaching Routines and Rules—Getting Ready to Learn

The very idea that a heterogeneous, high-poverty, multicultural group of 25 children could learn to read by the end of kindergarten might seem like a pipe dream. It can be done, however. One secret (in addition to using a research-based program) is teaching the students rules, routines, and rubrics for behavior, before even thinking about lesson plans to teach PA. Paula Larson has been teaching kindergarten for 16 years and has perfected the following approach. She shares her expertise with those who are eager to teach them all to read.

Teachers must believe that five-year-olds (or any age students) can sit and wait for their turn, listen to others, and keep their bodies still for a full 20 to 30 minutes of PA instruction. I keep my expectations extremely high to have the results I do. Teachers must remember that if students are not attending, they are not processing the information and skills being taught. It is impossible to talk and listen at the same time, so I am really tough on my students. I nail them the first time they start squirming. But I also shower them with praise when they get it right.

I teach three nonnegotiable and consistently enforced rules to my students:

1. *When I am talking, you are not.* I ask my students to repeat that sentence with me often, until they reach the point of automaticity. When I say, "When I am talking, you are . . ." they answer, "*not.*"

2. *Sitting tall.* Most of my instruction takes place while students are sitting on the carpet. Rather than listing all of the things I want students to do while they're on the carpet, I teach them

(Continued)

(Continued)

exactly what I mean by the phrase "sitting tall." It means folded legs, hands in laps, mouths closed, eyes on me, and leave your shoe laces alone. Once I have modeled, we practice, and once they have mastered sitting tall, all I need to say at the beginning of a lesson or as a reminder is, "Sitting tall."

3. *Quiet hands.* I explain to my students that they can only answer a question if I call on them, and that in order for me to call on them, I must see what I call, *quiet hands.* Quiet hands are hands that are raised without students talking at the same time. I explain, model, and we practice how that works until they have it. I cannot and will not call on someone who does not have a quiet hand. In the beginning, my students say what they want to say the minute they put their hands in the air. I stop them. I remind them. Then I call on a student who is doing the right thing. I make positive comments about that student doing the right thing. And then the very next person I always call on is the student who was talking out of turn earlier. I praise that student profusely for using a quiet hand.

This process takes some time in the beginning of the year, but far less time than you might expect if you are consistent. I often say this during a question-and-answer time: "With a quiet hand, who can tell me what the setting of this story is?" Then I have communicated the expectation at the beginning, rather than taking time from the lesson.

Researchers who have investigated the relationship between reading failure and behavioral problems like poor task engagement and lack of self-control have found that children with reading problems in first grade were significantly more likely to display behavior problems in third grade. As well, students with attention difficulties in first grade were more likely to have reading difficulties in third grade (Morgan, Farkas, Tufis, & Sperling, 2008). The importance of teaching task engagement and self-control along with reading cannot be overestimated.

Source: Reprinted with permission of Paula Larson.

In a heterogeneous class like our imaginary one, differentiated instruction is essential to meeting every student's needs. The whole class will participate in the core reading program's lessons to benefit from phonemic awareness, phonics, vocabulary, and comprehension instruction. However, during other periods of the day, the instructional groups might look like this. Row 1 and parts of Row 2, depending on how advanced their reading levels are, will immediately begin to work on more child-managed, meaning-focused activities. The students in Rows 3–5 are carefully monitored during the early weeks of the school year and at the first sign of difficulty receive some kind of small-group intervention delivered by the classroom teacher while other students are working in centers or, in the case of the early readers, working with the media specialist on mini-research reports.

A block of time devoted to differentiated instruction must be scheduled into the daily reading block. In a study comparing the effects of a whole-group phonics and spelling instructional approach on students' writing, Williams and Hufnagel (2005) found that the one-size-fits-all approach had no impact on the writing of either the highest- or lowest-achieving students. Only the average-achieving students were able to transfer the skills taught during the treatment to their writing. The conclusion: Differentiation of instruction is essential for all students to maximize their academic potential.

Explicit, Systematic, and Supportive Instruction

Successful intervention studies tell us a great deal about what PA instruction should look like in kindergarten and first-grade classrooms. It is explicit, systematic, and highly supportive. It is most effective when the following conditions are present:

There are sufficient amounts of direct instruction and coaching before students are expected to do a task independently. The instructional sequence (I do it, we do it, you do it) is essential when teaching PA to students at risk. Figure 1.3 shows a brief sample lesson. Some PA instructional materials merely describe an activity. The teacher's manual may launch immediately into the "you do it" phase of a lesson without showing teachers how to model for and coach their students ("I do it" and "we do it").

The teacher supports new learning by modeling the correct answer, guiding students to give the correct answer, and then monitoring students as they give correct answers independently. Enhancements involving the "I do it" portion of the lesson help make strategies such as phonemic segmentation and blending more explicit for students. Enhancing a lesson by adding more "you do it" segments provides needed practice on essential sound production skills in both PA and letter–sound correspondence tasks.

Figure 1.3   I Do It, We Do It, You Do It, Apply It Lesson Plan

Step 1: I Do It	The teacher demonstrates. For example, the teacher introduces the sound for the letter *p* by showing the letter to the students and saying it for them. The teacher then stops to ask this critical question internally: Are the students ready to move on to Step 2?
Step 2: We Do It	The teacher and students do the activity together, with immediate feedback from the teacher. For example, the teacher practices saying the *p* sound together with the students. If students say the sound incorrectly, the teacher assists them so they say it correctly. The teacher then stops to ask, "Are students ready to move on to Step 3?"
Step 3: You Do It	The students do the activity independently, and the teacher gives feedback about how the students did. This step is a practice phase with the teacher still involved. For example, the teacher asks the students to look at the letter *p* and say the sound it represents. The teacher then has the students read words that have letters they already know except for the newly learned *p* sound. The teacher then stops to ask, "Are the students ready to move on to Step 4?"
Step 4: Apply It	The student applies the skill to a novel problem, cooperative group activity, or real-life situation. For example, the teacher has students play the Oh, No game, where a letter sound is called out. Students point their thumbs down if it's not the sound represented by the letter *p*. Their thumbs go up in the air whenever a *p* is called out. Several days later, the teacher will have students spell words that contain the letter *p*.

Source: McEwan & Damer (2000, p. 143).

Classroom Snapshot

Let's wander down the hallway and peek into a kindergarten classroom. It's the end of the school year and all of the students are sitting tall on the rug in front of the teacher. They are totally focused on the teacher and her presentation material on an easel. The teacher points to some words and word parts. "My turn," she says. She points to individual letters and makes their sounds. "Your turn, get ready," and the children chorally respond as she slides her pen underneath the letters. "Fast way," she says, and everyone says the word normally as she slides the pen quickly. Now she chooses another word or set of letters and the process repeats. The pace is furious. The only letup comes when the teacher senses that one or more children are behind the others and are repeating others' responses rather than formulating their own. The repetition, alternation, and sheer speed of the prompts and responses create a magnetic field around the teacher, drawing everyone irresistibly into the energy and excitement she generates for learning. One of the visitors with whom I'm watching says, "This is too mechanical for me. Where's the creativity and the fun?" Perhaps the process looks mechanical today, but there will be plenty of opportunities for creativity when all of the children in the class can read effortlessly and devote their full attention to the content rather than struggling to figure out what the words are.

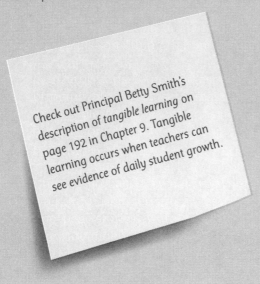

Check out Principal Betty Smith's description of tangible learning on page 192 in Chapter 9. Tangible learning occurs when teachers can see evidence of daily student growth.

Students have ample opportunities to practice the individual sounds after teachers have orally modeled the sounds. An important aspect of the practice phase for students is *feeling* the individual sounds when they say them. Some students may even need to see themselves or the teacher (or both) in a mirror to understand precisely what is happening to their lips and tongues when a specific sound is produced. Some programs (e.g., Lindamood & Lindamood, 1998) label the sounds that are made—for example, "lip-poppers," "lip coolers," and "tongue coolers"—to help children understand how a sound feels (p. 34).

Teachers frequently review and reinforce what has been taught previously. A 5-minute review session while waiting for a birthday treat or music class will pay enormous dividends for all students and especially for struggling students. Review sessions are not optional for those students who are seriously deficient. The most successful school intervention programs provide small-group, skill-based sessions with the classroom teacher to reteach and review lessons that were taught to the whole group.

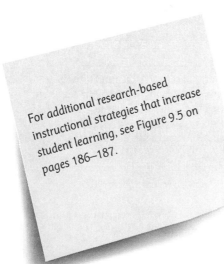

For additional research-based instructional strategies that increase student learning, see Figure 9.5 on pages 186–187.

Teachers consistently employ the following instructional strategies during their PA instruction:

- *Advance Organizers.* Prior to beginning a lesson, the teacher tells students what they will be doing during the lesson, why the activities are important, and how they are to behave during the lesson. A visual organizer is frequently presented along with a brief verbal description of what will happen during the lesson.
- *Unison Response.* The teacher signals all students to answer together to maximize practice and regularly monitor student progress. The teacher asks questions of individual students as an additional check of progress only after the whole group is correctly answering all of the questions.
- *Judicious Use of Teacher Talk.* The teacher presents the lesson in concise statements using language the students understand. The teacher does not present information unrelated to the task the students are to complete or provide verbose explanations. Nor does the teacher distract herself (or her students) with comments unrelated to the lesson.
- *Perky Pace.* There is a brisk presentation of questions or signals made possible by minimizing (a) the amount of time between activities (transition) and (b) the amount of time between a student's answer and the teacher's next question or prompt.
- *Increased Opportunities for Practice.* The teacher maximizes opportunities for student practice by increasing the number of practice items and finding additional time during the school day for practice.
- *Systematic Error Correction.* The teacher provides immediate corrective feedback to students by modeling the correct answer, guiding students to the correct answer as needed, and then asking the corrected student to give the answer independently. The teacher then uses delayed testing by asking the student to repeat the correct answer later in the lesson.
- *Cumulative Review.* The teacher adds examples of previously learned material to examples of newly learned material. Cumulative review teaches students to discriminate between new and old material and helps build student retention of previously learned material.
- *Example Selection.* The teacher uses instructional examples that include common skills students can use to read or write stories. The teacher also selects examples that allow for a high rate (95% accuracy) of student success by including an appropriate blend of new and previous learning.
- *Motivational Strategies.* The teacher strengthens appropriate academic and social behaviors by using positive reinforcement. The teacher increases social behaviors (e.g., staying in seat, raising hand before talking, keeping hands to self) by delivering consistent praise for those behaviors. The goal is to maintain a 3:1 ratio of praise for appropriate behavior to a correction for problem behavior. The teacher also delivers reinforcement to peers who are displaying appropriate behavior. For academic behaviors, the teacher adjusts the level of reinforcement to fit the difficulty level of the task. For example, the teacher provides constant praise when students are working hard on a new and difficult task. For familiar practice tasks, the teacher praises students after they have finished the entire task.

Intensive and Specialized Intervention

Students at risk of reading failure (the students in Rows 3–5) may need more intensive and specialized PA interventions than can be provided by the classroom teacher. An intervention is an enhanced opportunity to learn that provides struggling students with additional time added to what is provided during the regular reading block, a smaller group in which to learn, a more intensive approach to mastering PA skills or acquiring the alphabetic principle, and a teacher with more specialized skills, for example the speech pathologist or reading or special education teacher.

Teaching them all to read is a highly complex undertaking requiring the skillful management of time, data, instructional programs, and human resources at levels previously unseen in elementary schools. Several initiatives, models, and legislative mandates have helped some teachers and created confusion for others about what *must* be done and what *may* be done. They include response to intervention (RTI); Reading First, the three-tier framework, and Individuals with Disabilities Education Act (IDEA; 2004). An understanding of the way these various structures and mandates relate to one another is basic to providing instruction that is differentiated, explicit, systematic, supportive, intensive, and specialized.

Case Study

Learning to Read in Lake Wobegon—The Student in Row 5

Grace Haggerty* is a vibrant 12-year-old, a student at Lakeside Middle School in an affluent suburb of a large midwestern city. Grace loves to read, which is surprising given how much she hated it in first grade. Her current favorites are *A Single Shard* (Park, 2003), *The Westing Game* (Raskin, 1978), *Once Upon a Marigold* (Ferris, 2004), and *A View From Saturday* (Konigsburg, 1996). Grace's reading trajectory is a cautionary tale for educators who desire to teach them all to read.

Grace attended a Montessori School for three years and then enrolled in the first grade at Lake Wobegon Elementary School (LWES) in the fall of 2002. At that point, she was able to read the book, *A Pig Can Jig* (Rasmussen, 1985). Her parents noted that she was slow to acquire the color names and often could not retrieve words quickly during her conversations with them, but at that point, Grace was a beginning first-grade student, reading very simple kindergarten text. However, by November, her mother was deeply concerned because Grace's reading progress was stalled.

The teacher assured her, "Don't worry. Everything will be fine. Grace is just figuring things out." Sally Haggerty knew differently. Grace had become emotional and withdrawn and had lost her appetite. At mid-year, Grace's teacher finally became concerned.

She told the Haggertys, "Grace doesn't seem to understand the importance of school. She has her own time line for when she will finish work. I'm concerned for how she will manage in second grade." The Reading Recovery teacher (Reading Recovery Council of North America, 2008), however, deemed Grace ineligible for her program because she was able to self-correct while she was reading. Neither the classroom teacher nor the Reading Recovery teacher had any suggestions for how to help Grace.

In desperation, the Haggertys took Grace to a private reading clinic for an evaluation. The clinician was almost certain that Grace was dyslexic but first wanted to see how Grace would respond to intensive intervention.[4] Grace began one-to-one tutoring in 45-minute sessions twice a week, using a combination of strategies from the *Orton-Gillingham Approach* (Orton Academy, 2008) and *Wilson Reading System* (Wilson, 1988) programs. Within six weeks, Grace was happy again. She was confident, and she loved to go to reading. Grace's classroom teacher commended the Haggertys and said that whatever they were doing, they should keep it up, because Grace was doing much better in school. At the end of first grade, Grace was reading about 44 words per minute and gaining about .9 words per week.

After paying for private tutoring twice per week during most of first grade, Grace's parents began to feel the economic pinch. They also began to ask the hard question: Why should we pay for outside tutoring when our very affluent school system to which we pay tens of thousands of dollars in taxes every year should be teaching Grace to read? While Grace continued to learn to read with her twice-weekly tutor, her parents explored what it would take to get similar services in the Lake Wobegon School District. After many phone calls and meetings, a district administrator finally offered the following options for meeting Grace's needs: a guided reading group in the regular second-grade classroom at LWES, a transfer to another school to receive services from the resource room teacher, or occasional help from the district's traveling English language learner (ELL) teacher. Most disappointing to the Haggertys was the astonishing fact that no one in the district was trained to explicitly, systematically, supportively, and intensively teach students to read.

The stonewalling and circling of the educational wagons in Lake Wobegon can be seen in the stacks of forms, memos, and directives that district administrators used in an attempt to convince them that the district or school was right and the Haggertys were wrong about what Grace needed to become a successful reader. Finally, the Haggertys and their support team—the director of the reading clinic who taught Grace to read and their lawyer—convinced the superintendent, who was a very intelligent and reasonable man, that their daughter's needs could only be met at the reading clinic and that the district should pay for the tutoring. A schedule was developed, and Grace left school four days a week for one hour of one-to-one reading instruction. Grace thrived and adjusted to her new schedule quite nicely.

By November 2004, Grace's reading abilities exploded. She began reading the Lemony Snicket (Snicket & Helquist, various dates) books independently and requested *Little House on the Prairie* (Wilder, 1953) books for Christmas. She scored a personal best—80 words correct per minute—on a test of oral reading fluency.

At an end-of-year individual education program (IEP) meeting to discuss Grace's progress in third grade, the new principal at LWES remarked to the Haggertys, "You can't really know if Grace's progress was due to the services she received at the reading clinic or what we have done here at school." She seemed not to know that the teachers at LWES were unable to teach Grace to read.

After Grace's third grade, the Haggertys moved from Lake Wobegon to Lakeside, where Grace attended a small Catholic school for Grades 4–6 and did very well. She then begged her parents to let her attend the Lakeside Middle School where she is now thriving. The good news is that Grace did not fall through the cracks. What saved her was an intensive, specialized intervention taught in a systematic, explicit, and scaffolded way. The bad news is that the educators in the Lake Wobegon School District refused to shift their paradigms—even for a student who is seriously reading disabled sitting in Row 5.

* Pseudonym

Response to Intervention and Special Education

The term *response to intervention* has two distinct meanings about which educators must be clear as they seek to structure intensive and specialized interventions for readers at risk. The first meaning comes from IDEA (2004), which specifies that a local education agency "may use a process that determines if the child responds to scientific, research-based intervention as part of the evaluation procedures" (34 CFR §§300.307, 300.309, and 300.311). In this context, "response to intervention can be understood as a diagnostic approach for determining which students are entitled to special educational services" (Torgesen, 2007, p. 1). This meaning has specific special education requirements attached to it and applies to determining the eligibility for special education services of students at any grade level.

The reauthorization of IDEA (2004) put educators on notice regarding a shift from a remediation–special education paradigm to a focus on prevention through intervention. The new regulations under IDEA 2004 have changed from a discrepancy model that denied services to struggling students unless there was evidence of a significant discrepancy between their nonverbal IQ and level of school achievement.

The new model allows districts to use up to 15% of their Part B funds to provide support to students who have not been identified as eligible for special education services. This new category of services is referred to as *early intervening services* (EIS) and provides funds in the general education environment for students in Grades K–12, but with a special emphasis on Grades K–3. EIS include activities like professional development for teachers and other school staff to improve the delivery of scientifically based academic instruction and behavioral interventions and the provision of educational and behavioral evaluations, service, and support, including scientifically based literacy instruction. EIS gives educators resources and tools to immediately support struggling students. Now they can intervene early and intensively, instead of waiting.

Response to Intervention and the Three-Tier Model

The second meaning of response to intervention, and the one that is more commonly understood and used by educators, refers to a model for organizing early reading instruction developed by Sharon Vaughn (2005) at the University of Texas, commonly referred to as RTI. In the context of delivering early reading instruction at the elementary school level, the three-tier framework "is a way of thinking about instruction that emphasizes ongoing data collection and immediate intervention for any students who need it, not just those who are thought to be candidates for special education services. The RTI instructional model describes a general process that can be used with any grouping practices. Students can be grouped within class, within grade, or across grade as appropriate. The 3-tier framework can be used with any research-based program" (Vaughn, 2005, p.1). Although the three-tier framework was meant to be descriptive of how intervention services could be structured, many schools have interpreted the suggestions found at the University of Texas's Web site as a prescription that must be followed.

However, since the three-tier framework is not a reading program with a specific curricular content or a set or recommended instructional strategies, it can be viewed as one of many ways to organize a heterogeneous group of students with varying learning strengths and needs into homogeneous instructional groups that provide specialized opportunities for all students to learn at their differing instructional levels. Since the days of the one-room school, effective teachers have organized students, irrespective of their ages or grade levels, into need-based groups.

The danger of implementing RTI and the three-tier framework as a mandate or prescription is that educators will lose sight of the big idea—meeting the needs of students at risk—and forget to use their own common sense and deep knowledge of their students, themselves, and the programs, bowing instead to artificial time lines and decision points as recommended by Vaughn (2005). The three-tier model often differentiates in the following way, but it doesn't have to (Foorman & Nixon, 2005):

- *Tier 1.* High-quality general education classroom instruction
- *Tier 2.* Small-group instruction delivered in the context of general education
- *Tier 3.* Individualized problem solving and special education eligibility determination as found in the RTI model (p. 26)

Hall (2008) advises, "The best implementations of RTI occur when leaders begin with a more fluid view of the tiers" (p. 110). Tier 3 of the three-tier model (or

Tier 4 in some models) is where response to intervention becomes a diagnostic approach for determining whether a specific student is entitled to special education services. However, "the validity of the RTI diagnostic approach for identifying students with learning disabilities depends critically on the quality of the RTI instructional model as it is implemented in a school or school district. If students do not receive high quality initial instruction, and do not have available to them reasonable interventions if they struggle in the classroom, then far too many students will be judged to have learning disabilities when they are clearly victims of weak instruction" (Torgesen, 2007, p. 1). In the absence of differentiated, explicit, systematic, supportive, intensive, and specialized reading instruction, RTI and the three-tier model becomes a more complicated and expensive means of getting the same results we have always achieved. If RTI is well implemented, the number of special education referrals should dramatically decrease, thereby giving special education teachers fewer students with whom to work and an opportunity to design and execute more effective instruction. The best model is one in which general education and special education services are provided in a seamless and integrated way.

Figure 1.4 describes the three-tier model in more detail.

Figure 1.4   The Three-Tier Model

Core Reading Program (Tier 1 Instruction)	The *core reading program* is the basic program in which all students receive instruction during the reading block. This program must include instruction in the big five components of reading identified by the National Reading Panel (NICHD, 2000; phonemic awareness, phonics, fluency, vocabulary, comprehension), as well as spelling and writing to ensure that students meet or exceed grade-level standards. A core program should address the instructional needs of the majority of students in a respective school or district. Most Reading First schools chose a basal reading series as their core program.
Supplementary Reading Program or Instruction (Tier 2 Instruction)	*Supplementary reading programs or instruction* go beyond the instruction provided by the core program because the core program does not provide the kind of instruction or enough practice in a key area to meet the needs of the students in a particular classroom or school. For example, teachers may observe that their core program does not provide enough instruction in vocabulary or PA to adequately meet the needs of the majority of their students and then design a classroom intervention to meet those needs.
Intervention Reading Program (Tier 3 Instruction)	*Intervention reading programs* are intended for students who are reading one or more years below grade level and who are struggling with a broad range of reading skills. They include instructional content based on the five essential components of reading instruction with explicit strategies, coordinated instructional sequences, ample practice opportunities, and aligned student materials. They are more intensive, explicit, systematic, and motivating than the instruction students have previously received but are aligned with them and reintroduce the skills or knowledge. Intervention programs are generally taught by specialists, and students are pulled out of the classroom.

Response to Intervention and Reading First

Reading First was the largest federal–state initiative ever conducted to prevent early reading difficulties. The budget was approximately 6 billion dollars over six years (2003–2009). To receive funds, states were required to submit applications that met specific requirements with regard to the nature of instruction, assessments, professional development, and school leadership. Approximately 5,200 schools in 1,550 districts in every state received awards. The Reading First legislation was written to require states to use instruction consistent with "scientifically based research in reading." Reading First funds were used primarily for professional development, curriculum materials, early assessments, and classroom and school libraries (Torgesen, 2007). RTI and Reading First are compatible in both philosophy and structure. However, many Reading First schools were slow to implement any intervention groups at all. The task of implementing new core programs with fidelity as mandated by Reading First was an almost insurmountable task for the lowest-performing schools because of lack of teacher knowledge about effective reading instruction (Hall, 2008). The goals of Reading First were far more ambitious than could be realized in such a short period of time. In 2007, more Reading First schools began implementing Tier 2 (classroom interventions that build on the core program) and Tier 3 instruction (specialized and intensive interventions that focus on a specific skill deficit and use a supplemental program). However, as noted by Torgesen (2007), teachers need to be highly effective, with the skills to use data to make decisions about student placement in intervention groups.

■ GUIDELINES FOR IMPLEMENTING PHONEMIC AWARENESS INSTRUCTION

Implementing a PA program in your classroom, school, or district should be undertaken only with careful planning, a thorough assessment of students, ample staff training, and comprehensive on-site coaching. The following guidelines will increase your likelihood of success:

• Choose a program that focuses on the two most important goals of PA training: (a) helping children to notice the phonemes in words (i.e., to discover their existence and distinctness) and (b) helping children to make the connection between the phonemes in words and the letters of the alphabet (Torgesen & Mathes, 2000, p. 43). Make sure that adequate attention is given to *segmenting, blending,* and *detection.*

• Be cautious about the use of activities that have not been field tested with students or activities that purport to be literature based. These activities are often developed around a poem, story, or favorite food without regard for the importance of a specific instructional sequence; they can easily confuse students at risk.

• Begin assessing students' progress in acquiring PA skills at the middle of kindergarten. Assessments are less reliable until students are acclimated to kindergarten. The following skills have been identified as valid predictors for the identification of students at risk of reading failure at various points along the primary reading continuum: PA and identification of letter sounds, rapid naming of letters, vocabulary knowledge, and word reading, especially word-reading fluency (Fletcher et al., 2002). These various skills have been incorporated into early screening instruments, such as those shown in Figure 1.5.

Figure 1.5 Assessments to Determine Phonological Awareness Skills and Processing

Test	Testing Time	Age or Grade Range	Publisher
Dynamic Indicators of Basic Early Literacy Skills (Good & Kaminski, 2000)	1–5 minutes	Grades K–3	Sopris West
Lindamood Auditory Conceptualization Test LAC (Lindamood & Lindamood, 1979)	10 minutes	Suitable for any age of individual who understands the concepts of *same* and *different*, numbers to four, and left-to-right progressions	PRO-ED
PALS-PreK (Invernizzi, Sullivan, Meier, & Swank, 2004)	10–15 minutes	Between the ages of 4 and 5	PRO-ED

Source: Adapted from Lonigan, McDowell, and Phillips (2004).

• Provide quality training and ongoing support for teachers. Any PA instruction program will benefit from the presence of a literacy coach or, at the very least, classroom support from the speech pathologist, to achieve maximum effectiveness. Teachers will need intensive training in both hearing and saying the individual sounds, for few, if any, teachers have had adequate preservice training to prepare them for teaching PA skills. Teachers will need opportunities to practice speaking more slowly and carefully so that students can hear and distinguish the sounds. A trainer or supervisor should test all teachers on their competence with the sounds before the program is launched.

• Provide expert assistance to teachers in adapting core reading program materials for use with large numbers of students at risk. They will need help in adapting, supplementing, and choosing which of the myriad suggested teaching activities really do support the development of PA.

• The mere presence of the terms *phonological awareness* or *phonemic awareness* in a catalog or sales brochure does not guarantee that a program will get results.

• Make sure that the sequence of activities moves from words to syllables to sounds and that students are also taught the letters of the alphabet, but only after the sounds have been mastered. Make sure that teachers are provided with adequate scripts and ample practice exercises. Beware of programs that do not offer alternatives and enhancements for children who need them.

• Anticipate that some children will not respond to whole-group instruction and will need more intense small-group or even one-to-one instruction. Be ready to intervene before these students fail.

• Acknowledge frustration and listen to teachers' concerns during the beginning weeks of instruction.

■ SUMMARIZING CHAPTER 1

PA instruction ensures that students are able to identify and manipulate sounds, an important prerequisite for mastering the spelling–sound correspondences and learning to decode. Students will require different amounts of PA instruction, depending on their needs. However, no student needs to fail to learn to read because of a phonemic deficiency. We have 20 years of research to show us how to teach PA, even to the readers most at risk. When you are tempted to give up on a student, remember Grace Haggerty, the lone student in Row 5.

■ NOTES

1. The *onset* is the part of the syllable that precedes its vowel. The *rime* is the part of a syllable (not a word) that consists of its vowel and any consonant sounds that come after it. Said another way, the onset consists of the initial consonant or consonant cluster in a syllable, and the rime is the vowel and remainder of the syllable. For example, in the word, *phonological,* the first syllable or onset-rime is *phon.* The onset is *ph-* and the rime is *-on.*

2. There are two other roadblocks: (1) failure to acquire the verbal knowledge and strategies that are specifically needed for comprehension of written material and (2) absence or loss of the initial motivation to read or failure to develop a mature appreciation of the rewards of reading (Torgesen, 2002, p. 89).

3. Teaching of the sounds of letters before teaching the letter names is recommended. Students who are at risk are more likely to come to school unable to identify the letters of the alphabet by name. Learning the letter names and the sounds at the same time is very confusing for these students (Bursuck & Damer, 2007, p. 70).

4. In 1995, the International Dyslexia Association proposed and adopted a new definition for dyslexia, one of several distinct learning disabilities. It is "a specific language-based disorder of constitutional origin characterized by difficulties in single word decoding" (Lyon, 1995, p. 5).

2

Phonics

Phonics is an understanding of the alphabetic principle (that letters either singly or in combination represent various sounds) and the ability to apply this knowledge in the decoding of unfamiliar words.

The great debate regarding the role of explicit phonics instruction in learning to read has been ongoing for decades.[1] Unfortunately, there have been no winners. Only losers—the students who passed through the primary grades without explicit, systematic phonics instruction. Oh, most students learn some phonics in school, but for many, it was just enough to be dangerous. These students gave the appearance of being able to read, but when called upon to retrieve a solid orthographic image of a word to read or spell independently with no coaching or context to give them a clue, they come up blank.

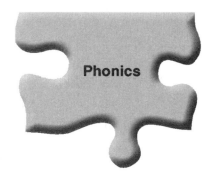

I was shocked not long ago to discover that my granddaughter who was recommended for placement in Fifth-Grade Advanced Language and Arts and Math by her fourth-grade teacher, was only reading at the third-grade level at the end of this so-called enriched experience. How was she able to keep this astonishing lack of reading ability under wraps for so long? I'm assuming that she did it with clever guessing, highly developed social and verbal skills, well-above-average writing skills, a little help from her friends, and a total lack of accountability for understanding anything she read by her teachers.

An online reading test, given as an afterthought in her fifth-grade Language Arts classroom, revealed this appalling academic deficiency. The teacher was stunned and embarrassed but had no suggestions for how to remediate the problem. The school had no programs to help her, either during the summer *or* the regular school year. Days before school was to adjourn for the summer, her mother called in a panic. My husband and I dropped everything and flew to the Midwest. I gave Abigail some simple tests and then had her tested by an expert. She confirmed what I already knew: Abigail didn't know all of her long and short vowels and was vague about quite a few consonant blends and digraphs as well. She readily admitted that she hated to read and hadn't read a complete book for more than two years. Her fluency, word and world knowledge, and comprehension were all stuck in third grade.

She was a whiz at soccer and softball, wrote fabulously imaginative stories, and was well liked by a wide circle of friends, but nobody was holding her accountable for comprehending what she read. She was getting by on sheer bravado. Abigail's mother ended up paying for private tutoring throughout the summer. Although she complained bitterly about attending summer school, Abigail filled in one of the missing pieces of *her* reading puzzle over the summer—phonics. However, catching up on the fluency, word and world knowledge, and comprehension pieces will be more difficult. All of her peers have passed her up. Once the Matthew effect kicks in for struggling readers, catching up is extraordinarily difficult. The term *Matthew effect* was first coined by sociologist Robert Merton (1968) and later picked up by Walberg and Tsai (1983) to describe an educational phenomenon. The term has its origins in the New Testament parable of the talents, in Matthew 25:29, in which according to Merton's initial interpretation, the rich get richer and the poor get poorer. As used by Stanovich (1986), the term describes the effect of reading deficits from which poor readers almost never recover—despite our most valiant efforts to remediate.

Watch for future references to the Matthew effect in Chapter 5 (page 101) and in Chapter 7 (pages 141 and 147). Difficulties in recovering from the Matthew effect make it imperative for educators to catch children before they fall through the cracks.

Abigail was what is called a confused decoder, a reader who demonstrates an overreliance on context usage, seeming to know a word one day and forgetting it the next (Carnine, Silbert, Kame'enui, & Tarver, 2004, p. 324). I call this approach to reading *the guessing syndrome.* It results from a disjointed approach to reading instruction characterized by the following: (1) lack of systematic and explicit phonics instruction so that students end up knowing some of the letter–sound correspondences and how to blend sounds to create words, but not deeply understanding the relationship between the arrangement of the letters in a word and its pronunciation; (2) the use of the three-cueing strategy (Does it make sense? Does it sound right? Does it look right?), which encourages students to use everything *but* their letter–sound knowledge to identify words, thus creating an insidious guessing habit that too frequently results in dysfluency and poor comprehension; and (3) an approach to reading instruction that eschews the regular assessment of discrete reading skills, like knowledge of letter–sound correspondences, preferring a holistic approach that allows students like Abigail to fall through the cracks. How can you prevent students from catching this dreaded syndrome? I'll explore the answer to that question in this chapter.

■ WHAT IS PHONICS AND HOW DO STUDENTS LEARN TO DECODE?

> *Decoding and comprehension . . . are the two halves of reading. But the two halves are not added together. Reading does not equal the sum of decoding and comprehension, for neither decoding in the absence of comprehension, nor*

PHONICS **39**

comprehension in the absence of decoding, leads to any amount of reading. A child who cannot decode cannot read; a child who cannot comprehend cannot read either. Literacy—reading ability—can only be found in the presence of both decoding and comprehension. Both skills are necessary; neither is sufficient.

—Gough, Hoover, and Peterson (1996, p. 3)

There are more instructional programs, workbooks, software, and videos on the market for teaching phonics than for any other aspect of reading. There are programs for parents, teachers, and even for adult nonreaders to teach themselves to read. If you had not noticed, phonics is popular. But what kind of phonics to teach is the big question for educators.

Heward, Wood, and Damer (2004) present a humorous but highly instructive workshop called Faux Fonics in which they describe several types of so-called phonics instruction that do not actually teach phonics at all. They define faux fonics as "any activity presumed to be phonics in which students are not expected to match letters to sounds or sounds to corresponding letters" (p. 9). In contrast, they offer these examples of genuine phonics instructional activities: (1) students are presented with a letter and say the corresponding sound or select the corresponding written representation of the sound or (2) students hear a sound and select or write the corresponding letter. Knowing the difference between a genuine research-based approach to teaching phonics and a poor imitation is important. Figure 2.1 compares

Figure 2.1   A Comparison Between Systematic and Nonsystematic Phonics Programs

Systematic Phonics Programs	Nonsystematic Phonics Programs
• Help teachers explicitly and systematically instruct students in how to relate letters and sounds, how to break spoken words into sounds, and how to blend sounds to form words	• Embed phonics in reading and writing activities
• Help students understand why they are learning the relationships between letters and sounds	• Teach letter–sound relationships incidentally
• Help students apply their knowledge of phonics as they read words, sentences, and text	• Focus on whole-word or meaning-based activities
• Help students apply what they learn about sounds and letters to the correct spelling of words in their own writing	• Pay limited attention to letter–sound relationships
• Can be adapted to the needs of individual students, based on assessments	• Provide little or no instruction in how to blend letters and pronounce words
• Include alphabetic knowledge, phonemic awareness, vocabulary development, and the reading of text, as well as phonics instruction	• Begin by teaching students a sight-word vocabulary of from 50 to 100 words, delaying instruction in the alphabetic principle until these have been mastered

Source: Adapted from Armbruster et al. (2001, pp. 16–17).

the characteristics of explicit, systematic phonics instruction with so-called phonics instruction that likely won't get results with readers at risk.

Phonics instruction that focuses solely on the letters and sounds of words and how they are related is known as *synthetic phonics*. Most synthetic phonics programs begin instruction by first teaching the letters of the alphabet (graphemes) and then matching those letters to the various sounds (phonemes) they represent. However, most students at risk arrive in kindergarten without any letter name knowledge, so beginning instruction with the sounds and then matching the sounds to letters is a far less confusing way to begin. That is why at least two popular Tier 3 intervention programs focus on teaching students to hear and reproduce the sounds before they match the sounds to the letters: (1) *LiPS* (Lindamood & Lindamood, 1998) and (2) *Phono-Graphix* (McGuinness & McGuinness, 1998).

Here's how matching sounds to spellings works in the *Phono-Graphix* program. There are 43 phonemes (separate sounds) of the English alphabet code as represented by approximately 100 letters and letter combinations in the *Phono-Graphix* program (McGuinness & McGuinness, 1998). It teaches the majority of these sound–spelling correspondences in two levels. Level 1 teaches the basic code (i.e., one sound to one letter correspondences with no digraphs). Skills covered in the lessons include phoneme analysis, segmenting, blending, reading, and spelling. These skills are practiced to mastery in simple three-sound words and words containing consonant clusters. Level 2 teaches the advanced code that includes consonant and vowel digraphs followed by phonemes with multiple spelling (i.e., one sound to many letters) as well as code overlaps, instances where the same set of letters make several different sounds.

When referring to the sound (phoneme) represented by a grapheme, researchers and curriculum developers commonly place slashes before and after a letter, like this: /f/. When the letter stands for a grapheme, the letter is enclosed with single quotes, like this: 'f'.

For students who do not know the letter names when they enter school, teaching a sound first and then anchoring the sound to a grapheme (letter group or letter sequence) is more logical (Moats, 1998). For example, the sound /f/ would be associated with four graphemes, 'f', 'ph', 'ff' and 'gh'. The keyword examples are *fish, phone, stiff,* and *tough.* Many parents have told me of their success using *Phono-Graphix* (McGuinness & McGuinness, 1998) to either teach their children to read at home before they enter school or to help their older-age children learn the sound–spelling correspondences they need to master in order to remediate the guessing syndrome. Many schools use the program as a third-tier phonics intervention (Florida Center for Reading Research, 2008).

A second program that works intensively with sounds before matching them to letters was developed by a speech pathologist, Nancy Lindamood, and her linguist husband (Lindamood & Lindamood, 1998). In the *LiPS* program, students receive intensive instruction in differentiating the sounds and learn to label the sounds that are made—for example, "lip-poppers," "lip coolers," and "tongue coolers"—to help them understand how a sound feels (p. 34). The program, originally developed for one-to-one clinical settings, has been adapted for use in classrooms and whole districts with great success (Sadowski & Willson, 2006).

Despite the variety of ways that phonics programs are organized and taught, there are only four possible ways to identify (read) words during the reading of connected text (Ehri, 1991a; Gaskins, 2005): (1) contextual guessing, (2) phonemic decoding, (3) analogy, and (4) sight. Figure 2.2 describes each of these ways in more detail.

Figure 2.2 The Four Ways to Read Words

Way to Read Words	Description
Contextual guessing	Guessing is the strategy of choice for *struggling readers*. They look at the pictures. They look at the first letter in the word. Then they make their best guess. Using context is an excellent strategy for determining word meaning. Beyond third grade, guessing to identify words leads to bad habits that are difficult to break. An extensive body of research shows that skilled readers do not guess. In fact, the ability to identify words in the absence of semantic cues is one of the defining characteristics of skilled readers (Share & Stanovich, 1995). Heed the warning of Marilyn Adams (1990) if you contemplate using predictable books for repeated reading or reading practice by readers at risk: "Where context is strong enough to allow quick and confident identification of the unfamiliar word, there is little incentive to pore over its spelling. And without studying the word's spelling, there is no opportunity for increasing its visual familiarity" (p. 217).
Letter–sound decoding (also called *phonemic decoding*)	Beginning readers who have mastered their letter–sound correspondences use this way to read words when the word is brand-new to them. The process may take a few seconds, but once a word is decoded correctly, readers have taken the first step to making that word one of their sight words. Some students will need as many as 10 sounding outs to acquire a word.
Analogy	Reading words by analogy only works when students have stored a body of analogous words (key words) in their long-term memories in a fully analyzed way (Ehri, 1991a). The key words must have been processed letter by letter and sound by sound to develop a complete and accurate mental orthographic image before they are useful for reading by analogy (Gaskins, 2005).
Sight	Reading words by sight is the ultimate goal of the word-learning process, whether that process is letter–sound decoding or analogy. Skilled readers read sight words in a split second. The conscious and deliberate process of decoding works fine for the first few sounding outs of a new word, but the ultimate goal is instantaneous word recognition. The more sight words that readers know, the more fluent their reading becomes.

Understanding the subtle differences between the four ways to read words is basic to evaluating phonics programs and instructional approaches as well as helping you appreciate and remediate the problems your students face on the road to becoming fluent readers. The bottom line of fluent reading is instant sight-word access.

The term *sight word* has two different meanings. For the purpose of discussing how students become fluent readers, a sight word is "a word that is immediately recognized as a whole and does not require word analysis for identification" (Harris & Hodges, 1995, p. 233). Sometimes, the term *sight word* is used to refer to phonically irregular words or exception words (e.g., *Wednesday, was, the*) that must be memorized as whole words. But do not confuse whole-word memorization with the acquisition of sight words that leads to fluent reading. In this book, the term *sight word* always refers to words that have been phonemically decoded multiple times and eventually imprinted and stored as mental orthographic images (MOIs) in long-term memory. Once learned, these sight words are instantly accessible whenever the reader encounters them in text. Becoming a skilled reader with a huge repertoire of sight words requires knowledge of phonemic segmentation, letter–sound correspondences, and spelling patterns (Ehri, 1980, 1995, 1998; Rack, Hulme, Snowling, & Wightman, 1994; Reitsma, 1983; Share, 1999). Once students have begun to create their personal lexicons—storehouses of words and meanings in their long-term memories—they will no longer need to rely solely on their knowledge of sound–spelling correspondences. However, these correspondences are crucial to success in the beginning stages of reading *and* whenever students encounter unfamiliar words. With the ability to decode, some students can acquire new sight words in as few as four quality encounters (i.e., sounding out and blending), whereas without decoding, 30 or more encounters with a word might be required to memorize the word as whole. Whole-word memorization ought to be reserved for exceptional words with irregular and unique spelling patterns. Using whole-word memorization for every word is inefficient and very difficult if not impossible for those without exceptional visual memories.

The view that children can become fluent readers only if they learn to skip words, sampling the visual information in text to support their hypotheses about its meaning, is erroneous. Within this view, teachers are supposed to encourage guessing about words to help children become free from their so-called bondage to print. With skilled guessing, students can make it to about fourth grade before their guessing catches up with them. There are tens of thousands of upper-grade students with the guessing syndrome. Until she mastered phonics, my granddaughter, Abigail, was one of them.

In fact, the understanding of skilled reading that emerges from the past 20 years of scientific research is, again, just the *opposite* of the view of skilled readers as word skippers. Two important facts about the way that skilled readers process text are relevant to this new understanding. The first of these is that skilled readers fixate, or look directly at, almost every word in text as they read (Rayner & Pollatsek, 1989). Skilled readers read rapidly, not because they selectively sample words and letters as they construct the meaning of text, but because they read the individual words rapidly and with little effort. They have solid orthographic images of these they can instantly retrieve.

Look for more detailed information about MOIs and how to help students acquire them on pages 58–64 in Chapter 3. Carefully read the MOI think-aloud on pages 62–63 to see how an expert does it.

A key piece of knowledge here, and the second important fact relevant to our understanding of skilled reading, is that good readers use information about all the letters in the words, even when they recognize them at a single glance (Just & Carpenter, 1987; Patterson & Coltheart, 1987). Because many words are differentiated from one another by only one or two letters, a global or gestalt image of a word is not sufficient to help recognize it reliably. Instead, the MOI used in reading words by sight must include information about all, or almost all, the letters in a word's spelling. Even when reading very rapidly, the good reader extracts information about all the letters in a word as part of the recognition process.

Adams (1991) summarizes these facts about word recognition processes in skilled readers this way:

> It has been proven beyond any shade of doubt that skillful readers process virtually each and every word and letter of text as they read. This is extremely counter-intuitive. For sure, skillful readers neither look nor feel as if that's

what they do. But that's because they do it so quickly and effortlessly. Almost automatically; with almost no conscious attention whatsoever, skillful readers recognize words by drawing on deep and ready knowledge of spellings and their connections to speech and meaning. (p. 207)

WHEN SHOULD PHONICS BE TAUGHT?   ■

The most pervasive and invaluable benefit of phonics is that, through experience, it creates the infrastructure in memory that enables readers to identify new words with ease and to retain them distinctly and enduringly as sight words. Phonics provides the infrastructure for acquiring sight words, and reciprocally, the acquisition of many, many sight word enriches that infrastructure and affords decoding automaticity.

—Adams (2008, pp. 287–288)

Phonics can be taught whenever students have the prerequisite PA skills to identify and manipulate the various sounds (phonemes). Phonics instruction can begin in kindergarten if students are ready; however, first grade is traditionally where the most intensive phonics instruction takes place. Students who read fluently at a second-grade level or above when they enter kindergarten often benefit greatly from specialized and accelerated instruction in the sound–spelling correspondences, such as that found in *SPELL—Links to Reading & Writing: A Word-Study Curriculum* (Wasowicz, Apel, Masterson, & Whitney, 2004). This program enhances reading, vocabulary acquisition, spelling, and written language skills by integrating five linguistic processes within a highly structured and sequential spelling instruction.

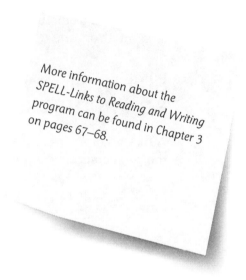

More information about the SPELL-Links to Reading and Writing program can be found in Chapter 3 on pages 67–68.

Be aware that many students who appear to be strong readers in the early grades later turn out to have decoding and spelling problems. They seem to be strong readers early on because they have impressive oral vocabulary skills and are good at using context to identify words. They are using what is called by some the "guess-and-go" or partial cueing strategy. They are not using full cue analysis to decode words, which is critical for developing strong decoding, spelling, and reading skills, particularly fluency. Usually at around fourth grade, these so-called strong readers suddenly develop reading problems because they can no longer rely on their existing vocabulary knowledge and story context to identify (i.e., guess) a word when reading (J. Wasowicz, personal communication, September 23, 2008).

THE ROLE OF PHONICS   ■
IN SKILLED READING

Letters do not make sounds; they represent sounds. This is no subtle distinction.

McGuinness & McGuinness (1998, p. 13)

Think of phonics as specialized instruction that enables beginning readers to crack a very complex code—the English language. Cracking the code enables them to extract meaning from the hundreds of thousands of unintelligible written messages they encounter everywhere—sign boards, cereal boxes, and printed pages in their books. What comes to *your* mind when you hear the word *code?*

I think of my father-in-law who was a master of the Morse code and ventured behind enemy lines during World War II to transmit radio messages to Allied intelligence officers. When the dots and dashes of a reply came clattering through his headset, he was able to decode them instantaneously into the letters of our English alphabet. Jean-François Champollion, the Egyptologist who broke the code of Egyptian hieroglyphics from studying the Rosetta stone, comes to mind as well. Champollion had to figure out the hieroglyphic code all on his own. He didn't have a first-grade teacher to help him. The code that is most important to students who do not know how to read is the English alphabet code. If nonreaders are to experience the thrill of deciphering the indecipherable and figuring out what those mysterious squiggles on the page mean, they need to acquire an accurate knowledge of the code: the conventionally accepted way in which letters or groups of letters correspond to spoken sounds in our language. *Your* knowledge of that code has enabled you to gain meaning from the text you have read thus far.

■ SCIENTIFIC EVIDENCE FOR PHONICS INSTRUCTION

Although most educators and publishers have concluded that phonics *should* be taught, the proliferation of phonics programs on the market is confusing, even to a relatively knowledgeable educator. Once you have decided to teach phonics, what kind should it be? For an answer to that question, look first to the major reviews of the phonics research such as Chall (1967/1983), Adams (1990), the National Research Council (Snow et al., 1998), and the *Report of the National Reading Panel: Teaching Children to Read* (NICHD, 2000). Taken as a whole, these meta-analyses leave no doubt about the critical role that phonics plays in beginning reading instruction. To summarize, explicit, systematic, supportive phonics instruction, taught as a stand-alone instructional component but within the context of a print-rich classroom environment with a significant literature base, is an absolutely essential (although certainly not sufficient) piece of the reading puzzle—particularly for students at risk. The critical question facing practitioners is, What does this research have to say about the likelihood of phonics instruction working for me, in my classroom, district, and school?

When a substantial body of experimental and quasi-experimental research is available (as is the case with phonics instruction), a meta-analytic approach is the ideal way to answer many of the questions regarding the generalizability of a particular method to your setting. In a reexamination of the National Reading Panel report, Ehri, Nunes, Stahl, and Willow (2001) quantified the effects of systematic phonics instruction compared to unsystematic or no phonics instruction on learning to read (i.e., learning to decode) in 66 treatment–control comparisons found in 38 experimental and quasi-experimental studies. The strength of this meta-analysis lies not only in the variety of students, settings, treatments, and outcomes considered, but also in the fact that all of the studies appeared in peer-reviewed journals.

The studies took place in regular school settings (as opposed to lab or university clinic settings) that enrolled students from a range of socioeconomic levels (low, middle, and varied). The students came from various achievement and grade levels: students who are normal achieving, at risk, reading disabled, and low achieving from

Grades K–6. Instructional settings included whole class, small group, and tutorial. The treatments included both synthetic phonics (systematic sound–spelling instruction) and analytic phonics (in which larger phonetic units of instruction are used)—many delivered via commercially available programs. The control groups included basal readers, a regular district curriculum, whole language, whole word, and a miscellaneous category. The outcome measures included decoding both real and pseudowords, spelling words, reading text orally, and comprehending text.

The overall effect of phonics instruction on reading, when *all* ages and types of readers in *varying* sizes of instructional groups were taught with *different* phonics programs, was moderate with an effect size of .41. You, however, are interested in exactly when and with whom phonics instruction is most helpful. Effects are larger when phonics instruction begins early (.55) as compared to after first grade (.27). While phonics is helpful as a remedial tool, its role in preventing reading difficulties is even more powerful. Perhaps you are also considering a phonics tutoring program as a Tier 2 intervention. Small-group instruction produced statistically larger effect sizes than tutoring or whole classrooms. Your decision to invest in a one-to-one program may be ill-advised if you can achieve similar outcomes in small instructional groups or even in the whole group. You may be wondering whether one type of phonics program is superior to another. The meta-analysis found that there are many curricula that provide effective systematic phonics instruction, and no one program is superior to another. Most critical to positive student outcomes in word reading ability is the systematic and explicit nature of the instruction.

You will not likely find another area of reading instruction in which there is more convergence regarding a positive answer to the does-it-work question than in the area of phonics instruction, but you are wondering if phonics can meet all of your students' needs. Critics of phonics instruction often point to the lack of significant effects of phonics instruction on reading comprehension (.31).[2] Although this is not an outcome to which phonics instruction is generally directed, it is nevertheless the overall goal of reading instruction. Many of the studies found positive effects for phonics instruction when combined with meaning-based approaches to reading instruction as compared to programs emphasizing only a meaning-based approach. These findings suggest the need for a skillful combination of phonics instruction with activities that immediately require students to apply their decoding skills (the goal of phonics instruction as measured in the studies) to the reading of real text to build fluency, increase comprehension skills, and acquire knowledge (adapted from McEwan & McEwan, 2003). Phonics is just one piece of the reading puzzle and should never supplant intensive, meaning-based comprehension instruction.

The evidence for phonics instruction is most persuasive for students who begin first grade with weaker PA skills (Foorman et al., 1998), weaker reading skills (Juel & Minden-Cupp, 2000), or weaker letter–word recognition (Connor, Morrison, & Katch, 2004), or are at higher risk for reading difficulties (Hatcher, Hulme, & Snowling, 2004). However, we must not overlook students who begin first grade with strong letter–word reading skills. Is traditional synthetic phonics the best approach for them as well?

New research suggests not. In a series of studies, Connor and various colleagues have shown that although children who begin first grade with below-average letter–word reading skills demonstrate greater improvement with greater amounts of time in explicit teacher-managed

The dilemma for teachers who are wedded to whole-group instruction is how best to provide differentiated instruction that meets the needs of students at the extreme ends of the reading continuum. Flexible instructional groups are the answer. See more about both further in the chapter, on pages 48–49, and on pages 189–192 in Chapter 9.

code-focused instruction, students who begin school with strong letter–word reading skills make more improvement in their overall reading ability when they spend less time in code-focused activities (Connor, Morrison, Fishman, Schatschneider, & Underwood, 2007; Connor, Morrison, & Katch, 2004; Connor, Morrison, & Petrella, 2004; Connor, Morrison, & Slominski, 2006; Connor, Schatschneider, et al., 2008).

■ EFFECTIVE INSTRUCTIONAL PRACTICES FOR TEACHING PHONICS

For students at-risk of experiencing reading difficulties, how we teach is equally as important as what we teach.

—Santoro, Coyne, and Simmons (2006, p. 124)

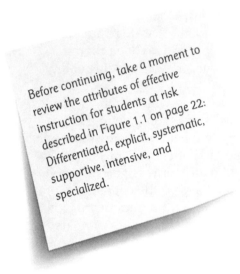

Before continuing, take a moment to review the attributes of effective instruction for students at risk described in Figure 1.1 on page 22: Differentiated, explicit, systematic, supportive, intensive, and specialized.

The widespread belief that creativity is the essence of effective teaching seduces many an excellent teacher off task. "This attitude is misdirected and can have ultimately disastrous consequences" (Heward & Dardig, 2001, p. 44), especially for students at risk. When teachers are tempted to make creativity and discovery their ultimate goal, the time for explicit instruction and real reading disappears. Beware of thinking that school should entertain either the teacher or the student. Instruction should be designed so that students have the opportunities they require to learn to read. Schmoker (2001) refers to the time that is devoted to activities that have little relationship to acquiring the ability to read as "the crayola curriculum" and recommends that educators take a hard look at what's *really* happening during reading instruction.

Two aspects of the first attribute of effective instruction for students at risk noted in the adjacent sticky note, *differentiated,* are especially critical in phonics instruction: flexible skill grouping and text at students' instructional levels.

Flexible Grouping

Differentiated intensive instruction is most effective when delivered in small, skill-based groups or in some instances one-to-one tutoring. There's a new term being used to describe across-classroom skill grouping: *walk to reading.* One Reading First district came up with a clever acronym for their plan, the ISBE (intensive, strategic, benchmark, enriched) Shuffle. At the same time every morning, all of the students in Grades K–3 shuffle themselves into a variety of small, skill-based groups to receive reading instruction targeted specifically to their needs (Whipple, 2008). There are three secrets to making walk-to-reading successful: (1) a collaborative effort by all teachers to deliver the same quality of instruction in each group, (2) thorough teaching of routines to students to reduce wasted time during transitions, and (3) a commitment by each teacher to obsessively adhere to the clock so as not to inconvenience students and fellow teachers.

Back in the late 1950s, skill-based grouping across grade levels was called the Joplin Plan, after the Missouri school district that first implemented grouping students across grades so that they could work in small groups with others who shared similar reading levels. At that time, students received the majority of their reading instruction in their skill-based group. Joplin's success with cross-grade grouping was actually featured in an article in the *Saturday Evening Post* on October 26, 1957, titled "Johnny Can Read in Joplin" (Tunley, 1957). Although very little experimental research was done at the time to evaluate the efficacy of this grouping arrangement as compared to other models of instructional delivery, the two experiments and the follow-up study cited promising effects on achievement (Hillson, Jones, Moore, & Van Devender, 1964; Jones, Moore, & Van Devender, 1967; Morgan & Stucker, 1960). In the 1960 study, 180 fifth-grade and sixth-grade students were randomly assigned to either the experimental Joplin Plan group or to one of the control whole-group classrooms. The 1964 study was a longitudinal study following a group of first-grade children for three years. Again, these students were randomly assigned to the Joplin Plan treatment and a comparison group of whole-group classrooms.

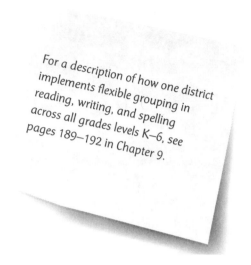

For a description of how one district implements flexible grouping in reading, writing, and spelling across all grades levels K–6, see pages 189–192 in Chapter 9.

The 1960 study of fifth and sixth graders produced reading improvements with an effect size of .33. In the first-grade study conducted after 18 months (Hillson et al., 1964), the students were tested in interpreting paragraph meaning, word meaning, and overall reading. The effect size of .55 on the comprehension of paragraph meaning was the smallest of the effect sizes. A follow-up study after three years (Jones et al., 1967) showed that the differences between the two groups—Joplin Plan students and whole-group students—had narrowed, but that the Joplin Plan students still outscored the whole-group students with an effect size of .27. Hopefully, more experimental research will be conducted on the cross-grade plans being used in today's classrooms, given the promising outcomes of these two studies.

Other grouping structures should include whole-class instruction for teacher read-alouds, book discussions, and the introduction of new vocabulary and strategies; mixed-ability cooperative learning groups in which students assume different roles and support each other in learning; flexible skills grouping for instruction on specific skills, such as blending and segmenting phonemes or making a story map; and pairing of children for activities such as oral reading, peer editing, and word study activities, such as sorting and making words with movable letters (Texas Reading Initiative, 2002, p. 24). I would personally avoid the term *ability* in any discussion of instructional groups. Harvard scholars Mosteller, Light, and Sachs (1996), in an excellent review of skill-grouping research, explain it this way:

> We prefer the expression "skill grouping" rather than "ability grouping" because the latter suggests a sense of permanence in a quality we believe might be modified by education, training, and practice. Skill grouping on the other hand, suggests that students are grouped together for purposes of instruction. (p. 799)

Case Study

Differentiating Instruction With Centers in First Grade

Candace Darling, Michelle Judware, and Darlene Carino comprise the first-grade team at Barringer Road School in Ilion, New York. They do almost everything together at school except teach. Each one teaches a heterogeneous group of first graders. Their class sizes average about 20 each year. I asked them to describe how they differentiate centers in their classrooms to make every minute count for teaching them all to read. Note the variety of ways that students are grouped for instruction and practice.

We call the block of time when our students work independently at various centers based on The Big Five (PA, phonics, fluency, vocabulary, and comprehension)—workshop time. We believe that a strong foundation in The Big Five will strengthen our students' overall reading ability, as well as allow them to become more independent in applying the strategies they have learned in our classrooms. We set up six to seven centers that remain constant for the entire year. As the year progresses, the intensity and expectations within those centers increases to meet the needs and levels of our students.

Before a new school year begins, we plan a schedule for the introduction and teaching of each new center, as they are introduced one at a time. The students are then taught the procedures for that particular center. We use the "I do it, we do it, you do it" lesson plan to introduce each individual center. We look ahead to anticipate possible problems that might arise within a center. We then do little skits that model the various ways that students might handle these little problems on their own without disturbing the teacher who is working with other students.

Once we feel confident that our students understand the objectives of a center and will be able to find independent success within that center, we move on to introduce the next one. Once we have introduced a few centers, we allow the students to begin rotating through the centers taught thus far. We carefully observe the students as they are working to ensure they are making the most of the materials and activities. Once the students have been carefully taught all of the rules and routines, the centers are essentially child managed while we work with students who need additional teacher-directed instruction. The secret to creating totally child-managed centers lies in spending enough time to thoroughly teach the routines and the rules of each center.

Following are the centers in our classrooms and examples of the activities in which students are engaged:

- *Word Play Center (ABC).* Becoming fluent with reading sight words (a list derived from *Open Court's* high-frequency word list, some of which are decodable and some of which are high-frequency exception words); becoming proficient with writing that same list of sight words; practicing spelling words and phrase wall phrases; and creating sentences using verbs, nouns, and adjectives.
- *Listening Center.* Developing listening skills, reinforcing print awareness and tracking, modeling reading fluency and expression, identifying details from the story, comprehending story elements, listening for enjoyment, and working cooperatively.
- *BEAR (Be Excited About Reading) Center.* Reading on students' independent levels, learning how to choose appropriately leveled books, developing comprehension strategies and story elements, and reading with a partner to build fluency and expression.
- *Fluency and Performance Center.* Reading and rereading Reader's Theater scripts and poems; working with new vocabulary, parts of speech, and sight words; performing in front of an audience; receiving exposure to various text genres; building listening skills; and working cooperatively.
- *Writing Center.* Building phonics and phonemic awareness through the use of alliterative sentences and writing lists, writing complete sentences, practicing writing skills, building ownership (as author-illustrator), and staying on topic.
- *Computer Center.* Building phonemic awareness skills, integrating technology into reading, developing listening skills, following directions, and sequencing.
- *Traveler or Group Center.* Teacher-directed center based on the individual needs of students within the group [Tier 2 interventions].

If we find that a center or a certain activity is not working as planned, we simply stop everything and teach a mini-lesson. If all goes well, after a few days of rotation, more centers are introduced. Workshop time in our classrooms is at least an hour a day. If our schedules allow, we try to fit in more time. During this time, the students rotate through two 30-minute centers. We chart everything out to be sure that the majority of our students visit each center at least one time per week. This workshop time also includes Group Center, which is a chance for all students to work in a small, teacher-directed group that is based on the specific instructional needs (whether above, below, or at benchmark) of the students in the group. We use various assessments and classroom observations when planning for these groups. This time is also when our Tier 3 intervention students are pulled out for smaller, more individualized groups with the reading teacher. Because some of our students are out of the classroom for a 30-minute period each day, they have less time to explore the centers within our classrooms. Therefore, we make sure that they go to the centers that target their areas of greatest need.

Each center is differentiated. Because we form heterogeneous student groups for moving through the centers (with the exception of the teacher-directed Group Center), each activity can be adapted to meet the individual needs of each student that visits that center. For example, the BEAR Center is set up as a Library Center where students choose books to read and discuss based on their library card bookmarks. These cards are color coded to the independent reading level of the student. For example, the yellow basket contains books that have one word per page with a corresponding picture clue. One student may be able to read from the green basket and another from the blue, yet both students can share their book choice with anyone they choose [they read it aloud for someone else in their group after they have read it on their own]. This gives less proficient and more proficient readers opportunities to work together and learn from each other. We make sure that each of our centers can easily be adapted for any student level; thus students are able to differentiate for themselves in many cases.

At the Computer Center, the programs are based on each individual's mastery of the taught skills. The computer will not allow them to move on until they have completed or mastered a specific task. The skills are also scaffolded.

In the Writing Center, our expectations for the amount and quality of writing are dependent on students' writing skills to that point. We always pair a more advanced writer with a less advanced one so they can help and learn from each other. This allows us (the teachers) to have two 30-minute sessions of completely uninterrupted group time with struggling students.

We use a wide variety of materials when planning for our centers. Some of our materials are purchased; however most activities are developed from ideas we have read about, adapted, or created, based on our professional development. Each summer, we sit down as a first-grade team and discuss what worked well during the past year and then decide what centers we need to change for the upcoming year. We bounce ideas off one another and incorporate things we have learned from our summer reading. Then as a team, we begin the setup of our centers. We try to have all materials (pencils, crayons, etc.) at students' fingertips and ready to go so that there is no wasted time.

We teach almost the entire core program to all of our students now. We have used *Open Court Reading* (Adams & Bereiter, 2002) in our school for seven years and have learned to incorporate more and more of the core program into our school day. We definitely see a difference in our students' progress to higher reading levels when we can keep coming back to an important skill several times during each day. We feel that our core program is very closely tied to the beliefs of the Reading First initiative that we have been focused on in the past four years. It also fits in nicely with The Big Five. As with any purchased program, we tweak our core program instruction to meet our own students' needs, as well as our own teaching styles. If we feel that the core program is not spending enough time on something, then we add to it. If our students have mastered something else, then we may not spend much time on it at all. We have taken the core program and made it our own. We are not teaching a program; we are teaching our students.

We create an atmosphere that allows us to differentiate the lesson by using a variety of questioning techniques. After the core lesson has been taught to the whole group, we use the 30-minute Group Center to reteach, modify, or extend to the next level for all of our students. We also try to fit in booster moments throughout the day where we may read with a student or do a five-minute mini-lesson with 2–3 other students.

Text at Students' Reading Levels

The types of words which appear in beginning reading texts may well exert a more powerful influence in shaping children's word identification strategies than the method of reading instruction.

—Juel and Roper-Schneider (1985, p. 151)

Choosing texts for beginning readers is one of the most important things that primary-grade teachers do. As Juel and Roper-Schneider suggest in the foregoing quotation, the text that teachers select impacts the kind of word identification strategies that students eventually adopt in their everyday reading. For example, students who read a preponderance of decodable texts develop a phonemic decoding strategy based on spelling–sound correspondences. Students who read from texts that are primarily constructed around high-frequency words will primarily employ a visual strategy for word identification. Students who use a preponderance of predictable literature will readily memorize the patterns, repetitive language and rhyme, but are unlikely to acquire strong phonemic decoding skills. If your goal is to provide daily high-success reading experiences for students, match the text to your students' growing abilities to phonemically decode text.

Most core programs offer a menu of text choices, including (1) literature anthologies, (2) decodable books, and (3) leveled books that have been written or selected according to the criteria developed by Reading Recovery (Peterson, 1991) and Guided Reading (Fountas & Pinnell, 1996), providing little guidance as to which types of text pose the biggest challenges to readers at risk. Within these three categories of books there are many different types of words. They are described in Figure 2.3. Each type of text has its own unique qualities. For example, in core program literature anthologies, the words may be rare, multisyllabic, high imagery, and nonrepetitive. This kind of literacy vocabulary may be difficult for many readers at risk unless they have an enormous amount of instructional support and proceed through the lessons at a much slower rate than the usual one story per week.

The words in core program decodable books may or may not be decodable by the students who are using them since in order for a book to be decodable, students must have mastered the sound–spelling correspondences contained in the words in the books. So if the person who wrote the curriculum didn't collaborate with the author of the decodable books, the text may still be inaccessible for your students most at risk. However, most decodable books have a tightly controlled vocabulary with lots of high-frequency words that are frequently repeated. Reading these kinds of texts helps students build fluency. Then there is a third category of texts: leveled books that have a mixture of predictable text and story structures, rare and multisyllabic words, and words that are used only once. These texts pose considerable challenge to readers at risk, since only one exposure to a new word reduces the likelihood that it will become a sight word for these students.

Which books offer beginning readers the best chance of developing fluent word identification skills? Menon and Hiebert (2005) sought to determine the answer to that question by comparing the skills of students reading a basal literature anthology to those of students reading a set of little books, called *Ready Readers,* that purported to balance phonics content and high-frequency words along with the criteria developed by Reading Recovery. The 15-week intervention was conducted in four first-grade classrooms of an inner-city school in a large urban district. Two classes were assigned to the intervention group, reading little books (20 texts at each of seven levels) especially selected from the larger series of 300 books for the text

Figure 2.3 Types of Words Used in Primary Texts

Type of Word	Definition of Word
Decodable	Words that can be sounded out by students because they have mastered the spelling–sound correspondences found in the words. Decodable books are those in which at least 70% of the words can be sounded out because the letter sounds and combinations comprising these words have been mastered by the students. Decodable books contain a relatively small proportion of previously learned, high-frequency sight words. A decodable book is readable or appropriate for instruction when a student can read the text with at least 90% accuracy (Bursuck & Damer, 2007, p. 321).
Controlled vocabulary	A set of words known to be familiar at certain grade levels. Text is written based on the parameters of this vocabulary (Hiebert & Fisher, 2005).
High frequency	Words that are among the most frequently encountered in written English. Half of the first 25 of the words on this list have vowel patterns that are irregular. However, these words needs to be recognized quickly if students are to become fluent readers since this list accounts for one-third of the total number of words in texts (Carroll, Davies, & Richman, 1971).
High repetition	Words that are used multiple times in a text so as to build fluent word identification skills.
High leverage	Words used in texts that are almost certain to be recognized by readers at certain grade levels, thereby increasing the likelihood that students will be able to read and comprehend them. For example in Level A of one Fluency Curriculum, the 300 most frequent words contain consistent short and long vowel patterns (Hiebert, 2008a).
Rare and multisyllabic words	Words that students have never encountered and are likely to have a high degree of difficulty reading. Unless words like this are repeated over and over in the text, students will not likely acquire them as sight words. Literacy texts (children's literature, trade books) have a high proportion of words that appear a single time (Hiebert, 2008b).
Singleton	A word that only appears once in a story or article (Foorman, 2007). See also rare and multisyllabic words.
High meaning (high imagery) multisyllabic words	Words for which readers are able to produce a mental image, like *elephant* or *tiger* or *hamburger*. Students may be able to incorporate these words into their sight-word mental lexicon more quickly than highly decodable words that are less meaningful to them (Laing & Hulme, 1999; Metsala, 1999).
Content specific	Words that are absolutely essential to comprehending content text (e.g., landform, photosynthesis, chrysalis, polygon, geography). These words are found in content standards.
Conceptually complex	Words that require learning new factual information or a related system of concepts (e.g., *divide* as "the boundary between drainage basins" requires information about river systems).
Conceptually accessible	A new word that has a synonym for which the concept is understood by the reader.
Literacy vocabulary	Words found in children's literature and trade books (e.g., *flustered, rambunctious, yelped*). These words are often rare and multisyllabic.
General academic vocabulary	Words that are used in a variety of academic settings (e.g., explain, summarize, infer, trace).

support they offered readers in terms of linguistic content (the types of words, whether high frequency or decodable) and cognitive load (the number of different words and the number of repetitions per word in the text). Two classes were assigned to the comparison group, reading the literature-based program anthology. Pretests and posttests were administered using word lists and graded passage from the *Qualitative Reading Inventory-4* (Leslie & Caldwell, 2005). Children in the intervention classrooms reading books with less challenging linguistic content and a more controlled cognitive load performed at significantly higher levels on the posttests than did their counterparts in the comparison classrooms who read selections from the literature anthology.

Keep in mind before you put in a requisition for this set of little books that researchers analyzed the 300 little books provided by the publisher with the TExT Analyzer (Hiebert & Martin, 2002, 2003), to determine the linguistic content and cognitive load of each. Average classroom teachers have neither the time nor the expertise to evaluate the materials provided by publishers.

Although publishers go to great lengths to assure prospective purchasers that their basal reading programs have been empirically validated, that assertion is suspect. For example, Cunningham (2005) found that leveled texts, such as those used in Reading Recovery and available as a part of most basal reading programs, provide only a moderate amount of support for word recognition instruction and almost none for decoding instruction in the use of onsets and rimes. Also the leveled texts do not consistently increase in word demands as their levels increase. Foorman, Francis, Davidson, Harm, and Griffin (2004) analyzed textbooks that were adopted for use in Texas in 2000, finding that 70% of the words were taught as single units with the percentage reaching 84 in six-week blocks of several programs. Foorman and colleagues questioned how beginning readers could be expected to acquire and apply sound–letter correspondences when only 20% of the words in texts are repeated two or three times.

Recall the students at risk in Rows 3 and 4 of our hypothetical class in Chapter 1. They are facing an uphill reading road made even more difficult by being given texts that are too difficult for them to read without extensive instructional support. Hiebert (2008a) makes the following recommendations for scaffolding too-difficult texts:

- Provide more in-depth instruction in decoding strategies with morphologically complex words (Nagy, Berninger, & Abbott, 2006).
- Provide extensive reading: Readers self-select materials from a collection of graded readers (books that have reduced vocabulary range and simplified grammatical structures) with the goal of reaching specified target times of silent, sustained reading (Taguchi, Takayasu-Maass, & Gorsuch, 2004).
- To the greatest extent possible, use texts that match the curriculum (Wilson, Erickson, & Trainin, 2007).
- Use technology to assist in reading instruction to provide more opportunities for students to acquire phonemic decoding skills (Adams, 2006).

Here are other suggestions:

- Adapt the core reading program to meet the needs of struggling students by slowing down the pace of instruction.
- Teach for mastery, not for coverage.
- Add multiple opportunities for practice of new words and story rereading during every day.

Intensive Interventions for Struggling Beginning Readers

Intensive instruction for students at risk can take place in three different dimensions:

- *Time intensive,* meaning that two to three times as much instruction would be required to teach students at risk to read.
- *Teacher intensive,* meaning teachers with more specialized training or at the very least strong and supportive embedded professional development are needed.
- *Content intensive,* meaning a more extensive, thorough, and perhaps more specialized exposure to the skills and knowledge is needed.

Torgesen (2002), in a review of six intensive interventions for seriously reading-disabled students, translated the achievement gains made by students in each of the six studies into standard score points per hour of instruction for three measures of reading skill: phonemic decoding, word identification, and passage comprehension. The interventions were designed for students with severe dyslexia (verbal intelligence in the average range and standard scores of phonemic decoding and word reading ability of 67 and 69) and ranged from 30 hours of instruction with a 1:4 teacher–student ratio to 67.5 hours with a 1:1 teacher–student ratio. Standard score gains per hour of instruction ranged from .41 to .30 on phonemic decoding, between .23 to .18 on word identification, and between .15 to .12 on passage comprehension (p. 100).

Torgesen (2002) concluded, "Given the right level of intensity and teacher skill it may be possible to obtain these rates of growth using a variety of approaches to direct instruction in reading" (p. 100). The challenge for educators is creating instructional settings that combine the right levels of intensity with high levels of teacher skill. It is all too easy to assume that students with severe reading difficulties should be heading off to the resource room for their reading instruction, but Vaughn, Moody, and Schumm (1998) identified the following reasons that students do not learn to read in resource room placements: (1) Teachers were carrying heavy case loads, which precluded intensive instruction; (2) little direct instruction was given in PA and decoding, with most instruction focused on phonics worksheets completed independently; and (3) no direct instruction in comprehension skills, which is an effective form of instruction for older children with reading disabilities (Mastropieri & Scruggs, 1997).

The implementation of intensive interventions takes time, teacher skill, and a willingness to change the instructional paradigm for seriously disabled readers.

SUMMARIZING CHAPTER 2 ■

Phonics is an essential piece of the reading puzzle that enables students to phonemically decode words by matching graphemes (the letters of the alphabet) to phonemes (the sounds the letters represent). Phonics instruction is most effective when it is part of a well-rounded program that includes word and world knowledge, spelling, fluency, comprehension, reading a lot, and writing. Most students need explicit systematic phonics instruction to fully master the code, but the type and amount of phonics instruction that individual students need to become fluent readers may vary. The students most at risk need intensive and specialized decoding instruction.

Decoding is one of four ways to identify words. Although it is not the fastest way, it is the most accurate way for students to build strong mental orthographic images of words that are essential for instant word identification as well as for correct spelling. Once mastered, the skill of phonemic decoding will only be used when readers encounter words they do not recognize by sight. For skilled readers who have enormous sight word dictionaries stored in their long-term memories, phonemic decoding may seem a relatively unimportant reading skill. However, for my granddaughter, Abigail, and tens of thousands of students like her, mastering phonemic decoding is like a life preserver to a struggling swimmer.

■ NOTES

1. Jeanne Chall and Marie Carbo debated phonics in the pages of *Phi Delta Kappan* in the late 1980s (Carbo, 1988; Chall, 1989). Carbo later backed off her antiphonics position, however (Carbo, 1996). Gerald Coles and Reid Lyon took up the debate in the late 1990s in *Education Week* (Coles, 1997; G. R. Lyon, as cited in Mathes & Torgesen, 1997). Gerald Coles (2000a) and Louise Spear-Swerling (2000) exchanged salvos when Spear-Swerling reviewed Coles's (2000b) book, *Misreading Reading: The Bad Science That Hurts Children.*

2. An *effect size* is a numerical indicator of the power of a treatment on an experimental group. The effect size of .31 noted here for phonics instruction may not seem like much. However, an effect size of .30 corresponds to about 30 points on an SAT verbal or mathematics standardized test (Cohen, 1977). While this might not seem like a notable gain for one student, for an entire population of students, the cumulative gains will be impressive.

3

Spelling

Spelling is "recognizing, recalling, reproducing or obtaining orally or in written form the correct sequence of letters in words" (Graham & Miller, 1979, p. 76).

Spelling is the third piece of the reading puzzle. It is a far more critical piece than most educators realize. The Report of the National Reading Panel (NICHD, 2000) did not include spelling in its list of essential components of a reading program. At the time, spelling was considered an adjunct of PA, and scholars may have hypothesized that explicitly taught PA and phonics would produce proficient spellers as well as skilled readers. However, there is a new body of compelling research indicating that although PA and phonics instruction in the primary grades are essential to laying a strong foundation for reading and spelling,  they are not sufficient to produce solid and enduring spelling proficiencies as students advance to the upper grades (Mehta et al., 2005). Poor spellers are also likely to be dysfluent readers and struggling writers.

The lack of a solid mandate or even a modest stamp of approval from the National Reading Panel (NRP) for direct and systematic spelling instruction gave educators little impetus to add one more subject to an already overloaded reading block. In anticipation of writing this chapter, I conducted an informal e-mail survey of educators on my mailing list, asking if their schools or districts used a formally adopted spelling program and, if not, how spelling instruction was provided to students. A Virginia principal said, "Our district has an adopted spelling program, but the teachers do not use it. The books are all packed away." A Washington state principal who confesses that he is a terrible speller himself and depends on a combination of Spell Check and his wife to ensure correct spelling said, "I have come to believe that the best way to teach spelling is with a strong phonics program. But we can't stop sending that list home every week because the public would complain."

Some educators do have programs to guide spelling instruction, but don't find them to be effective. A third-grade teacher using the district-adopted *Sitton Spelling* (Sitton, 1996) is dissatisfied with its organization. "One thing I don't like about this program is that it focuses on four to five spelling words a week that don't have a common pattern. I teach a third-grade gifted cluster and find myself creating extra challenge words for my students. I usually pull words that we've used during the week, such as math terms, reading vocabulary from our current text or story, or themed words from current events or holidays."

In many elementary schools, the following teacher's experience is the norm: "Every teacher at my school does something a little different. Due to limited instructional time throughout the day, very little spelling is actually 'taught.'"

In addition to spelling's omission from the Report of the National Reading Panel (NICHD, 2000), there are other likely reasons for spelling's low profile on the literacy landscape. There are no high-stakes spelling tests to hold educators accountable for spelling achievement, unless you count the annual Scripps National Spelling Bee. In fact, in some places, misspelled words get a pass. Although correct spelling is part of the Texas Assessment of Knowledge and Skills scoring rubric for writing in response to reading, few points are subtracted for poor spelling if the errors do not interfere with the reader's ability to understand the content. There is little incentive for teachers to focus on spelling instruction.

With the emphasis on invented spelling in many primary classrooms, the popularity of journal writing that goes largely unread or uncorrected by teachers in upper-grade classrooms, and the emphasis on prolific self-expression without regard for the conventions of spelling and grammar, instruction in spelling is often so implicit that it is hard to find. Where spelling instruction is found, it is likely to be taught from poorly designed curricula. A central office administrator said, "We use the spelling program that comes with our basal reading series. It's not a very solid program." Many elementary schools don't have formal spelling programs at all, preferring to "integrate" spelling instruction with reading and writing. A midwestern principal described his program this way: "Teachers work with students to select words from content areas (math, science, social studies) or from leveled reading books, but I feel too much time has been spent on learning lists for a test and forgetting them as soon as the test is completed."

In spite of the casual way that spelling is taught in a great many schools, society in general and employers in particular look upon the ability to write using correct spelling as the mark of a well-educated individual. In this era of instant text messaging where speed outweighs accuracy, there are still employers who sort job applications into two stacks: Good Spellers and Poor Spellers. A report by the National Commission on Writing for America's Families, Schools, and Colleges (2005) concluded that in 8 out of 10 cases, an application that is poorly written or contains many misspelled words will likely be eliminated from consideration. Unfortunately, even Spell Check programs cannot deliver correct spelling on demand to those new high school or college graduates who are completing a handwritten, on-the-spot job application. Given the importance of knowing how to spell in the real world and the power of orthographic knowledge to improve reading and writing skills, educators must move spelling to the instructional forefront to produce fluent readers and writers.

■ WHAT IS SPELLING AND HOW DO STUDENTS BECOME GOOD SPELLERS?

To the average person, spelling seems like a straightforward skill—"the ability to recognize, recall, reproduce or obtain orally or in written form the correct sequence of letters in words" (Graham & Miller, 1979, p. 76). But this definition hardly does justice to the complexity and sophistication of spelling in the 21st century. Spelling is in the process of becoming a brand-new subject for inclusion in the reading block—*word study*. *Word study* is specific and focused attention to the encoding (spelling) and decoding (word-level reading) of words using one's knowledge of the linguistic properties of words (Apel, 2007, p. 1). *Word study* is far more complex than merely studying a list of unrelated words for a weekly test or copying definitions from the dictionary.

This new approach to spelling is a multifaceted discipline encompassing the following linguistic skills: (1) PA, (2) orthographic knowledge, (3) morphological awareness, (4) semantic knowledge, and (5) mental orthographic images (Apel & Masterson, 2001; Apel, Masterson, & Niessen, 2004). Figure 3.1 defines each of the five linguistic skills that are needed to spell proficiently.

Students become good spellers in much the same way they become skilled readers—through explicit, systematic, supportive instruction using a research-based program that directly teaches them how to analyze and study words using the five linguistic skills. This approach is contrary to the way many of us were taught spelling or may still be teaching it—writing each spelling word 10 times. That approach is one of the least effective ways to teach spelling (Templeton, 2004).

The new spelling also stands in direct contrast to some of the more contemporary spelling programs that eschew spelling rules and select the weekly words based on their frequency of use in the English language rather than paying attention to the similarity of their patterns or common roots. This method presupposes that the spelling system of the English language makes no sense and rote memorization is the only way to become a skilled speller. Nothing could be further from the truth. When words are studied from the five linguistic perspectives cited earlier, spelling is

Figure 3.1 Linguistic Skills Needed for Proficient Spelling

Linguistic Skill	Description
Phonemic awareness	The ability to think about, talk about, and manipulate speech sounds
Orthographic knowledge	A set of skills necessary to translate language from spoken to written form; the application of spelling rules and patterns
Morphological awareness	The awareness of the semantic aspects of a root or base word and its corresponding inflections and derivations, including morphological units (the base word *cat* and the letter *s* that makes it plural), morphological forms (*ly*, *ed*, and *tion*) that alter the meaning of root words; modification rules (*hope*, *hoping*), and the relationship between words and their derived forms (magic, magician, magically)
Semantic knowledge	Knowledge of the effect of spelling on word meanings, such as in homophones (e.g., *bear* and *bare*, *won* and *one*, and *which* and *witch*)
Mental orthographic images	Clear mental images of words or morphemes stored in long-term memory

Source: Adapted from Apel (2007).

transformed into a multilinguistic study of words, their origins, meanings, and spellings that improve students' reading and writing capabilities at the same time as their spelling abilities.

■ WHEN SHOULD SPELLING BE TAUGHT?

Spelling instruction that is carefully and intentionally integrated into a beginning reading program can help students improve both spelling and reading skills.

—Santoro et al. (2006, p. 122)

Treiman (1993) recommends that "[children] should learn as soon as possible that every word has a conventional spelling . . . and that even if they do not yet know a word's conventional spelling, they will learn it when they get older" (p. 290). She also points out that phonological training will have a beneficial impact on spelling. Foorman (1995) suggests that direct instruction in spelling begin by midyear first grade rather than later for two reasons: (1) those students at risk of falling through the cracks will have the most difficult time with spelling, and (2) the teacher cannot assume that the knowledge gained from reading will automatically transfer to spelling without direct instruction (p. 382).

Too frequently, educators assume that spelling will develop naturally as students do more reading and writing. However, just as those students who enter school without PA will not develop it without direct instruction, students who are poor spellers as beginning readers will not likely grow into good spellers with only a casual and incidental exposure to words.

■ THE ROLE OF SPELLING IN SKILLED READING

Researchers agree that reading and spelling are highly interdependent (Ehri, 1991b), if not almost identical skills (Ehri, 1997). They draw from the same sources of knowledge in long-term memory: (1) knowledge about the alphabetic system and (2) knowledge about the spellings of specific words. Reading and spelling differ from one another in that students actually need *more* information in memory to spell words accurately than to read them, thus making spelling instruction a must, especially for readers at risk. More recent research has shown that although word reading, reading comprehension, and spelling are highly interrelated across Grades 1–4, reading instruction does not transfer to spelling proficiency (Mehta et al., 2005).

In addition, students can often appear to be better readers than they are through skillful guessing and sheer bravado. The processes of reading and writing are more tolerant of inaccuracies or intelligent guesses, whereas in spelling, a word is either right or wrong. For example, in writing, students have the option to choose a word that is similar in meaning but easier to spell than the originally selected word. In reading, there is always a chance that context might provide a clue to the meaning of the word or passage. Spelling is unforgiving. A student who tries to spell a word without an accurate mental orthographic image (MOI) of that word in long-term memory is like the adult trying to gain access to his online bank account when he can't remember his password. What is needed for spelling words correctly as well as summoning the exact password for a Web site is a detailed and exact mental model.

The multilinguistic model of spelling instruction offers teachers a way to help students become more conscious and intentional about constructing MOIs.

Teachers who encourage students to make educated guesses about words based on the first letter or letters of the word (e.g., train, trunk, or trap) or even context when they are unable to quickly identify a word are interfering with students' ability to develop adequate MOIs.

SCIENTIFIC EVIDENCE FOR SPELLING INSTRUCTION

Spelling was considered to be one of the most researched topics in the language arts 30 years ago (Allred, 1977). However, during the first half of the 20th century, research focused primarily on identifying which words should be included in the study of spelling based on how frequently they appeared in written text, analyzing students' spelling errors to determine which words were more difficult to spell, and identifying the best ways to teach spelling.

In the second half of the 20th century, research began to examine the alphabetic, syllabic, and morphological characteristics of words as well as hypothesizing that spelling was a developmental process of stages through which most learners predictably progressed on their way to becoming skilled at spelling. More recently, spelling research has focused on its multilinguistic structure and the impact of spelling instruction on reading and writing. The following brief review of spelling research focuses on that topic.

The Relationship Between Spelling and Reading

As I have mentioned, reading and spelling are closely related skills (Apel & Masterson, 2001; Berninger et al., 2002). In fact, scholar Linnea Ehri (1997) demonstrates how reading and spelling are one and the same, almost. They are the same because they draw from the same linguistic knowledge sources in long-term memory that individuals begin constructing as they learn to read and spell. Reading and spelling are different, however, in the kind of information they draw upon from long-term memory.

If you were asked whether identifying a word or spelling it required the retrieval of more information from long-term memory, you would no doubt choose word identification. After all, everything teachers do in the primary grades is focused on teaching word identification, while spelling is an add-on or an afterthought. Surprisingly, however, the act of reading a word involves only one cognitive response (identifying the whole word) while the act of spelling requires multiple responses (writing several letters in a correct sequence). Although reading (decoding by mapping sounds to letters in order to identify words and comprehend written text) and spelling (encoding by mapping letters to sounds in order to spell and write) seem to be two sides of the same coin, they differ dramatically in the demands they make on our long-term memories.

Spelling is the most exacting and objective measure of the literacy-related skills because it requires careful attention to a word's exact conventional form (Apel, 2008). Consider this personal example: I can always read the words *embarrassment* and *commitment* fluently when I encounter them in text. I never mistake either of them for any other word, identifying both in a split second. In the act of reading, I need not pay close attention to the bedeviling double consonants in these words. *Embarrassment* and *commitment* have been glued into my mental sight-word lexicon for decades. On the other hand, spelling these words takes far more time out of my life than it ought because I do not have solid MOIs of these words affixed in my long-term memory.

The Importance of Spelling Instruction

Consistent use of proper decoding strategies—combined with encoding that requires more detailed attention to the individual letters of words than required for reading—establishes clear and complete mental orthographic images of words in long-term memory.

—Wasowicz (2007, p. 5)

Educators once thought that explicit PA and phonics instruction would facilitate the development of spelling skills in readers at risk, but such is not the case. Teaching students to read without also teaching them to spell may in fact result in students who are not only less skilled readers, but also poor spellers (Ehri, 1997). The kind of spelling instruction that produces strong readers and spellers is far different from choosing a few words from the core program or a high-frequency word list and expecting students to memorize them for the following week. That kind of spelling instruction is guaranteed to frustrate students at risk and drive their parents to distraction. Even teachers cannot understand how students can supposedly memorize a word for a test and not be able to retrieve it during writing. The problem is this: Students simply do not have enough language knowledge in their long-term memories to enable them to spell some words correctly. Students with acute visual memory skills may remember the words forever. Some of the students may remember them long enough to get A's on the test. The rest of the students won't be able to spell the words at all until we include actual spelling instruction in the reading block.

Effective spelling instruction integrates PA and the alphabetic principle (Adams, 1990; Ehri, 1997; Moats, 1995; O'Connor & Jenkins, 1995) and is known to impact students' abilities to read in the following ways:

- Spelling instruction that strengthens students' abilities to segment words increases their word recognition abilities (Bradley & Bryant, 1983; Ehri & Wilce, 1987; Hatcher, Hulme, & Ellis, 1994; O'Connor & Jenkins, 1995).
- Practicing letter–sound correspondences in the context of learning to spell is more effective in terms of increasing students' word reading abilities than practicing sounds in isolation (Vandervelden & Siegel, 1997).
- Learning letter–sound correspondences in the context of learning to spell is more effective than embedding phonics instruction in the context of a literature-based program for improving word-reading skills and reading connected text, an effect that extends into the upper grades (Roberts & Meiring, 2006).

Effective spelling instruction includes learning to write the letters of words, a practice that is known to impact students' reading and spelling abilities in the following ways:

- Handwriting is not merely a motor process, and learning to write the letters of words while also learning to spell them helps students to construct more solid MOIs (Berninger, 1999).
- Time spent in letter name instruction during handwriting and spelling activities has a beneficial impact on students' reading abilities (Santoro et al., 2006).

- When students are spelling words (orally and in writing) while they are learning to read, the instructional redundancy may contribute to more fluent and automatic word identification skills (Treiman & Bourassa, 2000a).
- Spelling and reading taught simultaneously results in increased word reading accuracy (Apel, Masterson, & Hart, 2004; Apel, Masterson, & Niessen, 2004; Ehri, 1983, 1991a, 1991b; Ehri & Wilce, 1987; Santoro et al., 2006; Treiman, 1993, 1998).

Multilinguistic Spelling Instruction

A multiple linguistic approach to spelling instruction recognizes that skilled reading and writing depends on having knowledge about words from the five different linguistic knowledge sources: PA, orthographic knowledge, morphological awareness, semantic knowledge, and mental orthographic images (Adams, 1990; Apel & Masterson, 2001; Apel, Masterson, & Niessen, 2004; Kelman & Apel, 2004; Roberts & Meiring, 2006; Treiman, 1998; Treiman & Bourassa, 2000b).

Most reading programs teach the basics of PA in kindergarten and then move on to teach orthographic knowledge in the course of phonics instruction. However, incidental instruction is rarely enough for students at risk of reading failure or students who are reading disabled. Well-designed Tier 2 interventions that boost up some struggling students generally fail to help the most disabled of students master the intricacies of the English language system. In order to fully assemble their reading puzzles, these students need explicit, systematic spelling instruction that recognizes the critical role of spelling in learning to read and write.

When spelling is taught from a multiple linguistic perspective in which students are required to pay detailed attention to the individual letters, patterns, and other linguistic properties of words, it is likely that word-reading abilities will improve as well. However, for all students, multiple linguistic spelling instruction is more effective than traditional spelling instruction for improving spelling (Apel, Masterson, & Hart, 2004; Nagy et al., 2006).

EFFECTIVE INSTRUCTIONAL PRACTICES FOR TEACHING SPELLING

Hundreds of readings of the spelling of a word do not guarantee correct spelling.

—Bosman and Van Ordern (1997, p. 184)

The Dos of Effective Spelling Instruction

- Provide direct instruction offering many examples (and nonexamples) as appropriate, while at the same time encouraging students to suggest words with similar linguistic patterns.

- Model for students how to develop a clear and complete mental image of a word to hold in their long-term memories. Then lead students to use these mental images of correct spellings to inform their reading and writing. See Figure 3.2 for a think-aloud script in which a teacher is working with a student to create an MOI of a word. Expect students to use all of their senses during spelling instruction, providing multiple opportunities to hear sounds or words pronounced properly, produce the sounds or say the words correctly, write the letters or words that the sounds are spelling, and visualize the correctly spelled letters or words, in order to create an MOI.

Figure 3.2   Script for Teaching a Mental Orthographic Image

When students display a partial or complete misspelling of a word, they may not have an accurate MOI of the word stored in long-term memory. The following think-aloud, presented as a table, shows how a teacher can lead a student to build that image. The target word is *approach,* and the student has spelled it *aproach.* The word has five phonemes or sounds: *a/pp/r/oa/ch.* The student didn't represent the second phoneme correctly in the spelling, spelling the /p/ sound with only one "p." Visualizing orthographic images is not memorizing. Visualizing MOIs is especially helpful for exception words for which other sources of linguistic knowledge (PA, orthographic knowledge, morphological knowledge, or semantic relationship knowledge) are not available or words for which these knowledge sources are incomplete.

Steps to Developing an MOI	Teacher Script	Teacher Actions	Student Response
Explain the purpose of the activity.	Sometimes you won't be able to spell one or more parts of a word correctly unless you have a clear picture of the word stored away in your mind. I'm going to show you one way to create those clear word pictures.		
Discuss the characteristics of the word.	Let's look at the word *approach.* Take a close look at the word. Now look at each of the letters.	Teacher points to the word on the printed page.	Student points to each letter in the word and says it aloud.
Spell the word with the printed form present.	Now let's spell the word.	Together the teacher and the student slowly spell the word while looking at the printed form of the word.	
Visualize the word.	Now take one more careful look at the letters in the word because in a moment, I am going to ask you to close your eyes and then I will ask you some questions about the letters in this word. OK, I want you to close your eyes now and picture this word inside your head. Do you see the word? Let's look and point at each letter individually. As we say the letter together, stand up on your tiptoes if the letter is a tall one. Stay in a normal position if the letter is a short one, and crouch down if the letter goes below the line.	Teacher and student stand up. Teacher models for student how to go up on tiptoes for tall letters, stay in a normal position for short letters, and crouch down for letters that go below the line (e.g., *y, g,* and *p*).	Student remains in a normal position for the letter *a,* crouches down two separate times for the two occurrences of the letter *p,* returns to the normal position for the letters *r-o-a-c,* and stands up on tiptoes for the letter *h.*
Spell the word without the printed form present.	Open your eyes now. Do you still have a picture of the word in your mind? Look over my right shoulder. Do you see the word floating there? Look at each of the letters in the word and count the number of	Teacher removes or covers the printed form of the word.	Student looks over the right shoulder of teacher, looking out into the space very intently. If possible, have student gaze at an empty wall when doing this.

Steps to Developing an MOI	Teacher Script	Teacher Actions	Student Response
	vowels. How many do you see? From left to right, what are they? Now count the number of consonants. How many? Can you still see the word in your head? Can you see any words inside the word? What are they? Spell the word backwards. Now say the word, use it in a sentence that shows you understand its meaning, and write the sentence in your notebook. Attaching word meaning to the MOI is very important.		Student counts three vowels and identifies them by name (*a, o,* and *a*). Students counts five consonants and identifies them by name (*p, p, c,* and *h*). Student spells the word backwards *(h, c, a, o, r, p, p, a)*. Student says the word and writes it in a notebook.

If students have difficulty answering any of the questions in the second column, their MOI is not firmly fixed in their memory. Go back to Step 4—visualize the word.

Sources: Masterson, Apel, and Wasowicz (2002, p. 44) and J. Wasowicz (personal communications, August 4, 2008, October 21, 2008, and January 2009).

• Provide organized and sequential instruction. The scope and sequence should follow a natural word order that corresponds to phonological development as well as to the sounds and words being learned during reading instruction. If needed, supplement the core reading program with a multilinguistic spelling program. The spelling programs associated with core reading programs likely will not meet the needs of Tier 2 and 3 students.

• Begin by teaching phonemic strategies (i.e., teaching words in the primary grades that have predictable sound-to-spelling correspondences, such as *man, flat,* and *hit*). Then move to teaching morphemic strategies for words made up of prefixes, suffixes, and bases (e.g., *disjoined, unreliable,* and *worried*) in the upper grades and as appropriate, teach words that must be taught as wholes because they are neither phonemic nor morphemic (e.g., *restaurant, Wednesday,* and *was*). Use grade-level-appropriate passages in which words have intentionally been spelled incorrectly so that students can practice proofreading. Encourage students to call up their own mental images of correct spellings so they can immediately recognize spelling errors.

The Don'ts of Effective Spelling Instruction

• Don't teach spelling using self-constructed lists of dissimilar words that have not been analyzed for their various linguistic properties. Randomly selected words do not provide the scaffolding students need to become skilled spellers based on word knowledge.

- Don't ask students to write each spelling word several times. This practice is actually one of the least effective ways to assist students in learning to spell new words because it becomes a rote activity that does not focus their attention on the critical attributes of a word or on spelling patterns found in large numbers of related words.

- Don't expect your students to pick up spelling skills from doing lots of reading and writing. There may be a few students who seem to pick up new words effortlessly, but this is the exception rather than the rule.

- Don't teach each week's vocabulary list from reading as spelling words. Because these words are introduced in isolation without careful attention to their linguistic characteristics, the words will be memorized for the test and immediately forgotten by all but a few students. Teach spelling for the future, not for Friday.

- Don't fall into the trap of thinking that Spell Check is the answer to the world's spelling problems. Only 63% of spelling errors are detected with spell checkers (MacArthur, Graham, Haynes, & De La Paz, 1996), and Graham (2000) notes that overreliance on spell checkers may actually be detrimental to spelling development. Furthermore, Spell Check is not that helpful unless one has some sense of what the correct spelling ought to be.

- Don't blame your lack of spelling instruction on the supposed irregularity of the English language. In reality, only about 13% of English words are classified as exception words, words that don't follow any predictable pattern. Fifty percent of English language words are predictable and can be decoded and spelled by students who have the alphabetic principle. The remaining words consist of more complex spelling patterns that can be explicitly taught (Foorman et al., 1998).

- Don't skip the writing step during spelling instruction. Writing the word once while concentrating on its critical attributes and saying it quietly can be a powerful way for students to cement the correct spelling in their long-term memories where it will always be at the ready when needed in the course of reading or writing. Writing a word 10 times while watching TV or listening to music is not helpful.

- Don't develop your own spelling program or use one written by someone who lacks a deep knowledge of the linguistic aspects of spelling. The secret to effective spelling instruction is to tap into the expertise of those who have studied the English spelling system. These experts work in a variety of disciplines and have conceptualized spelling to make it more amenable to explicit and systematic instruction. They include speech–language pathologists like Wasowicz et al. (2004), the authors of *SPELL-Links to Reading & Writing;* reading and human development experts like Louisa Moats, coauthor with Rosow (2002) of *Spellography;* and language arts curriculum specialists like Bear, Invernizzi, Templeton, and Johnston (2000), authors of *Words Their Way: Word Study for Phonics, Spelling, and Vocabulary Development.* Take direction from these experts, and your students will become skilled spellers and more expert readers and writers as well.

■ INTENSIVE SPELLING-BASED READING INTERVENTIONS

Spelling deficits related to the five critical areas of linguistic knowledge cited earlier directly impact students' ability to read fluently and then write about what they have read using conventions of grammar and spelling. Consider Blake Hendez*, a fifth-grade student who scored Below Basic on the fourth-grade state reading assessment. Blake received PA and phonics instruction in kindergarten and first grade, participated in a fluency-building program in second grade, received a Tier 2 coaching intervention on the use of cognitive strategies in third grade, and attended a year-long afterschool program that focused on test-taking strategies, including writing practice in preparation for the state assessment. Blake seems to have had multiple opportunities to learn.

Although we do not know the quality of the programs or instruction Blake experienced, he has been in school every day since kindergarten, and his teachers seem to have been doing all of the right things. Although Blake made progress each year K–3, he lost ground in fourth grade as the textbooks grew longer and more complex and the reading and writing load increased. Blake scored Below Basic on the state reading assessment. There is always the temptation to put someone with Blake's profile into a remedial reading program, like *Corrective Reading* (Engelmann, Hanner, & Johnson, 1999) or *Language!* (Greene, 2004). However, doing that without further investigation would be akin to a doctor prescribing an antibiotic without knowing precisely where an infection is located. In Blake's case, we must determine the root cause of his comprehension difficulties.

We first administer the *TOWRE* (Torgesen, Wagner, & Rashotte, 1999) Sight Word Efficiency Test (takes 45 seconds) and discover that for his grade level, Blake scores well below the 39th percentile (a cut-off point recommended by Torgesen & Hayes, 2003). Blake's word-reading accuracy and fluency are low. In order to determine the source of Blake's dysfluency, we administer the *TOWRE* (Torgesen, Wagner, & Rashotte, 1999) Phonemic Decoding subtest (45 seconds). Blake once again scores below the 39th percentile. His phonemic decoding is very low, so we give him the Elision subtest from the *Comprehensive Test of Phonological Processes* (Wagner, Torgesen, & Rashotte, 1999) and discover PA deficiencies. In Blake's case, these three standardized tests produced a fairly accurate picture of his deficiencies. However, many standardized tests produce false negatives for students like Blake who have scattered and very specific deficits (e.g., phoneme segmentation deficits for word-final 'st' clusters only and vowel discrimination deficits for short vowel 'a' vs. short vowel 'e' but normal segmentation and discrimination for all other phonemes).

After administering these various subtests to Blake, we have some very specific diagnostic information. If we keep giving Blake more of the same kind of instruction he has had since kindergarten, we are likely to get the same results. I suggest that we test Blake with a prescriptive spelling assessment that will tell us precisely which areas of linguistic knowledge he lacks, based on the errors he makes in a computerized spelling assessment, which is more sensitive and thus able to identify specific deficits that are interfering with reading and spelling. The *SPELL-2: Spelling Performance Evaluation for Language and Literacy*® (Masterson, Apel, & Wasowicz, 2002) evaluates students based on their own spelling errors, and a program of remediation is then customized based on those errors. Following the assessment, which is administered by the speech–language pathologist or other reading and language-learning specialist, letters are sent to Blake's parents and his teacher. A copy of the teacher letter is shown in Figure 3.3.

SPELL-2 is a prescriptive assessment that not only pinpoints the language skills where Blake needs work, but it also tells the speech pathologist who will be working with Blake and precisely which lessons he needs to master. Since Blake has failed to achieve Basic on the state assessment, Blake is now officially enrolled in a Tier 3 intervention where the intervention staff (speech–language pathologists trained in

---

* Pseudonym

Figure 3.3 SPELL-2 Spelling Performance Letter to Teacher

SPELL-2

Spelling Performance Evaluation for Language and Literacy™

Student: Blake Hendez

Date of Birth: 4/25/1996

School: Dawes Middle School

Date of Test: 4/26/2007

Grade: 5

Age: 11 years, 0 months

Level of SPELL-2 Administered: 2

Examiner: Jonas Garcia

Dear Teacher,

I used SPELL-2: Spelling Performance Evaluation for Language and Literacy to measure Blake's spelling ability and underlying language knowledge and skills. SPELL-2 is a computer software program that assesses spelling and related skills and helps determine what type of spelling instruction is needed to improve literacy skills.

Spelling is a complex written language skill that draws upon on a number of different types of language abilities and knowledge. These include:

- **Awareness of components of spoken language (Phonological Awareness).** The ability to think about spoken words, and the ability to think and talk about the syllables, rhymes, individual speech sounds, and syllabic stress of words in spoken language.

- **Knowledge of English phonics and spelling rules or patterns (Orthographic Knowledge).** The knowledge of and ability to use specific letter-sound relationships and common letter patterns and spelling rules (for example, a long vowel sound in a one-syllable word that ends with a consonant sound is almost always spelled with two vowel letters) to spell words that follow English spelling conventions.

- **Knowledge of word parts and related words (Morphological Knowledge and Semantic Relationships).** The knowledge of and ability to use meaning to spell certain word suffixes such as "walk<u>s</u>, walk<u>ing</u>, walk<u>ed</u>", and certain word prefixes, such as "<u>dis</u>continue" and "<u>il</u>legal"; the knowledge of and ability to use familiar, related words to spell more complex words, for example, using "magic" to help spell "magician".

- **Memory for word images (Mental Orthographic Images).** The ability to store and recall clear and complete visual images of known words.

All of these factors are important for spelling and each affects how well a student spells. When a student struggles with how to spell words correctly, other aspects of his or her writing, such as grammar, organization and clarity, may be compromised. Language-based spelling instruction leads to significant improvement not only in spelling and writing, but also leads to significant improvement in reading skills.

SPELL-2 required Blake to spell a set of words and possibly to complete a series of additional tasks that provided further information about his underlying language knowledge and skills. SPELL-2 indicates that Blake needs to do the following to improve his spelling skills:

1. Awareness of components of spoken language (Phonological Awareness)
   - Blake needs phonology-based spelling instruction to improve spelling of
     - Short Vowel: u / ^ /
     - Long Vowel: o — Vowel digraphs and other spellings

2. Knowledge of English phonics and spelling rules or patterns (Orthographic Knowledge)
   - Blake needs pattern and rule-based spelling instruction to improve spelling of
     - Consonant Digraph(s) & Trigraph(s): Final 'ch, ten'
     - Consonant Digraph(s) & Trigraph(s): 'ck'

3. Knowledge of word parts and related words (Morphological Knowledge and Semantic Relationships)
   - Blake needs semantic and morphology-based spelling instruction to improve spelling of
     - Silent Letters: Non-conditioning silent 'e' and silent consonants

4. Memory for word images (Mental Orthographic Images)
   - Blake needs to develop clear and complete word images to improve spelling of
     - Consonant(s): Soft 'c'
     - Consonant(s): Soft 'g'
     - Consonant(s): Flapped 'tt, dd, t, d'
     - Consonant Digraph(s) & Trigraph(s): Final 'ch, tch'
     - Within-Word Consonant Doubling: 'pp, bb, tt, dd'
     - Long Vowel: a — Vowel digraphs and other spellings
     - Long Vowel: e — Vowel digraphs and other spellings
     - Long Vowel: u spelled 'u'
     - Long Vowel: u spelled 'u_e'
     - Long Vowel: u — Vowel digraphs and other spellings
     - Syllabic Vowel Sounds: Syllabic-l as in "bottle"
     - Silent Letters: Non-conditioning silent 'e' and silent consonants

I am including a list of suggestions for implementing these recommendations into your language arts curriculum. I hope you will find this information helpful.

Thank you, Jonas Garcia

Source: Reprinted by permission of Jan Wasowicz. Learning by Design.

the program) will provide direct instruction to Blake for one hour daily. The *SPELL-Links to Reading & Writing: A Word-Study Curriculum* (Wasowicz, Apel, Masterson, & Whitney, 2004) provides differentiated instruction driven by data-based decision making and frequent progress monitoring required under IDEA (2004) regulations. Blake's response to this diagnostic intervention will determine whether he is eligible for special education services. However, the speech pathologist who has worked with students like Blake in the past is confident that after this intervention, Blake will have improved in the following language skills: reading decoding, fluency, comprehension, vocabulary knowledge, accuracy and complexity of written language, and writing fluency. In addition, Blake will see improved academic performance across the curriculum and increased job potential and career success. Blake, his teacher, and his parents are eager to begin. This case study is based on information drawn from the following sources: Apel, Masterson, and Hart, (2004); Kelman and Apel (2004); Masterson et al. (2005); and Torgesen and Hayes (2003).

■ SUMMARIZING CHAPTER 3

Spelling and reading are almost the same in that they draw upon the same linguistic knowledge sources in long-term memory. They differ in only one way—spelling is a more exacting skill than reading. The integration of explicit, systematic spelling instruction with reading instruction is beneficial for all students, but especially for those who have sketchy and incomplete language knowledge and therefore experience difficulty in developing strong MOIs. Spelling instruction is an essential piece of the reading puzzle.

4

Fluency

> Fluency is the ability to read so effortlessly and automatically that working memory is available for the ultimate purpose of reading—extracting and constructing meaning from the text. Fluency can be observed in accurate, automatic, and expressive oral reading and makes possible, silent reading comprehension (Harris & Hodges, 1995, p. 85; Pikulski & Chard, 2005, p. 510).

I fully expected that my son Patrick would come home from kindergarten early in the fall of 1977 and announce that he had learned to read that day. After all, his older sister by two years had done just that. Because Patrick had enjoyed virtually identical literacy experiences since birth, it seemed a foregone conclusion to me that he would become a fluent reader at exactly the same time as his sister had. He did not, however. Oh, he satisfied all of the kindergarten expectations, according to his teacher, but he couldn't pick up just any book and read it when he was promoted to first grade. Nor did he demonstrate fluency at the end of first grade. Oh, Patrick was well grounded in phonics and could read simple decodable books with no difficulty, but he hadn't achieved automaticity in his reading.

Fluency

Although his second-grade teacher, Patty Taylor, looked like a mild-mannered suburban school teacher, she stepped into her closet every morning before school, slipped out of her teacher togs, and turned into Wonder Woman. Of course, the principal and parents never witnessed this transformation, but my son wrote an essay in high school describing how she magically endowed him with the power to become an honors student. You see, Patrick read 1,087 books in second grade. That was a noteworthy achievement for him, but what was even more remarkable was that Mrs. Taylor motivated him to do it. She marveled at the simple reports that he wrote, listened with wide-eyed fascination as he summarized the stories for her, and then recorded every book on a chart for all to see. Wonder Woman, to be sure! She even pinned a construction paper star to his T-shirt every time he read another 10 books.

When Patrick was ready for a new book, Mrs. Taylor was there to recommend one, slightly more difficult than the previous title but not so hard as to discourage a sensitive second grader. Gradually, the books that Patrick read became more challenging, and by the end of second grade, he was reading chapter books by E. B. White, Beverly Cleary, and Laura Ingalls Wilder with ease and enjoyment. Patrick had his nose in a book almost every waking moment during second grade. His transition from a novice to a skillful reader took place almost imperceptibly, but it was no less miraculous than his sister's pronouncement that she had learned to read at school on one day in October.

Many students fall through the cracks at precisely this point on the road to literacy. Even those students who know how to phonemically decode can fail to develop fluency if the books they choose or are given to read do not support their current reading levels or they do not engage in sufficient amounts of practice to acquire automaticity and accuracy in word identification.

■ WHAT IS FLUENCY AND HOW DO STUDENTS BECOME FLUENT READERS?

Until fluency was brought to the forefront of the reading instruction agenda in the Report of the National Reading Panel (NICHD, 2000), it was the forgotten piece of the reading puzzle. Oh, there were a few individuals who knew how important it was and occasionally wrote an article to remind educators (Allington, 1983; Anderson, 1981). Today, there are dozens of books and programs on the market to help educators build fluency in their classrooms.

In the first edition of *Teach Them ALL to Read* (McEwan, 2002a), fluency was defined as "automaticity and flow in the act of reading." In this edition the definition of fluency has expanded to include two additional concepts: (1) the ability to read with the kind of expression that indicates the reader understands the text and (2) the ability to make the transition from fluent oral reading to fluent silent reading comprehension.

Some fluency experts have begun to examine the role of prosody, "a series of features including pitch or intonation, stress or emphasis, and tempo or rate and the rhythmic pattern of language, all of which contribute to an expressive rendering of text" (Kuhn & Stahl, 2003, p. 6). Prosody, more simply, is reading with expression that indicates that the reader fully understands the meaning conveyed by the author. However, scholars are uncertain whether prosody causes readers to comprehend more readily or whether training in prosody improves comprehension.

Fluency encompasses at least five different components (Torgesen, Rashotte, & Alexander, 2001):

1. The proportion of words that are recognized as orthographic units; that is, sight words that can be immediately retrieved from long-term memory

2. The variation in speed with which sight words are processed either because they have not yet been fully fixed in the reader's long-term memory or because the reader has some difficulties with processing speed

3. The speed of the processes that are used to identify novel words that have never been encountered previously by the reader (such as phonemic decoding, analogy to known words, or guessing from the context or meaning of the passage)

4. Use of context to speed word identification, which is largely dependent on extensive vocabulary knowledge

5. Speed with which word meanings are identified (p. 337)

Of these five aspects of reading fluency, one stands out as the biggest roadblock: problems identifying individual words fluently. Therefore the major fluency objective in most classrooms today is increasing students'"rate and accuracy in oral reading" (Hasbrouk & Tindal, 1992). Increasing the number of words correct per minute that students can read orally as measured by the *DIBELS (Dynamic Indicators of Basic Early Literacy Skills;* Good & Kaminski, 2000) is the bottom line. More teachers than ever are paying attention to students who are unable to read fluently; however, some have forgotten that the purpose of fluency building is to prepare students to read silently for their own enjoyment and edification. Frankly, I am concerned about teachers who are so focused on easy answers to fluency that they have no time to do the real kind of fluency building that Mrs. Taylor did with my son Patrick. The authentic way to build fluency is by putting accessible books into the hands of students so they can increase their own fluency by doing lots of independent reading—orally at the beginning of the process and silently later on. The National Research Council (Snow et al., 1998) concluded, "Adequate progress in learning to read English (or any alphabetic language) beyond the initial level depends on sufficient practice in reading to achieve fluency with different texts" (p. 223).

WHEN SHOULD FLUENCY BE TAUGHT?   ■

The act of reading text is like playing music and listening to it at the same time.

—Atwood (2003, p. 50)

The question of when fluency should be taught presumes that fluency *can* actually be taught. However, upon deeper reflection, you may conclude as I have: fluency cannot be taught. At least not in the same sense that PA and sound–spelling correspondences are taught, with a careful progression of explicit, systematic lessons. *Fluency must be facilitated.* Teachers must do everything in their power to make the process of reading easier. How does a teacher make the process of reading easier for a struggling student? By making the text as accessible as possible. By scaffolding instruction with explicit phonics instruction as needed to help students decode new words. By providing generous blocks of time for structured oral repeated reading of accessible text.

Second grade has generally been the point at which teachers have concerned themselves with fluency building. The conventional wisdom has been that when students understand the alphabetic principle and are able to read first-grade passages accurately and at a rate of at least 40–50 words correct per minute, they are ready to focus on fluency (Good, Kaminski, & Howe, 2005). However, Hiebert and Fisher (2006) suggest that second grade may be too late and that "fluency from the first" should be the goal. An adaptation of their lesson plan for facilitating fluency in first grade can be found in Figure 4.5 later in the chapter.

Once achieved, fluency opens a window to the wonderful world of reading. Fluent readers are able to identify sight words in a split second. Understanding how students make the transition from painstaking decoding to fluent reading is critical to facilitating fluency for your students. As you may recall from earlier discussions, the secret lies in the independent sounding-out process that beginning readers go through with every unfamiliar word they encounter. The number of sounding-outs needed to know a word solidly is different for each student. Some students may need only three or four readings of a word to create a strong MOI and fix it solidly in their long-term memories for automatic retrieval. Students who readily acquire sight words will not need to read the same text repeatedly. Expect these students to read more books and increasingly more challenging books (both fiction and nonfiction)—taking care to monitor and periodically assess their fluency and comprehension in more difficult texts.

Other students may need upwards of 10 to 15 sounding-outs of a word to master it. They will benefit from repeated oral readings of familiar controlled text. The students who are most at risk of reading failure may need up to 30 repetitions of a word before it becomes a part of long-term memory. These students must orally reread accessible text that is at their independent levels many times to gain the fluency they need to become literate. Recall that accessible text is not predictable text. Predictable text does not make reading easier. It makes rote memorization easier. Accessible text gives students repeated encounters with high-frequency words, enabling them to build their own mental lexicon of sight words—words they can instantly retrieve from long-term memory.

■ THE ROLE OF FLUENCY IN SKILLED READING

> *If words are not identified accurately in sufficient numbers of repetitions, then accurate orthographic representations are not formed, and words must be recognized through analytic means (phonemic analysis, analogy, context) that take more time than recognition on the basis of a unitized orthographic representation. One of the principle characteristics of most children with reading disabilities after the initial phase in learning to read is a severe limitation in the number of words that can be recognized instantly.*
>
> —Torgesen, Rashotte, et al. (2001, p. 348)

Fluency plays a critical role in skilled reading, serving as the bridge between word identification and comprehension (Pikulski & Chard, 2005). Automatic and accurate sight word reading enables readers to focus all of their cognitive energies on the meaning of what they are reading. Here's how one exasperated fourth grader explained the process to his equally distraught reading teacher as she tried in vain to help him extract meaning from a single sentence of the paragraph they were reading together:

> I don't have enough brains left at the end of the sentence to tell you what it means. I've used them all up just figuring out what the words are.

The working memory of the human brain has limitations regarding how much it can process at one time, much like the desktop of a computer. When students are forced to devote all of their brain power to painstakingly sounding out every word, it's no wonder they lose track of meaning.

As you might expect, fluency is highly correlated (.80) with the ability to comprehend what is read (Fuchs, Fuchs, Hops, & Jenkins, 2001; Fuchs, Fuchs, & Maxwell, 1988; Good, Simmons, & Kame'enui, 2001). In fact, measures of oral reading fluency have been found to be *more* highly correlated with reading comprehension scores than were measures of silent reading rates in a sample of children whose reading skills varied across a broad range (Jenkins, Fuchs, Espin, van den Broek, & Deno, 2000). As students develop fluency in their oral reading, their comprehension scores will often also improve (Calfee & Piontkowski, 1981). Fluent oral readers are better able to understand what they read than are their dysfluent peers, given similar knowledge of the vocabulary and concepts in the text.

Lest you conclude that fluency problems are relatively rare—a concern for special education or remedial reading teachers to handle—consider the results of a large study of fluency achievement in the United States (Pinnell et al., 1995). Conducted as part of the National Assessment of Educational Progress, the study examined the fluency of a national sample of fourth-grade students. It found that 44% of students tested were dysfluent, even when reading grade-level stories that they had already read under supportive testing conditions. Until you actually assess the oral reading fluency of your students, whatever their grade level, you will not know what part of their comprehension difficulties are actually the result of slow and inaccurate reading. However, enrolling a dysfluent reader in a comprehensive fluency-building program without first discovering and remediating the underlying problem is not the wisest use of instructional time. Tackling gaps in word identification skills must come first. Fluency difficulties are directly attributable to the inability of readers to identify words quickly and accurately (Lyon, 1995; Torgesen, Rashotte, & Alexander, 2001; Wise, Ring, & Olson, 1999).

SCIENTIFIC EVIDENCE FOR FLUENCY INSTRUCTION

The National Reading Panel (NICHD, 2000) focused its review of fluency research on fluency building with repeated oral reading of text in students in the second and third grades, concluding that children improved in their reading fluency or comprehension when orally reading the same text repeatedly. In order for repeated reading to be effective in building fluency, three conditions must be present: (1) oral reading and rereading text a specified number of times or until the student achieves a specified fluency criteria (number of words correct per minute), (2) an actual increase in oral reading practice in a supported context using tutors or peers, and (3) various types of feedback concerning the accuracy and fluency of reading. Precisely how these three conditions act and interact to produce fluent reading is not known with certainty, but most research indicates that repeated reading impacts individual word reading efficiency more than any other aspect of fluent reading (Faulkner & Levy, 1999; Levy, 1999).

The benefits of repeated oral reading of text can only be realized if the text that is given to students provides repeated exposures to texts with controlled vocabularies. Of the fluency studies reviewed by the National Reading Panel (NICHD, 2000), 74% used texts with controlled vocabularies. Four of these studies used literature for repeated reading. Only one of those four literature-based studies reported any improvement in students' fluency, and in that study, treatment and comparison groups did not differ significantly. What is crucial for practitioners to know is that *the effect size for fluency reported by the National Reading Panel came from the studies that used text with controlled vocabulary* (Hiebert & Fisher, 2005). In other words, the magnitude of the effect of repeated oral reading with controlled vocabulary text on students' fluency levels overcame the lack of effect of repeated oral reading using literature on students' fluency levels. More recent research has examined the following aspects of fluency instruction:

- The critical role of accessible text in building fluency (Foorman et al., 2004; Hiebert, 2008a; Hiebert & Fisher, 2005; Hiebert & Martin, 2002)
- The impact of facilitating fluency as part of the daily reading lesson, along with word study and comprehension instruction (Stahl & Heubach, 2005)
- The relationship of practice to developing fluency (Kuhn & Stahl, 2003)
- How to effectively facilitate fluency in younger students who are most reading disabled and older struggling readers (Torgesen & Hudson, 2006)
- The power of fluency-building in late first grade (Hiebert & Fisher, 2006)

Just ahead I undertake a more comprehensive description of the most effective instructional practices to facilitate fluency in K–3 classrooms.

■ EFFECTIVE INSTRUCTIONAL PRACTICES FOR FACILITATING FLUENCY

There are four ways to facilitate fluency for all K–3 students:

1. Facilitate fluency during the reading block for all students.

2. Use small-group fluency interventions for students who need scaffolded instruction with more accessible text to build fluency.

3. Use a wide variety of repeated-reading techniques to keep students engaged in various kinds of repeated oral reading throughout the school day.

4. Use more intensive, specialized fluency-building interventions for the students most reading disabled or most at risk of reading failure.

Facilitate Fluency During the Reading Block

Facilitate fluency during the reading block on a daily basis by including the following experiences:

- Fluency-based reading instruction

- A large volume of independent reading characterized by high levels of success

- A motivational at-school–at-home recreational reading component that is closely monitored and supported by the classroom teacher

Fluency-Based Reading Instruction

The most important thing we can do to improve children's reading achievement is to have them read as much connected text at their instructional level as possible.

—Stahl (2000, p. 9)

Students who are reading at late first-grade or second-grade levels benefit from scaffolded instruction in daily repeated oral reading of text to build fluency. There are at least two schools of thought regarding how best to deliver fluency-based reading instruction: (1) with a whole-class, heterogeneous group of students using the core reading program's weekly selection from the core program's anthology or (2) in a smaller skill-based group using more accessible texts than those available in the anthology.

FORI (fluency-oriented reading instruction) is a fluency-based lesson plan for whole-class instruction using the core program's anthology (Stahl & Heubach, 2005). The five-day implementation schedule as adapted from Walpole and McKenna (2007) is shown in Figure 4.1. While this model is attractive, care must be taken to scaffold repeated reading practice for the most at-risk readers in smaller skill-based groups. The activities for each day of implementation are accompanied by some critical issues to think about as you plan to use FORI.

When students at risk of reading failure are not developing fluency at an appropriate rate, consider using more accessible text and substituting SAFER (Successful, Anxiety-Free Engaged Reading; Bursuck & Damer, 2007, p. 184) in place of the teacher read-aloud for students' first reading of the text. As you consider the SAFER method described in Figure 4.2, remember that in order to benefit from this method, students must have scored 50 phonemes per minute or more on the *DIBELS* Nonsense Words Assessment with at least 15 read as sight words (as opposed to phonemically decoding) or they should be reading second-grade or higher leveled text. Attempting SAFER reading with students who do not meet these criteria will not result in anxiety-free reading. Those students need increased word identification instruction. The steps to SAFER reading shown in the middle column will take place during the first reading of a new story and include some components not found in the FORI model. The notes in the third column offer further explanation for each step.

Real, High-Success, High-Volume Independent Reading Experiences

Extensive exposure to text through wide and deep reading practice is essential to growth in the number of words that children can recognize orthographically [by sight].

—Torgesen, Alexander, et al. (2001, p. 34)

The second essential component of the reading block is independent reading. Independent reading experiences in Grades K–3 ideally have the following characteristics:

- They are *real*, meaning that students are independently processing text during oral reading (unassisted by an adult) or silent reading, as opposed to doing anything else that may seem like reading, but isn't.
- They are *high success* so that students do not experience frustration or failure as they read unassisted.
- They are *high volume*, meaning there are large numbers of real, high-success reading experiences.

Real Reading

Children can learn a great deal about the language and content of texts through listening to experienced readers read texts aloud but, unless children's eyes are making contact with print and translating that print into language, they can't be described as reading.

—Hiebert (2008a, p. 1)

Real reading takes place when students identify words independently, either analytically (through phonemic decoding, analogy, or context) or increasingly as they

Figure 4.1   Fluency-Oriented Reading Instruction, Five-Day Implementation Plan

Day	Activities	Suggested Enhancements to FORI
1	Read the selection aloud to the class as they follow along in their own books. Then lead a comprehension discussion.	Bursuck and Damer (2007) recommend using text at students' instructional level, a minimum of 90% word reading accuracy on a "cold read." A "cold read" can only be successful if students are grouped according to their reading levels. The use of FORI with a heterogeneously grouped whole class has the potential for letting some students fall through the cracks. Anytime students are expected to read frustration level text they experience high levels of anxiety and do not achieve the desired reading gains. When text is first read aloud to students, they do not have the opportunity to employ their individual decoding skills to read the more challenging new words, because they hear them read first. When students' accuracy reading the words is less than 90%, comprehension activities should be integrated as students read the text.
2	Lead the students in Echo Reading (see page 84) with a classmate. Students take the selection home to read with a caregiver.	To provide additional opportunities to learn at school, assign a repeated reading of the selection for an after- or before-school tutoring session or a recess "book break" activity. Teach the students an error correction procedure to use with their partner for misread words and monitor whether they consistently use it. Feedback on word errors is important because when students learn to read a word incorrectly, reteaching that word takes so much longer that valuable time is wasted.
3	Lead the students in reading the selection chorally (see page 85). Students again take the selection home to practice with a parent, peer, or caregiver.	Schedule a "book-buddy" break sometime during the school day in which students read the selection to an older student (a book-buddy). The goal of repeated reading is not to have students memorize the text. There is a distinct difference between students' memorization of words as wholes (the word learning that is necessary for exception words) and the word learning that is essential for recognizing words orthographically after repeated sounding-outs. Consider how best to monitor students. If FORI is not accompanied by explicit, systematic phonics instruction, even the best students will falter as they encounter increasingly large numbers of new and more difficult words.
4	Lead students in paired reading with peers (see page 84). Students have a final chance to practice at home.	Build in a Read-Think-Share activity before or after paired reading with a peer to enhance comprehension of the text.
5	Students do extension activities. While they work independently, the teacher assesses the fluency of each child individually by having them read the story aloud.	If students are making too many errors in word identification, consider modifying the amount of time they are reading without any error correction by a teacher. Because behavior problems increase when students are working independently for long periods of time without direct teacher instruction, teachers need to use their time efficiently in assessing students' reading. For a quick fluency test use the one-minute *DIBELS* ORFs every other week. Students' whose ORF (oral reading fluency) scores are not progressing are not making gains in reading and the teacher should further assess to determine why.

Source: Five-Day Schedule was adapted from Walpole and McKenna (2007). Suggested enhancements are the author's.

Figure 4.2   Steps to SAFER Reading

Step	Description	Some Things to Think About
1	Call on individual students randomly and have them read between 1–3 sentences of the story.	Although Step 1 may appear to be Round Robin Reading, it is not. What makes SAFER reading different is that all of the students in the SAFER group have the skills needed to read the text independently. There will be no embarrassment or hesitation from students. They will be tuned into the text, knowing that they will be called on and feeling confident that they are ready. In the typical Round Robin reading session, there are students at multiple reading levels with varying degrees of engagement with the text. High-level readers are skipping ahead. Struggling readers are avoiding the eyes of the teacher, hoping they won't be called upon to "read."
2	Expect students to follow along in the text with their pointer fingers.	This simple technique enables students to focus on the text and keeps them from losing their places.
3	Call on students quickly and avoid unnecessary tangential teacher talk by focusing comprehension questions to key ideas, vocabulary, and supporting details.	Make this aspect of your SAFER reading as perky and brisk as you can. Resist the temptation to engage in teacher talk (meandering side trips that create mindless reading).
4	Write missed words on the board. At the end of the story have students sound out each missed decodable word and read it. If the missed word is an exception word, tell the student the word.	In addition to telling students missed exception words, encourage them to visualize the word with their eyes closed and then orally spell it using the visualization method described in Chapter 3. The error correction aspect of SAFER reading is important because when immediate and corrective feedback is provided, accurate word reading and comprehension significantly improve (Pany & McCoy, 1988).
5	Note any obvious error patterns to determine if reteaching is needed.	
6	Explain to students that their goal is 97% accuracy. Reread the story once more before having students pair up and read the story to each other. Monitor for accuracy as students read.	At this point, students should engage in a variety of repeated oral readings until the fluency goal of 97% accuracy is achieved. The FORI lesson plan offers a variety of ways to structure the remaining days of the week.

Source: The steps to SAFER reading have been adapted from Bursuck and Damer (2007). SAFER is based on procedures for instructing group oral reading originally developed by Carnine et al. (2004). The things to think about are the author's reflections and observations on the SAFER approach.

gain fluency, through the rapid identification of words stored in their mental dictionaries as sight words. Although the following literacy activities are beneficial for building word and world knowledge in the earliest literacy experiences, they do not qualify as real reading because they do not provide reading practice that builds fluency: (a) rereading and memorizing predictable big books; (b) listening to read-alouds; (c) writing predictable books as a class, based on predictable books that have been read aloud; (d) looking at pictures in books; (e) drawing pictures about stories that have been read aloud; (f) dramatizing books; (g) sharing student-authored books; and (h) creating language experience charts.

In order to become fluent readers, students *must read independently.* They must personally process the text, decoding unfamiliar words enough times through repeated oral readings to store the words in their long-term memories as sight words. Each student will move through the stages from slowly sounding out and blending words to fluent silent reading on a slightly different timetable, but there are far too many students who will never achieve fluency because they have not engaged in enough real reading. See Figure 4.3 for a description of the four stages of reading development.

High-Success Experiences

The most effective instructional practice for building fluency is the provision of what Allington (2006b) calls high-success reading experiences. Novice readers are sensitive to the slightest failures and give up easily in discouragement. The difficulty of basal or core reading programs, as documented by Hiebert (2006a) and Foorman and her colleagues (2004), makes the provision of scaffolded instruction essential, either on an individual or small group-basis. A critical factor in guaranteeing high levels of success for students is the accessibility of the text. The benefits of repeated oral reading can only be realized if the text that has been chosen gives students repeated exposure to a controlled vocabulary. That makes the on-grade-level core

Figure 4.3   Stages of Development in Learning to Read Words by Sight

Stage	Description	Example
Prealphabetic	No understanding of the alphabetic principle (the idea that there is a systematic relationship between the sounds of our language and the written letters)	Prereaders use visual clues in print, such as the shapes of letters, to "read" words.
Partially alphabetic	Some understanding of the relationship between letters and sounds	Prereaders make associations between the initial consonant in one word like *dog* and then begin to generalize what they know about the letter and the sound to identify all words beginning with *d* as *dog*.
Fully alphabetic	Complete understanding of the alphabetic principle, resulting in the accurate processing of print and the rapid acquisition of increasing numbers of sight words	Readers rapidly add sight words to their mental lexicons, including information about the spellings, pronunciations, and meanings of words (Ehri 1998, pp. 11–12).
Consolidated alphabetic	Ability to recognize whole words instantly as well as letter patterns	Readers are able to rapidly process sound–spelling correspondences and can also readily process onset-rimes, a faster way to decode than blending each individual phoneme (sound). Readers in this stage are poised to become fluent readers *if* they continue to read a lot and add lots of word and world knowledge to their long-term memories while also acquiring a repertoire of comprehension strategies.

Source: Adapted from Ehri (1995).

curriculum *or* leveled fiction books suspect as recommended text for building fluency. Figure 4.4 defines three levels of reading: instructional, independent, and frustration. Knowing precisely where each student is performing and how to match text to student is an important prerequisite for providing high-success experiences for every student.

High Volume of Reading

Unfortunately, the students who need the *most* reading practice actually get the least during an average school day, especially when compared to their more accomplished peers (Allington, 1977, 1980). Children in low-reading groups read as few as 16 words in a week, while their more linguistically rich classmates in higher reading groups read as many as 1,933 words per week (Allington, 1984). Nagy and Anderson (1984) reported that proficient readers read about 1,000,000 words per year in and out of school while their less skilled classmates are reading as few as 100,000 during a year. Cunningham and Stanovich (1998) found a similar chasm between the reading volume of good and poor readers. A student at the 90th percentile of reading ability may read as many words in two days as a child at the 10th percentile reads in an entire school year outside the school setting. Closing the achievement gap will be impossible unless we find ways to increase reading volume for readers at risk.

More recently, Allington (2006b) has suggested that a critical step in designing interventions for struggling readers should begin with making sure they have as many real reading experiences in school as their more successful peers. He recommends that students spend 90 minutes a day reading either at their instructional levels with teacher support or their independent levels unassisted.

Figure 4.4   Choosing Text for Building Fluency

1. Instructional Reading Level	Choose text at students' instructional level when the goals are building word and world knowledge and scaffolding comprehension strategies that have previously been taught. When text is at their instructional levels, students need teacher support to read the text with understanding. Instructional text is text that students can read at first reading with at least 90% accuracy. No more than 1 in 10 words should be too difficult for students to read on their own.
2. Independent Reading Level	Choose text at your students' independent reading level for repeated oral reading to build fluency, for oral reading to increase comprehension of text, or for independent reading at home. When text is at students' independent levels, they can generally read the text with ease and fluency. Texts at this level can be read with at least 95% accuracy on a first read. No more than 1 in 20 words should be too difficult for the student to recognize through analytic means (phonemic decoding, analogy, context). Many words should already be sight words, instantly retrievable in a second or less.
3. Frustration Reading Level	Students have less than 90% accuracy in text at their frustration level. When expected to read text at their frustration level, students tune out, talk to their neighbors, distract the teacher, and find excuses to move about the room.

Source: Adapted from Harris and Sipay (1985); Armbruster et al. (2001); and Bursuck and Damer (2007).

Teachers in the primary grades *cannot* assume that fluency will develop for all or even most of their students in the absence of a structured and well-monitored program that includes both repeated oral reading and reading in a variety of other ways. Teaching students how to read is of no value if there is not a simultaneous effort to encourage them to assiduously practice their newly learned skills with some expectation of accountability for learning new words and writing about what they have read.

The question of how much time students actually spend in real reading during the reading block has always intrigued me. When I am working with a low-performing school that is looking for ways to notch up their students' reading performance, I do a walk-through during the primary reading block, spending about 10 minutes in every K–3 classroom. I am looking for real reading. If students are not engaged in real reading on their own, then teachers need professional development in precisely how to increase the amount of reading during the school day.

A group of researchers working with Reading First schools in Mississippi undertook a similar project. They wanted to increase the time that students spent reading accessible texts, but they first had to determine how much students were actually reading (Brenner, Tompkins, Hiebert, Riley, & Miles, 2007). They used a methodology that had been previously used to determine if students were reading: they intently watched the eyes of six students in each classroom to calculate the amount of time they had their eyes on the page, observing each child for 30 seconds every three minutes (Adler & Fisher, 2001). They then computed the amount of time that this selected sample of third-grade students (both boys and girls at three different achievement levels) in 65 Reading First schools in 32 districts in Mississippi spent in actual reading during the reading block. Using the data from their sample, they extrapolated the findings to a whole class. During the reading blocks, which ranged from 90 to 120 minutes in the various schools, the actual time spent reading averaged between 18 and 19 minutes, just 17.5% of the average time allocated for the reading block. Most distressing is that during one-fourth of the recorded observations, no reading at all was observed.

Having determined a baseline amount of reading, the team then set out to increase the amount of reading time in classrooms in these schools. They provided professional development for literacy coaches in the form of seven modules focused on varying topics related to how to increase the amount of time students read: partner reading, repeated reading, reading with a purpose, and the difference between reading-rich and reading-poor activities. Literacy coaches in turn presented the modules to their faculty members. During a follow-up assessment, the actual time spent reading went from 18 minutes to 29 minutes. Eleven minutes more per day times about 176 days of the year adds up to a lot more reading practice for students who need it most.

As part of their research, the team also carefully examined the various core reading programs being used in the various districts to determine how well they supported reading time for students. They discovered that the programs suggested many more reading-poor activities (what I call *unreal reading*), and there was little focus in the teacher's manuals on time spent reading.

In contrast, consider the real reading practices at Benchmark School. Irene Gaskins, founder of Benchmark, a private school for students who are severely reading disabled, and her staff have long been committed to increasing students' academically engaged time during seatwork. To that end, they eliminated the meaningless activities that inevitably creep into the reading block and increased the amount of real reading that students did. The reading was always on students' independent level, so it was accessible to them. Students could progress at their own rate and so everyone was reading from different books. Gaskins and Elliot (1991) describe how students were held accountable for what they had read during each high-volume 40-minute seatwork period:

> There was usually some kind of written response required after the completion of each story or chapter. Our guideline: 80% of the seatwork time should be spent reading and no more than 20% of the time on writing a response to what was read. These responses were not intended to be inquisition-like. Rather they were to provide the student with an opportunity to reflect on what was read. . . . A further guideline was that students were to be given feedback regarding their written responses sometime during the morning language arts period on the day the response was completed. (p. 12)

If students enter third grade reading fewer than 90–95 words correct per minute in grade-level text, their likelihood of having high-success reading experiences in school begins to diminish sharply. All too soon, for many students, their textbooks will be too difficult to read. Sometimes even the text found in supposed interventions is too difficult for students to read without major scaffolding support from their teachers (O'Connor et al., 2002). Not only are these students not having any high-success reading experiences, they are losing ground daily in the acquisition of standards-based-content and academic vocabulary.

The paramount goal of first-grade and second-grade teachers is the development of fluency through the provision of high-success reading experiences. This is not a program you can buy in a box or teach from a manual. It requires obsessive attention to every child's personal reading experiences, for it is only through intensive practice that reading becomes fluent.

A Motivational, Recreational Reading Component

In the third component of fluency building during the reading block, students choose whatever, wherever, and whenever they want to read. The minimum acceptable time students must devote to this component is 55 minutes—25 minutes at any time during the school day and 30 minutes at home. Students who devote more than the required 55 minutes are rewarded with points that are exchangeable for small prizes in the school store. Students are held to an honor system for their extra reading. Teachers and parents are required to sign off. For example, if a student chose to read during 10 minutes of a rainy-day indoor recess, the supervisor on duty would be responsible for signing the student's reading record. The only requirement is that students must read during any free time they have at school (even during recess and lunch if possible), and they must also read at home, both to and with parents, caregivers, older siblings or a pet (if that's the only living creature available to listen). Parents must sign off on students' home reading, and students must write two sentences about their reading on a form provided by the teacher.

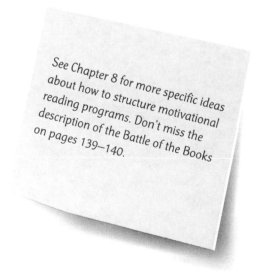

See Chapter 8 for more specific ideas about how to structure motivational reading programs. Don't miss the description of the Battle of the Books on pages 139–140.

Note that the *Accelerated Reader* program (Advantage Learning Systems, 2001) cannot take the place of a skilled teacher in building fluency in Grades 1–2. This important learning outcome of Grade 2 cannot be delegated. An exception to this rule can be made for students who are reading well above grade level and may be participating in a more advanced reading motivation program with the media specialist.

Even if students are reading a lot at school, just reading at school is *never* enough. Students *must* read voraciously, voluminously, and voluntarily outside of school as well (Shefelbine, 1999). Teachers and principals must communicate early and often with parents regarding the importance of engaging children in regular oral reading at home just as soon as a child acquires beginning decoding skills. Educators and parents need to support each other's efforts in this endeavor.

Most parents do not fully understand the importance of achieving fluency by the end of second grade, or third grade at the very latest. Educators must convey to parents the urgency of reading along with and listening to their children orally read books on their independent reading levels. Teachers must be accountable for helping students to select the just-right books to take home, or the system will break down as struggling readers grow frustrated with too-difficult text and parents do not know what to do. The key to maximizing these at-home reading experiences includes having just-right text and offering training for parents in how to help their students develop fluency.

Use Small-Group Interventions to Increase Reading Fluency

The SAFER (Bursuck & Damer, 2007) method was suggested earlier as one way to scaffold readers at risk during fluency development. Hiebert and Fisher (2006) describe a small-group intervention designed to both increase the number of words students read as part of their reading lesson and improve their reading fluency. Their intervention goals were based on the findings of two studies: (1) the amount of time that students read in the classroom is closely related to their reading achievement (Fisher & Berliner, 1985) and (2) low-performing first graders typically read approximately 27 words per half hour during the reading block (Allington, 1985).

Hiebert and Fisher's (2006) intervention to build fluency among ELL students during the last third of first grade took place during twenty-four 30-minute sessions over an eight-week period. One group did repeated oral reading from single-criterion texts (SC), a second group used multiple-criteria texts (MC), and a third group served as the control group.

The SC group orally read decodable books from the *Open Court* Program (Adams & Bereiter, 2002). The MC group used little books from the NEARStar program (Pacific Resources for Education and Learning, 2003). These books used three different types of words: words with common and consistent letter–sound patterns, high-frequency words, and high-imagery words.

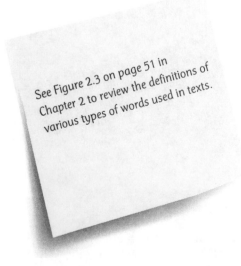

See Figure 2.3 on page 51 in Chapter 2 to review the definitions of various types of words used in texts.

The texts differed in the number and kinds of unique words. The SC program had 296 unique words, 70% with short-vowel patterns, and an additional 10% among the 100 most frequent words. Of the 145 unique words in the MC program, 58% had short-vowel patterns, and an additional 23% were among the 100 most frequent words.

The three groups had similar pretest results. In posttests, students in both of the intervention groups outscored the control group in words correct per minute (wcpm) on the Texas Primary Reading Inventory (Texas Education Agency, 1998). The students in the SC group made a gain of 2.9 wcpm on the TPRI for every week of the intervention while the students in the MC group made a gain of 3.4 wcpm for every week of the intervention. In both of the treatments, students read about 6,500 words over a 12-hour period, or approximately 270 words per half-hour. The intervention multiplied the number of words read times 10 over the amount they had previously been reading in their classrooms. Figure 4.5 is an adaptation of the lesson plan used in this first-grade fluency intervention.

Use a Wide Variety of Repeated-Reading Techniques

There are many ways to structure repeated oral reading in your classroom. Do not assume that older students or even more proficient students will not benefit from repeated oral reading of text. The following variations will motivate and engage students as you provide as many opportunities for repeated oral reading as you can during the school day. Use peers, older students, parents, and volunteer tutors to read with and listen to your students.

The Neurological Impress Method

The neurological impress method (NIM) was originally used after World War II to teach brain-damaged adults to read again and was first described in 1969 by Heckelman (1969). To implement NIM, the tutor sits slightly behind the student and reads aloud into the student's ear. Some practitioners of NIM recommend sitting nearest the ear that corresponds to the hand with which the student writes or eats. The tutor and student share a book, with the tutor holding one corner of the book and the student holding the opposite one. The tutor and the student read with one voice, so to speak, with the tutor's speed slightly exceeding the student's normal rate so that the student is forced to pay attention to whole words and sentences to keep up with the tutor. The tutor tracks words by running a forefinger under them while reading. After several *joint* oral readings of the text, the student then begins to lead the reading while the tutor guides the student's finger smoothly under the words as they are read. The tracking responsibility is also gradually given over to the student after repeated readings of the same text. When a specific passage can be read at the selected target rate (usually 85 correct words per minute), a new, slightly more difficult passage should be selected. NIM is also referred to as *duet reading* (Heckelman, 1969).

Figure 4.5   Sample Lesson for First-Grade Fluency Intervention

Activity	Description	Time Allocation
Word cards	These activities use two words with particular letter–sound correspondences from a text.	6 minutes
Repeated reading of a story	This encompasses three readings of a new book: a teacher-led read-aloud with retelling by the students, paired reading, and choral reading.	10 minutes
Writing words	This entails writing words on individual chalkboards.	5 minutes
More reading	Students read an additional book or reread books from previous lessons.	9 minutes

Source: Adapted from Hiebert and Fisher (2006).

Cross-Age Reading

Older readers who may be reluctant to engage in enough repeated oral readings of text at their instructional level to reach an 85-words-per-minute goal will usually jump at the chance to read aloud to younger students. In preparation for their read-aloud sessions, older readers must first engage in several repeated readings of their books without an audience and then read them aloud to as many listeners as they can find. Provide older readers with accountability forms on which the parents or teachers of younger students can sign off after the read-alouds are completed. Debrief with older readers following each set of read-aloud sessions regarding how their reading fluency improved between the first read-aloud and the last (Labbo & Teale, 1990).

Taped Reading

In this version of repeated oral reading, students read aloud once or twice short passages of text at their independent reading levels and then record the passage via a tape recorder. The tapes are then replayed, and students follow along with the text and monitor their oral reading. Students then record the passage again and listen for improvement. Students continue to read, record, and monitor their recording as often as needed to reach their goals.

Paired Reading With a Parent, Older Student, Sibling, or Tutor

This technique involves a family member, volunteer, or older student pairing with a dysfluent reader. Listening to repeated oral readings of text is a perfect assignment for senior or parent volunteers. Use the guidelines given earlier for choosing the text to be repeatedly read, or investigate commercially available programs. Tutors and readers can first read the text aloud together (shared reading). When students feel confident about reading on their own, they can then read the passage orally several times. Paired-reading contracts in which older siblings or parents agree to do repeated readings with students are a powerful way to make sure that students with fluency problems get adequate oral reading practice at home.

Paired Reading With a Peer

Paired reading with a peer is a variation of repeated reading in which peer partners who are on or about the same reading level each read a short passage aloud three to five times and then evaluate both their own and their partners' reading. The paired students take turns reading orally and keeping a record of the errors and time elapsed for their partner's reading (Koskinen & Blum, 1986).

Echo Reading

A parent, tutor, older student, or teacher orally reads the first line of the text, and the student then reads the same line, modeling the tutor's example. The tutor and the student read in echo fashion for the entire passage, gradually increasing the amount of text that either the tutor or the student reads at one time. The tutor should gradually increase the reading speed to push the student to identify words more quickly. Students can also do echo reading with peers who are more accomplished readers.

Do You Read Me?

This is just another name for assisted repeated reading in which students read orally, along with a commercial or volunteer-made tape that corresponds to a selected passage or book. Some schools set up an area in the media center for what they call *automatic reading* where students read along with a tape several times daily until they can read the story smoothly by themselves. Closely monitor the first few readings, however. Some commercially prepared tapes are read aloud at speeds that are too fast for dysfluent readers. The preparation of tapes using slightly slower readers may prove to be what is needed (Dowhower, 1989).

Choral Reading

Choral reading is the simultaneous oral reading of text by a small group or class of students. The text must be displayed on an overhead projector or everyone must have their own copies. Choral reading is an excellent way to give dysfluent students experience with more challenging text without the risk of embarrassment. Choose a poem or famous speech and read it repeatedly with the class over several days until the fluency, expression, and diction are near perfect. Then invite a guest to hear students perform before choosing another selection (Miccinati, 1985).

Readers' Theater

This method of repeated reading enables students to participate in the reading of a play without the props, scenery, and endless rehearsals. Students do not memorize lines or wear costumes. They just repeatedly read their parts orally in preparation for the performance. Play tapes of old radio shows to show students how powerful text can be when read fluently and with appropriate expression (Opitz & Rasinski, 1998).

Take It Home

Form partnerships with parents as early as possible in the school year. Invite them to school for a repeated-reading training session in which teachers demonstrate how to do it and how to measure oral reading fluency. Share research with parents that demonstrates how powerful repeated reading is and ask them to contract with teachers to listen to their child do 10 to 15 minutes of repeated reading three to five times per week combined with reading aloud more challenging text to their children. Many teachers have seen their students realize enormous growth in oral reading fluency when they enlist parents as their partners in achieving this goal (Topping, 1987).

Fluency Development Lesson

Fluency development lesson is a combination of reading aloud, choral reading, listening to students read, and reading performance and is implemented over an extended period. Students first listen to the teacher read a poem or other text to the class. They then read the text chorally, pair up and practice reading the text with a classmate, and then perform for an interested audience (Rasinski, Padak, Linke, & Sturdevant, 1994).

Keeping Track

This method of repeated reading involves having students graph their own oral reading fluency scores over a period of time. As older students become familiar with the process, they can work with a partner to do the timing and error counting. When students assess and monitor their own fluency, they are highly motivated to work harder for increased fluency.

Radio Reading

In radio reading, students independently practice selected portions of the text ahead of time by reading them orally as often as needed to develop expression and fluency. This type of repeated reading can be used in lieu of the teacher reading aloud to students. Small groups of students work together and prepare sections of a chapter to be read chorally. More proficient students might read parts of the chapter solo. Assign one student to be the announcer who reads the opening and closing portions of the chapter (Searfoss, 1975).

Read Around

This method of repeated reading is best used with older students. Students choose a favorite part of a story or book they particularly like; rehearse it until they read it fluently; and then read it for peers, a small group, or the entire class. Students can choose poetry, narrative text, or even the lyrics of a song they particularly like (be sure to have the lyrics preapproved by the teacher). Read Around can be a required activity or offered as an optional opportunity for students once or twice a week (Tompkins, 1998).

Teacher Modeling and Repeated Reading

Teacher modeling and repeated reading (TMRR) combines a number of features from previously mentioned variations of repeated reading. In TMRR, students first read their selected passage orally to a partner or teacher for one minute and determine the number of correct words per minute. Next, students read along silently while listening to an audiotape of the passage that models correct expression and phrasing. Using a one-minute timer, students then repeatedly read the passage until able to read it at a predetermined goal rate. Last, the teacher monitors the students' final reading of the passage determining the words correct per minute, and students graph the number of words read correctly *before* practicing and then again *during* the final testing (Ihnot, 1995).

Use More Intensive, Specialized Fluency-Building Interventions

In addition to informal fluency-building as part of the core reading program and skills-based fluency-building groups as Tier 2 interventions, there is also the option of structuring a classroomwide fluency-building program, either a packaged, published program or one of your own design. In order to implement such a program, you must have a thorough understanding of the technicalities and specific definitions that relate to building fluency using the repeated oral reading of specific passages.

The Measurement of Oral Reading Fluency

Oral reading fluency is measured by asking a student to orally read an appropriate passage about 250 words in length. Estimates of a text's grade level can be ascertained by using one of the following: (a) a readability formula (Chall & Dale, 1995), (b) classroom materials that have been graded by a publisher, or (c) a standardized measure of oral reading fluency that contains several testing selections for each grade level (e.g., the *Multilevel Academic Skills Inventory*; Howell, Zucker, & Morehead, 1994). If you are using passages from your own curriculum materials, select those that have minimal dialogue and no unusual names or words. If students are reading well below their actual grade levels, select text that is at their independent reading levels.

Prepare two copies of the passage—one for the student and one for the examiner. On the examiner's copy, indicate the number of words in each line. Use a stopwatch to time the student's reading. When one minute has passed, make a double slash mark after the last word read and stop the student. Different tests use different scoring methods, but generally, omissions, insertions, and self-corrections are *not* counted as errors. Substitutions and incorrectly identified words *are* counted as errors. The score that counts is the *number of words read correctly in one minute.* Subtract the errors and substitutions from the total number of words to determine the number of words read correctly.

A supplement to measuring oral reading fluency through passage reading should also include the periodic assessment of the accuracy and speed of a student's *word identification* skills (for both actual and nonsense words). There is no other classroom assessment that is as simple, quick, and sensitive to the smallest incremental changes in reading ability as a measure of oral reading fluency. If students improve by at least one to two words weekly in the number of words correct per minute they can read, teachers can be certain progress is being made in fluency and usually also in comprehension, given good listening comprehension skills. On the other hand, if a child's oral reading fluency remains unchanged, even after several weeks of intense instruction and practice, that child needs further diagnostic tests to determine what kind of additional instruction may be needed. Measures of oral reading fluency have powerful predictive value in identifying students who need help or, conversely, in confirming that students are making progress in their abilities to read. For example, Good et al. (2001) found that 96% of the students who met or exceeded a third-grade oral reading fluency benchmark also met or exceeded expectations on the Oregon Statewide Assessment, a high-stakes outcome measure. Keep in mind that a test of oral reading fluency measures progress or lack thereof. It cannot explain *why* a child is not making progress.

An Acceptable Level of Oral Reading Fluency

Oral reading fluency is a combination of accuracy *and* rate. The fluency score is reported as *words correct per minute.* To consider either accuracy or rate by itself is a meaningless exercise. For example, students who make no errors but read very slowly have as little likelihood of comprehending what they read as students who read very quickly but guess at and misidentify many words. According to Hasbrouk and Tindal's (1992) norms, second-grade students scoring at the 75th percentile read 82 words correct per minute in the fall of the school year, whereas those same students read 124 words correct per minute in the spring. In the fifth grade, students at the 75th percentile read 126 words correct per minute in the fall and 151 words correct per minute in the spring. Note that even in the upper grades, students who are progressing in reading continue to increase their number of words correct per minute. Although different authors and tests suggest varying target rates for students in Grades 1 through 6, based in part on differences in the difficulty of passages used and the variety of administration procedures, a score of 40 to 44 words correct per minute or less in the fall of second grade definitely flags a student who is at risk of reading failure (Davidson, 2000).

The minimum acceptable oral reading fluency rate for instructional purposes in grade-appropriate texts suggested by Lovitt and Hansen (1976) is 80 words per minute with two or fewer errors.

The Ceiling for Oral Reading Fluency

Reading fluency rates continue to be an excellent indicator of reading proficiency, including comprehension abilities, through sixth grade. Once a student has reached an oral reading fluency rate of 140 correct words per minute, however, the question of rate is moot. Faster at this point is not better. When students are able to read very rapidly as well as accurately, then they are able to focus their attention on improving expressiveness, voice projection, and clarity of speech in their oral reading.

Choosing Text for Repeated Oral Reading

Choose a selection of about 50 to 100 words that is on the students' *independent* reading levels (the highest level at which students can read without assistance, with few errors in word recognition, and with good comprehension and recall). All too frequently, students are given text to read that is at their *frustration* level. At this level, students' reading skills break down, their fluency disappears, errors in word recognition are numerous, comprehension is faulty, recall is sketchy, and signs of emotional tension and discomfort become evident (Harris & Sipay, 1985).

Time students' reading of the sample and note the number of correct words and the number of errors. If students take more than two minutes to read a passage or make more than five errors, the passage is too difficult. If students can read a passage at 85 words per minute with two or fewer errors, then the passage is too easy. Choose a more difficult one.

If a passage is deemed suitable for repeated reading practice, then go over any errors that were made. Ask students to repeatedly read the chosen passage until they are confident in their reading, able to read more quickly and fluently than they could at the beginning of their practice. The practice can take several forms, including reading orally to oneself, listening to an audiotape while reading along and then reading orally without the tape, or reading the selection orally to an adult or peer. Always take note of the correct words per minute. Teachers, aides, volunteers, or older students themselves can graph their progress over time on a chart. The goal is that students will improve their fluency in reading challenging material to at least 85 words correct per minute before moving on to a new passage (Gunning, 1998, p. 202).

There are currently four intensive intervention fluency-building programs reviewed on the Web site of the Florida Center for Reading Research (http://www.fcrr.org). Each review gives a brief description of the program, summarizes the research support for it, and details its strengths and weaknesses. If you are planning to adopt a commercially available intensive fluency-building program, make this Web site your first stop.

■ SUMMARIZING CHAPTER 4

Fluency is the ability to read text so effortlessly that all of the reader's cognitive resources can be devoted to extracting and constructing meaning from the text. Fluency is the bridge from word identification to comprehension and is ideally developed in the earliest grades through fluency-based instruction. Fluency, however, depends on students' abilities to phonemically decode words, hence the extreme importance of students receiving explicit systematic PA and phonics instruction in kindergarten and first grade. First grade, according to some researchers, is not too early to start repeated oral reading of accessible text at students' independent reading levels. Fluency can be facilitated through a variety of interesting repeated-reading techniques as well as through commercially available programs. The foundation of fluency is instant word recognition.

5

Word and World Knowledge

Word knowledge is knowing the meanings of words, knowing about the relationships between words (word schema), and having linguistic knowledge about words. *World knowledge* is having an understanding (background knowledge) of many different subjects and disciplines (domains) and how they relate to one another.

I was recently having a webcam chat with my daughter, Emily, when her three-year-old daughter Eri thrust a full-page photo of herself in front of the camera. She was pictured with a stunning Monarch butterfly perched on her outstretched hand. I immediately had to hear the story of Eri's butterfly. Later, I chatted with the teacher about how she brings word and world knowledge alive for preschoolers.

Word and World Knowledge

Maren Herman, teacher of the Young 3s at Shady Lane School in Pittsburgh, has always filled her classroom with creatures large and small to scaffold the acquisition of word and world knowledge for students. The butterfly cycle project is taught in the fall of each year. At the end of August, Maren and her sons tramp through the Pennsylvania woods and meadows in six state parks collecting Monarch butterfly eggs. Twenty-six caterpillars hatched in the classroom, one for each child plus a few extras. Young caterpillars need nourishment, and the Hermans gathered milkweed for them to munch on. Maren secures the milkweed stalks in ceramic and metal frogs or floral foam and then places the resulting bouquets in small containers filled with water inside aquariums around the classroom. The butterfly life cycle project is a tradition at Shady Lane begun by Donna Chase, who first taught Maren's son and then later partnered with Maren to teach her how to implement the project.

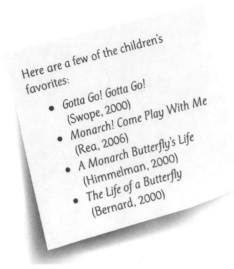

Here are a few of the children's favorites:

- *Gotta Go! Gotta Go!* (Swope, 2000)
- *Monarch! Come Play With Me* (Rea, 2006)
- *A Monarch Butterfly's Life* (Himmelman, 2000)
- *The Life of a Butterfly* (Bernard, 2000)

To build students' word and world knowledge, Maren and her teacher partner, Rachel Ripley, read aloud a variety of books about the life cycle of butterflies generally, and the Monarch butterfly specifically. Of course, *The Very Hungry Caterpillar* (Carle, 1981) is already a favorite of many of the students, but Maren goes deeper into this knowledge domain, sharing nearly a dozen other read-aloud books from the school's library.

She guides students to compare the creatures who hatch from eggs (like butterflies) with creatures who are born straight into the world without an egg or cocoon stage (like boys and girls). The children watch as the caterpillars stuff themselves with milkweed, crawl to the top of a stalk, and spin their cocoons. There they rest for about week. As each chrysalis turns black and then becomes transparent, the wings of the butterfly can be seen through the silky threads.

As the process of metamorphosis unfolds, the children are spellbound. One day in early September, seven butterflies emerged. Having 20-plus very hungry caterpillars turn into beautiful butterflies before your eyes builds background knowledge that cannot be duplicated anywhere, even in the pages of a book. Students and teachers watch the newly emerged butterflies hang upside down to dry their wings and carefully transport them to the playground where they release these beautiful creatures to fly off to find nourishment to sustain them on their long flight from Pennsylvania to Mexico.

Maren noted that some of the butterflies were lethargic when they emerged from their cocoons. Eri's butterfly was one of those and hence the photo opportunity. Maren and Rachel led the students in experimenting with various kinds of sweet fruits and juices to see if they could tempt the lethargic butterflies, since a hard frost had killed many of the flowering bushes around the school that provided nectar for those that hatched earlier. Finally they discovered a plant that worked.

Students do not fully process all of the new word and world knowledge immediately. For example, Eri told her mother about the chrysalis but had confused it with the word *Christmas.* They sounded the same to her. My daughter discovered this lexical mix-up when Eri pointed to the pocket chart hanging on their kitchen wall that contains photos of far-away family members, including one of Grandma and Grandpa holding Eri and standing in front of a Christmas tree. More language learning took place as my daughter explained the difference between *chrysalis* and *Christmas.* There's a limit to how much three-year-olds can process and integrate with prior knowledge in one instructional encounter. However, as the stories are reread and students are reminded of their classroom experiences with picture albums and art projects they have created, their word and world knowledge eventually is stored in their long-term memories.

Word and world knowledge acquisition at the elementary school level is similar. Students do not truly learn a word after hearing it and a definition for the first time. McKeown, Beck, Omanson, and Pople (1985) suggest that even as many as four teaching encounters with a word do not give learners enough knowledge to improve their reading comprehension in text containing that word. It may take as many as 12 experiences. Word and world knowledge is acquired incrementally, in bits and pieces here and there (Nagy & Scott, 2000), hence the need to recursively teach words to help students make the connections that will affix them and their associated world knowledge into long-term memory. But what of the students who do not have the benefit of high-quality preschool instruction or language-rich experiences in their homes? Just ahead, I examine the challenges of teaching word and world knowledge to students at risk of reading failure and provide some ways to implement the process in classrooms.

WHAT IS WORD AND WORLD KNOWLEDGE ■
AND HOW DO STUDENTS ACQUIRE IT?

Without strong knowledge about the big ideas that come from solid instruction in the sciences, arts, and humanities, students' reading (and writing) will ultimately suffer. Reading and writing must always be about something, and the something comes from subject-matter pedagogy—not from more practicing of reading "skills." Reading skills are important, but without knowledge, they are pretty useless.

—Pearson (2006)

The foregoing statements made by P. David Pearson in a letter to the editor of the *New York Times* make a convincing case for the relationship of word and world knowledge to skilled reading and writing. For example, as a group of third graders in Mrs. Wexler's class prepare to read *Grandfather's Journey* (Say, 1993), the first story in their Macmillan/McGraw-Hill literature anthology (Flood et al., 2001), she is faced with an overwhelming amount of word and world knowledge to teach her students. The story is a relatively short one, a memoir about the author's grandfather and his journey long ago from Japan to the United States. Most of the students have never traveled beyond their urban neighborhoods, although two newcomers have recently made journeys from other countries to live in the United States. Their English skills are limited, however, and they may not be able to share their background knowledge with fellow students or understand the stories themselves. Can the story be appreciated without knowing some facts about Japan and California and the Pacific Ocean and how one travels by steamship? Has anyone in the classroom ever experienced the ocean or homesickness? How many students even know their grandfathers? And what will Mrs. Wexler do about the war (WWII) that is mentioned in the story?

The teacher's guide suggests only six words to teach before students read the story: *scattered, journey, surrounded, enormous, towering,* and *astonished.* However, most of the students will need far more word and world knowledge to comprehend the nuances and poignancy of this finely crafted tale. Walsh (2003) found that none of the widely used core programs provide the amount and the depth of vocabulary instruction needed to result in comprehension, and that is certainly the case in this example.

Word Knowledge

Word knowledge in its narrowest sense is simply knowing the meanings of lots of words. In a broader sense, word knowledge includes the five linguistic facets of word study described in Chapter 3: phonological awareness, orthographic knowledge, morphological awareness, semantic knowledge, and mental orthographic images (Apel, 2007). Nagy and Scott (1990) call the information we store about specific words a *word schema,* and Crystal (2007) suggests that new word knowledge is not simply added to a list of words in long-term memory but rather integrated with prior knowledge to create a more complex schema.

Eri integrated the word *chrysalis* into her word schema of *Christmas* when she initially heard it because the words had some sounds in common. She was reminded of *chrysalis* when she saw the picture in the pocket chart and retrieved it quite nicely. However, when instructed by her mother, she had to make some mental adjustments. *Chrysalis* did not fit into her *Christmas* schema, which included presents, a tree, and a visit from Grandma and Grandpa. Confusion about new words is common, even in older learners, especially when they are English language learners (ELLs). Word learning requires multiple exposures with various kinds of cognitive processing.

World Knowledge

As mentioned, world knowledge is having an understanding and awareness of many different subjects and disciplines or knowledge domains. This kind of knowledge is often called *background* or *prior knowledge,* and teachers are encouraged to activate it in advance of a lesson. In Maren Herman's classroom, the specific knowledge domain was the life cycle of the Monarch butterfly. In Mrs. Wexler's third-grade classroom, the world knowledge included many unrelated bits and pieces of geography and history.

Contemporary educators who downplay the role of knowledge in schooling usually point out that they can't possibly teach children everything there is to know, so a far better use of instructional time is to teach students how to access and acquire information on their own. In the real world, however, knowledge is thought by most laypersons to be a byproduct of education, and the lack of knowledge is often a major contributor to poor reading comprehension (Perfetti, Marron, & Foltz, 1996). Some researchers have argued for a concept of comprehension that is unaffected by the reader's domain knowledge (Perfetti, 1989), but it is difficult to make a case that sports illiteracy will not affect one's ability to enjoy an article in *Sports Illustrated* or that ignorance of scientific word and world knowledge won't adversely impact one's understanding of articles in *Scientific American.*

Advantaged children have been acquiring knowledge in natural and implicit ways for five years before they enter kindergarten. Disadvantaged children are already so far behind when they enter school that they can ill afford to wait for natural and implicit acquisition to occur. Hirsch (1989) recommends that if educators want students to learn fast, they must be explicit and break down each domain to be learned into manageable elements that can be mastered.

Here are some of the ways effective teachers facilitate students' acquisition of word and world knowledge:

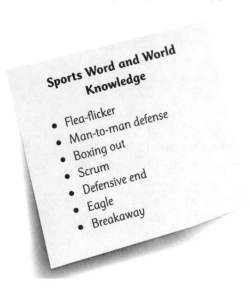

Sports Word and World Knowledge

- Flea-flicker
- Man-to-man defense
- Boxing out
- Scrum
- Defensive end
- Eagle
- Breakaway

- Helping students understand how language works (i.e., teaching the conventions of grammar in speech and writing in age-appropriate ways)
- Providing continuous and excellent conversational, reading, and writing models for students to emulate
- Continually expanding students' word and world knowledge through reading aloud, using new words during instruction and in conversation with students, directly teaching the meanings of new words, and exposing students to a wide variety of challenging texts

- Developing a knowledge base of word parts and foreign language cognates to which students can turn to figure out or remember the meanings of unfamiliar words
- Showing students the myriad ways in which language is constructed in texts, such as understanding story grammar in narrative texts or how cause and effect are used in expository text
- Stimulating excitement and interest in words—a word consciousness that serves to focus students' cognitive energies on learning and using word and world knowledge in their reading, writing, and speaking
- Constructing concept maps and word walls to show how words are connected to each other and used in a variety of ways in speaking and writing
- Providing background knowledge whenever it is needed to understand text or complete assignments

WHEN SHOULD WORD AND WORLD KNOWLEDGE BE TAUGHT?

The ideal time to teach word and world knowledge is from birth. One of the biggest hurdles that educators face in teaching all students to read results from the huge differences in language development that exist between various subpopulations of students. White and Watts (1973) were among the earliest researchers to contrast the home environments of advantaged and disadvantaged children, noting the marked differences in the amount of conversation directed to children in one environment as compared to the other. When parents, teachers, or day care providers seriously engage in dialogue with language-learning preschoolers, children develop language more rapidly. In many preschools and day care centers, where poorly paid and often untrained staff members do not have the word and world knowledge to teach and model for students, there is less likelihood that they will acquire what they need to access content text with ease in the upper grades.

In a later study of language in the home, Wells (1985) found a significant correlation between the total amount of talking adults do with children and the quality and gains in their language over time. In *Meaningful Differences in the Everyday Experience of Young American Children,* Hart and Risley (1995) present the most comprehensive picture to date of the gap that exists in language experiences between advantaged and disadvantaged children:

> To illustrate the differences in the amount of children's language experience using numbers, rather than just *more* and *less,* we can derive an estimate based simply on words heard per hour. The longitudinal data showed that in the everyday interactions at home, the average (rounded) number of words children heard per hour was 2,150 in the professional families, 1,250 in working-class families, and 620 in welfare families . . . Given the consistency we saw in the data, we might venture to extrapolate to the first 3 years of life. By age 3 the children in professional families would have heard more than 30 million words, the children in working class families 20 million words, and the children in welfare families, 10 million. (p. 131)

By the end of first grade, the word knowledge differences between linguistically rich and linguistically poor students amount to about 15,000 words. Linguistically rich first graders know the meanings of approximately 20,000 words, whereas their linguistically poor peers know the meanings of only about 5,000 words. Although we can teach most linguistically poor students how to read using best instructional practices, and although we can enable them to read and understand primary text with strong instructional support, the durability of their achievements is suspect (Chall, Jacobs, & Baldwin, 1990; Moats, 2001) unless we provide ongoing language development through direct and systematic instruction of word and world knowledge.

■ THE ROLE OF WORD AND WORLD KNOWLEDGE IN SKILLED READING

Vocabulary knowledge is knowledge; the knowledge of a word not only implies a definition, but also implies how that word fits into the world. Schemas for even simple concepts such as fish may be infinitely expanding from fish to specific fish, to the anatomy of fish, to broiled fish, to other sea creatures, to scales and gills, ad infinitum. The more we know about fish, the more words we will bring into our own understanding of the concept.

—Stahl (2005, pp. 95–96)

Language development is inextricably linked to reading success (Biemiller, 1999), and word and world knowledge are important predictors of reading comprehension. Those of us who have worked in schools serving high percentages of students at risk do not need research to tell us about the word and world knowledge gap between economically advantaged and disadvantaged students. However, when Becker (1977) first posited that the school failure of disadvantaged children was due to lack of vocabulary knowledge, it was a new idea that stimulated vigorous discussion and research regarding how many words students should be learning and how many they learn both from direct instruction and incidentally at school (Cunningham & Stanovich, 1998; Nagy & Anderson, 1984).

Although the idea of linguistically poor students is no longer a new one, solutions to the problem continue to frustrate educators. While we may be able to teach discrete reading skills, we are depressingly familiar with what often happens to linguistically poor and academically deprived students once they leave the cocoon of the primary grades. If these students are not consistently, directly, and intensively taught word and world knowledge from the moment they arrive at school, their hard-won achievement gains from the primary grades will begin to fade as they struggle to handle the demands of more difficult upper-grade texts. Low-SES students, racial and ethnic minority students, and non-native-English-speaking students are especially hard-hit by linguistic poverty (Moats, 2001, p. 8) and lack of academic background knowledge.

Linguistic Poverty

Linguistic poverty, as defined by Moats, includes partial knowledge of word meanings, confusion regarding words that sound similar but that contrast in one or two phonemes, and limited knowledge of how and when words are typically used. The gap in vocabulary knowledge between economically disadvantaged and advantaged children that begins in preschool persists through the school years and is a depressing correlate of poor school performance (Coyne, Simmons, & Kame'enui, 2004).

Knowledge Deficits

The lack of academic background knowledge is addressed by E. D. Hirsch (1989), who calls the world knowledge that is needed to understand reading anthologies and textbooks *cultural literacy*. He includes knowledge about mythology, geography, history, medicine, science, folk and fairy tales, poetry, and the arts, to name just a few. Cultural literacy seems a distant goal in many low-performing schools.

Teachers are struggling to increase reading and math achievement while the science and social studies books are gathering dust. A report from the Center on Education Policy (McMurrer, 2008) shows that since the No Child Left Behind Act of 2001 (2002) was passed, instruction time for language arts and mathematics has increased, while time for social studies and science has decreased significantly.

Skipping science and social studies instruction may seem to be the only choice for schools with large numbers of students at risk. However, the short-term gains to be realized in reading achievement may disappear when students reach the upper grades without the background knowledge and content vocabulary they need to understand and retain history, geography, biology, and chemistry.

SCIENTIFIC EVIDENCE FOR TEACHING WORD AND WORLD KNOWLEDGE ■

Classrooms where students receive sound word instruction are ones where lessons focus their attention on specific words and word-learning strategies, where opportunities to talk about words are many, and where occasions for applying what has been taught with engaging and content-rich texts and with motivating purposes occur with regularity and purpose.

—Kamil and Hiebert (2005, p. 10)

The National Reading Panel (NICHD, 2000) drew a number of conclusions about vocabulary instruction based on their review of 50 experimental and quasi-experimental studies (section 4-4). My italicized comments in the paragraphs to follow discuss the implications of these findings for classroom instruction.

There is a need for direct instruction of vocabulary items required for a specific text. *Students cannot be expected to comprehend text absent the word and world knowledge required to understand the text. It must be taught in advance.*

Repetition and multiple exposure to vocabulary items are important. Students should be taught new words that are likely to appear in many contexts. *When limited time is available to directly and systematically teach vocabulary, teach high-frequency words that students are likely to encounter repeatedly during the school year as well as in future academic contexts.*

Learning in rich contexts is valuable for vocabulary learning. Vocabulary words should be those the learner will find useful in many contexts. When vocabulary items are derived from content learning materials, the learner will be better equipped to deal with specific reading matter in content areas. *Students need many exposures and experiences with new words in order to fully understand them in new text or use them in writing and speaking. A rich context is one in which students both acquire definitions for words and are also taught how new words connect to formerly taught words and key concepts.*

Vocabulary tasks should be restructured as necessary. It is important to be certain that students fully understand what is asked of them in the context of reading, rather than focusing only on the words to be learned. Restructuring seems to be most effective for low-achieving students or those at risk. *Directly explain to students the purpose of learning new words: to be able to understand the meaning of the text. Demonstrate to them the power of words in reading and writing. Point out where in the text the new word will be encountered so that students will be motivated to remember the word.*

Vocabulary learning is effective when it entails active engagement in learning. *Active engagement means students are able to feel the teacher's excitement and enthusiasm for learning new words. Active engagement means that students have opportunities to see pictures, handle objects, and do experiments, as well as speak, read, and write using the new words they have learned.*

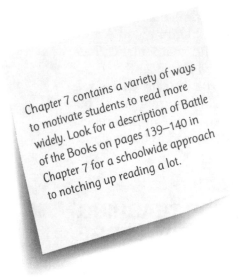

Chapter 7 contains a variety of ways to motivate students to read more widely. Look for a description of Battle of the Books on pages 139–140 in Chapter 7 for a schoolwide approach to notching up reading a lot.

Vocabulary can be acquired through incidental learning. Much of a student's vocabulary will have to be learned in the course of doing things other than explicit vocabulary learning. Repetition, richness of context, and motivation may also add to the efficacy of incidental learning of vocabulary. *Although vocabulary can be acquired through incidental learning, the fact that this does not occur for many students is troublesome. Educators must consider how to overcome this roadblock in the limited contact time they have with students and leverage their instruction by teaching high-frequency and academic content words and motivating students to read widely.*

Dependence on a single vocabulary instruction method will not result in optimal learning. A variety of methods was used effectively with emphasis on multimedia aspects of learning, richness of context in which words are to be learned, and the number of exposures to words that learners receive. *Creative teachers who recognize the importance of building word and world knowledge use multiple ways to facilitate word consciousness in their students.*

Stahl (2005, p. 96) identifies four problems that frustrate educators as they attempt to implement best practices in vocabulary instruction:

1. The sheer number of words that children need to learn so as to understand and use with proficiency both oral and written language

2. The differences in levels of word knowledge among children

3. The differences in levels of word knowledge that begin even before children enter school

4. The failure of traditional vocabulary instruction to teach children word-learning strategies and how to appreciate words

Despite the immensity of the task, many educators are creating word-conscious classrooms and schools and teaching word and world knowledge in robust ways.

■ EFFECTIVE INSTRUCTIONAL PRACTICES FOR TEACHING WORD AND WORLD KNOWLEDGE

The importance of vocabulary is daily demonstrated both in and out of schools. In the classroom, achieving students possess the most adequate vocabularies. Because of the verbal nature of most classroom activities, knowledge of words and ability to use language are essential to success. After schooling has ended, adequacy of vocabulary and knowledge are equally essential for achievement in vocations and in society (Petty, Herold, & Stoll, 1967, p. 7). Effective word and world knowledge instruction is an essential piece of the reading puzzle.

Build a Word- and World-Conscious School

An awareness of words, a love of words, and a curiosity about words don't just develop by themselves . . . As teachers we need to provide opportunity and access to sophisticated language so that all children can become aware of the power of words, and develop an awareness and curiosity about words that will facilitate their academic careers.

—Scott, Skobel, and Wells (2008, p. 12)

At Geil Elementary School in Gering, Nebraska, a Reading First school where 36% of students receive free and reduced-fee lunch, all of the students are excited about words. Principal Mary Kay Haun attributes this excitement to a rich curriculum that is packed with word and world knowledge taught by highly trained teachers with high expectations for students.

She reports, "We have a combined group of above–grade-level readers made up of fifth and sixth graders. Their vocabulary knowledge is amazing. Having completed all levels of the *Reading Mastery* curriculum (Becker & Engelmann, 1983), they are now reading expository text, *Understanding U.S. History: Through 1914* (Carnine, Crawford, Harness, & Hollenbeck, 1996), about 80% of the time and historical novels for about 20% of the time."

Following are the district's selected novels for this group of advanced students: *Roll of Thunder, Hear My Cry* (Taylor, 1976); *Ishi: Last of His Tribe* (Kroeber, 1973); *Night of the Twisters* (Ruckman, 1986); *The True Confessions of Charlotte Doyle* (Avi, 1992), *Johnny Tremain* (Forbes, 1944); *The Witch of Blackbird Pond* (Speare, 1958); *Across Five Aprils* (Hunt, 1964); *The Secret Garden* (Burnett, 1911/1998); *My Brother Sam Is Dead* (Collier, 1984); *The Red Badge of Courage* (Crane, 1895/2004); and two units of poetry. Teachers use *LitPlans* (Teachers Pet Publications, 2008) as their teaching guides.

The district's schools are also using *Vocabulary Workshop* (Shostak, 2005) to build word and world knowledge for advanced upper-grade students. Each Monday morning, a sixth-grade student introduces the school's word of the week over the intercom. The student says the word, spells it, gives a student-friendly definition, and uses it in a sentence of at least seven words. Throughout the school, teachers and students are jotting down the information.

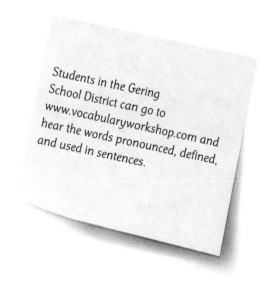

Students in the Gering School District can go to www.vocabularyworkshop.com and hear the words pronounced, defined, and used in sentences.

Mary Kay explains, "During the week, any student who comes to my office and shares a sentence of at least seven words that correctly uses the word (or a form of the word) receives a token that is part of the school's behavior and achievement program to be used toward participation in an all-school assembly and a recreational activity. Recently the word of the week was *peevish*. After the word was introduced, I happened to be observing in a first-grade classroom where the teacher was introducing the story for the week—*The Land of the Peevish Pets* from *Reading Mastery III.* The first-graders came unglued over having the word of the week in *their* story. Before this experience, I could never have imagined that a challenging word could generate such enthusiasm from beginning readers. I know that no student in that class will ever forget the meaning of *peevish.*

"The Word of the Week takes just a couple of minutes, but it has created an excitement and interest in words and their meanings at every grade level. One week the word was *scurried,* and a kindergarten student came to the office early in the week to tell me his sentence: *I scurried home.* I told him that was a good sentence, but it didn't have seven words. In order to get credit, he would have to think of more words to make his sentence longer. Sure enough, he came back later with a longer sentence."

Generative processing in which students take information about a word's meaning and create a new product like a sentence that expresses the word's meaning is one of the most effective ways to actively involve students in word learning. Mary Kay and her faculty are creating reasons for students to acquire word and world knowledge.

Raise Students' Awareness of Words

Vocabulary instruction is not just one of several important aspects of reading, it is a gift of words, a gift that one gives generously to others.

—Stahl (2005, p. 113)

Stahl's concept of words as gifts has been adapted by Scott et al. (2008) in their work with students. They define gifts of words as "artfully composed phrases found during reading that capture one's attention and make one want to write them down and remember them" (p. 8). As students read and are read to, teachers must model for them how to identify phrases that are wonderfully expressive. These phrases are gifts of words that authors give to readers. In some classrooms, rather than creating a word wall, students identify gifts of words to post on the wall.

I have always collected my own gifts of words. Before computers, I wrote them on backs of envelopes, shopping lists, and bookmarks and stuffed them into bulging file folders. Then I graduated to sticky notes that I stuck up on my bulletin board. Now I have technology to help me keep track of the gifts I collect and eventually pass on to others in my writing. I use the Notes feature on my iPhone, a sticky notes program on my computer that gives me an immediate place to jot down a phrase or quotation that particularly moves me, and a more comprehensive program called SOHO Notes in which I can store hundreds of different files in various categories, one being Quotations. Paul Auster (2006) gave me this gift of words: "Reading was my escape and my comfort, my consolation, my stimulant of choice: reading for the pure pleasure of it, for the beautiful stillness that surrounds you when you hear an author's words reverberating in your head." I have passed this gift on to my children and I hope . . . to my grandchildren.

Build Big Words Into Everyday Routines

Hiebert (2008b) suggests that teachers use big words when giving directions or sharing routine information. For example, instead of telling a student to write his or her name on the board, say "Please add your name to the list of those who will be receiving accolades at the end of the week." Or as students line up to go to the gym for an awards assembly, say, "This afternoon we have an assembly to give accolades to students." As students are moving through the end-of-the-day routine, ask, "What highlights of our school day will you impart to your family tonight?" Or as you prepare to read an after-lunch story, say, "I notice that many of you are quite lethargic after lunch." (For more ideas about building word play into the school day, see Dickinson & Tabors, 2001; Graves, Juel, & Graves, 2004; Johnson, Johnson, & Schlicting, 2004; and Stahl, 1999.)

Provide Definitional and Contextual Information About New Words

Simply giving students definitions of new words is not enough to improve their comprehension when they encounter those words in future reading (Stahl & Fairbanks, 1986). However, if students are provided with *both* definitional and contextual information about a new word, comprehension improves significantly (Stahl, 1999).

Definitional information includes teaching antonyms and synonyms for new words, rewriting or restating definitions in students' own words, providing examples and nonexamples of the word, and comparing and contrasting the word and related words. *Contextual information* includes giving students several sentences that illustrate the word being used in different contexts, creating a short story or scenario in which the word plays a role, acting out the word or drawing a picture for younger students, asking students to create their own sentences containing the word, or using more than one new word in a sentence to help students see relationships between words.

Provide Multiple Opportunities for Cognitive Processing

Students (and adults) remember new information more readily when they perform some type of cognitive operation on that information (e.g., rehearsing responses in anticipation of answering questions about a word; connecting the word and its meaning to prior learning or experiences; personally paraphrasing the definition of the word; or coming up with antonyms, synonyms, examples, and nonexamples of the word; Bransford, Brown, & Cocking, 2000; Craik & Tulving, 1975).

Content-specific words from science, social studies, and mathematics require multiple learning approaches (Pearson, Cervetti, Bravo, Hiebert, & Arya, 2005) that include (1) some kind of hands-on activity (conducting an experiment, seeing a video, looking at or drawing pictures, or handling an artifact), (2) a discussion about the word, (3) multiple opportunities to read the word in and out of context, and (4) opportunities to write the word. This "do it, talk it, read it, and write it" approach to acquiring word and world knowledge results in meaningful learning that is more readily retained in students' long-term memories.

Play With Words

Engage students in lively discussions to determine what experiences they have had with new or recently learned words. Freewheeling vocabulary discussions are particularly helpful for linguistically poor students or young learners who have partial or totally inaccurate definitions of words or who have confused the word with another similar-sounding one (e.g., jail and gel; Christmas and chrysalis). Share your students' excitement upon discovering an unknown word or a familiar word in a brand-new context. Stir their curiosities and motivate them to find out what new words mean. Help them collect new words in vocabulary journals and record other hearings and sightings of these words or their cognates in their journals.

One way to ensure that students remember key vocabulary is to build movement into lessons. Middle school educator Simone Kern has discovered that her students, all of them Hispanic and many ELLs, retain word meanings more readily when they design their own gestures, sign language, or body movements as mnemonics. The charter school in which she teaches has its own vocabulary program, but Simone has tweaked the program using the ideas of Beck, McKeown, and Kucan (2002) to provide robust vocabulary instruction and create a word-conscious classroom. She was frustrated about the fact that students weren't using the taught words in their writing and speaking. To motivate them, she purchased a tried and true sticker chart at the teacher's store, entered all of her students' names, and announced she would be giving stickers for each instance that students could describe a personal usage of the word outside of her classroom. She calls it the Real-World Vocab Challenge.

She says, "I have my English students for study hall, which is a perfect time to have our little 'word chats.' Students have to describe when they used the word, to whom they were speaking, and exactly what they said. They can only get credit for one word per day. Amazingly, with just this little motivation, my students are using words we studied weeks ago and even other teachers are noticing their vocabulary usage. One of my C students found this activity so appealing that he is on target to be the first one to reach the 30-word prize." Javier's latest example featured his mother: "I was talking to my mom, and she was getting all dressed up to go to the movies. I told her she looked luminous."

Note: All of Simone's students passed their Texas 2009 reading and writing tests.

Jennifer Dunn decorates her second-grade classroom with what she calls "juicy word" charts. They aren't fancy (a large piece of colored butcher paper on which students write big words they encounter in their listening and reading), but they pack a powerful punch when it comes to motivating students to discover and use big words. When they find a juicy word, students are expected to write it on one of the charts, first in *pencil* and then after the word has been checked in the dictionary and corrected (if needed), in marker. Jennifer says, "I'm not the only one who is teaching and using big words! My students constantly refer to these charts as they use 'juicy words' in their writing assignments" (McEwan, 2006, p. 45).

Teach Word and World Knowledge Recursively

Come back to previously introduced words over and over again—in different contexts, with slightly different shades of meaning, and with richer examples and nonexamples. There are practical limitations to the amount of word and world knowledge students can absorb in any one lesson or exposure. McKeown et al. (1985) found that 12 encounters with a word improved comprehension of the word in a newly encountered text, while four encounters did not.

Teach Word Parts: Prefixes, Suffixes, and Roots

When we acquire a new lexical item, we do not simply tack it on to the end of a list of already learned items. Rather, the new item has to find its place within the lexicon we have already acquired. . . . When we learn a new lexeme, we always make at least two gains in precision, not one.

—Crystal (2007, p. 198)

There is a way to make word learning less daunting: think in terms of meaning units called lexemes. For example, when the word *child* is a lexeme, students who know its meaning have access to a whole family of words: children, childlike, childhood, childbirth, childish, childbearing, childproof, childishness. When students know the meaning of a lexeme, they can readily add dozens of new words and expressions to their mental lexicons (e.g., child restraint, child support, child labor, child abuse). Two other morphologically rich families are based on the lexemes *create,* with 14 related words, and *interpret,* with 19 related words (Coxhead, 2000). If students are taught knowledge about morphology, 60% of the new words they encounter can be broken down into parts that give clues to their meaning (Nagy & Anderson, 1984).

Harness the natural redundancy of the English language to show students how many words they will automatically know by just learning one word or word part (Anderson & Nagy, 1992). For example, 14 prefixes account for 81% of all prefixed words (un-, re-, in-, im-, il-, ir-, dis-, en-, em-, non-, over-, mis-, sub-, and pre-) and 10 suffixes (–s, -es, -ing, -ly, -er, -or, -ion, -tion, -action, -ition) account for 80% of all suffixed words (White, Sowell, & Yanigihara, 1989). Teach these high-leverage word parts, and students will have an instant mental lexicon from which to retrieve meanings of new words.

Integrate Spelling and Vocabulary Instruction

Ehri and Rosenthal (2007) investigated whether encounters by lower-SES second and fifth graders with the written spellings of new nouns would improve their memory for the pronunciation and meanings of those words. The two grade levels were each taught two sets of words. The words were defined, depicted, and embedded in sentences. During study periods, the students were shown the written forms of only one set of words. Spellings were not presented for the other set.

Presenting the spellings of the words enhanced students' memory for the pronunciations and meanings compared to the words for which students did not have spellings presented. In both groups, students who were initially better spellers and readers did increasingly better than students who were poorer spellers and readers, suggesting a Matthew effect in which students who have more skills and knowledge at the outset will gain skills and knowledge at a far faster rate than their less skilled classmates, thereby creating an even bigger achievement gap (Walberg & Tsai, 1983).

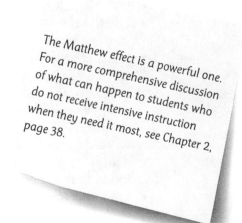

The Matthew effect is a powerful one. For a more comprehensive discussion of what can happen to students who do not receive intensive instruction when they need it most, see Chapter 2, page 38.

- However, the implications for practice of Rosenthal and Ehri's (2008) study suggest that teachers should include written words as part of vocabulary instruction and that students should spell words aloud as well as determine meanings when they encounter new vocabulary words. Use every sensory channel to increase vocabulary learning: have students see the word, say the word, and spell the word in addition to learning its meaning.

Use and Teach Content Vocabulary
Daily in a Systematic Way

If the goal [of vocabulary instruction] were to teach words in a way that would improve students' performance on multiple-choice vocabulary tests, the goal could be achieved through many simple and relatively undemanding methods. However, if the goal is to teach words in a way that will improve students' comprehension of text that contains these words, the methods become more labor- and time-intensive.

—Nagy (2005, p. 27)

Systematic vocabulary instruction has three characteristics: (1) it happens on a daily basis, (2) there are routines for how words are understood and practiced, and (3) students have multiple opportunities to cognitively process new words. Upper-grade teachers may think they are teaching systematic vocabulary instruction if they hand out a list on Monday, assign definitions to be copied from the glossary or dictionary to be turned in on Wednesday, and then give a test on Friday. Observations in 23 ethnically diverse classrooms found that only 6% of class time was devoted to vocabulary instruction, and in the core academic subjects, only 1.4% of instructional time was used for building word knowledge (Scott, Jamieson-Noel, & Asselin, 2003). Unless teachers bring words to life by directly teaching and talking about meanings and connections, students will memorize the definitions for the test and promptly forget them. Notch up the amount of time you spend teaching vocabulary, and you will find that students more readily understand and retain content knowledge.

Here's how to systematically teach words for mastery in the content classroom:

- Post the words in your classroom in their syllabicated forms (e.g., math-e-ma-tics) to aid struggling readers who have difficulty identifying and pronouncing multisyllabic words.
- Pronounce *and* spell each new word as you introduce it, as spellings of new vocabulary enhance students' memory for pronunciations and meanings (Ehri & Rosenthal, 2007; Rosenthal & Ehri, 2008).
- Provide a student-friendly definition of the word (avoid vague and circular dictionary definitions).
- Suggest synonyms or antonyms for the word (Simone Kern gives students two to three of each and lets students pick a favorite).
- Put the new word into a context or connect it to a known concept.
- Use the new word on multiple occasions and in multiple contexts (e.g., sentence starters, games).
- Have students prepare word cards to put on a metal ring so they can review vocabulary if they complete other work.
- Whenever you say the word in the course of instruction, run your hand or a pointer under the syllables of the written word on the wall as you pronounce it, quickly cueing struggling readers to associate your spoken word with its written form.
- After you say the word, have the class chorally read and spell the word or ask individual students to read the word to make sure everyone is processing it.
- Place several new words into a shared context by using them together in a sentence that requires students to answer a question.
- Ask questions that contain the new words so students must process their meanings in multiple ways.

- Teach students how to construct semantic word maps for new vocabulary (see Figures 5.1–5.3 for a sample lesson for teaching semantic word maps, a sample semantic word map, and a blank form to use in your classroom).
- Give students extra credit points for hearing, seeing, or using new vocabulary in speaking or writing outside the classroom.

Figure 5.1 Sample Lesson for Teaching a Semantic Word Map

Lesson Template for Teaching Semantic Word Map	Teacher Script, Notes
1. Show students several models of semantic word maps (two well-constructed samples and two poorly done nonexamples). Explain the purpose of constructing semantic word maps and how it can be used to understand and remember the meanings of words.	
2. Introduce a key word or concept from an upcoming unit and tell students you are going to model for them and think aloud about how you construct a semantic word map.	
3. Model for students how to brainstorm a list of related words. Then think aloud about how you decide which words are important and should become major categories and which words are examples of those categories. Put the words in the appropriate boxes on a large organizer on the overhead or LCD (I Do It).	
4. Choose another concept (an easy one with which students are already familiar from a prior unit). Activate students' background knowledge about the word by asking them to think of as many related words as they can. Then ask them to suggest categories and possible words for you to place in the appropriate boxes on a large organizer. (We Do It)	
5. Choose a third concept from an upcoming lesson and ask students to first activate prior knowledge (brainstorm a list of related words) as a whole class and then complete the organizer in pairs. (You Do It)	
6. Post the students' semantic word maps around the classroom and ask them to carefully review them. Debrief with students about their conclusions regarding the maps and provide time for them to add/delete items from their maps before turning them in.	

Figure 5.2 Semantic Word Map: The Brain

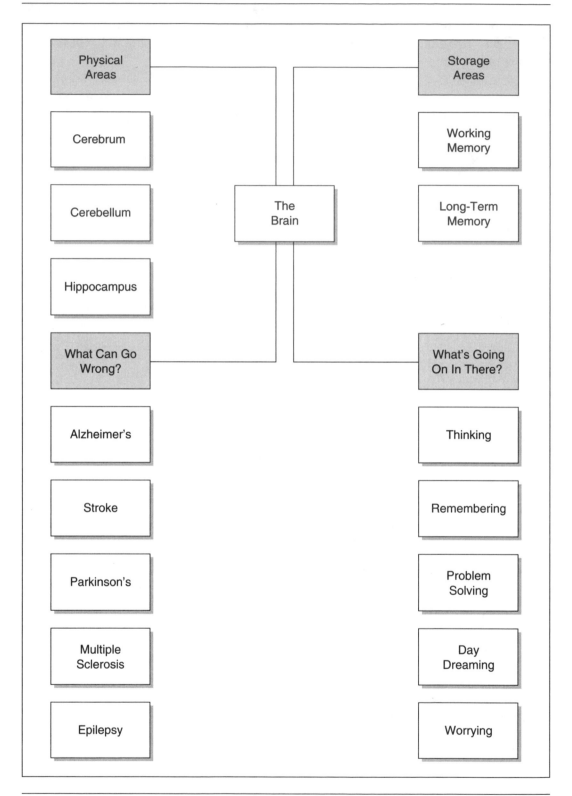

Figure 5.3   Blank Semantic Word Map

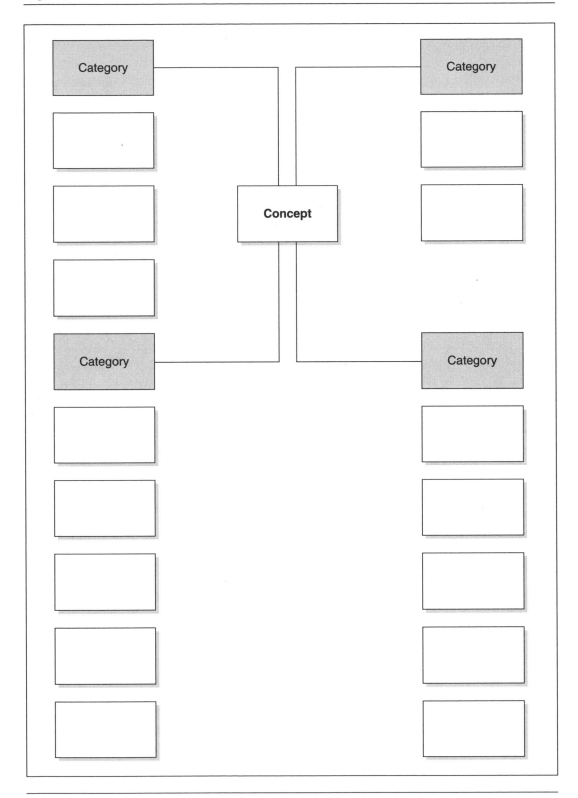

Accelerate Vocabulary Knowledge for Advanced Students

It is true that not all of the words that appear in students' environment will be learned. But, then again, if students do not encounter new words, there is no possibility of learning them.

—Beck et al. (2002, p. 118)

When Farrell Becking was hired to teach sixth grade in the Gering Public Schools, she was an experienced educator. However, she had never used any of the Direct Instruction curricula and teaching methodologies. On a school tour before she was hired, she was astounded to see upper-grade students reading on and well above grade-level textbooks and then writing essays to answer questions from their reading.

She says, "That was a whole new experience for me. The students weren't just decoding big words. They were comprehending what they were reading."

As Farrell began to work with her own *Reading Mastery-VI* group, she discovered that they were critical thinkers, open to new ideas, and willing to take risks. "They boldly stated their opinions and then came up with facts to support them. It was truly amazing."

When Farrell's multiage reading group of advanced students was about to complete the final levels of *Reading Mastery* and *Reasoning and Writing,* she knew they would need challenging text in which to expand their reading and writing abilities. She and a district colleague, Becky Michael, whose students were similarly advanced, researched the options and found a unique text that teaches history along with writing and critical thinking skills, much like those found in the *Reasoning and Writing* curriculum: *Understanding U.S. History: Through 1914* (Carnine et al., 1996). Although the title was a bit intimidating, the minute Farrell and Becky saw the structure of the text and the opportunities it provided for writing and thinking, they wanted the district to adopt it. They presented their idea to the School Board Curriculum Committee and were approved for a new set of advanced programs, including *Vocabulary Workshop* (Shostak, 2005) and a collection of historical novels to be alternated with history units.

Advanced fifth and sixth graders in Gering are acquiring word and world knowledge in amazing ways. Figure 5.4 is an example of how one student got excited about the new words he was learning in *Vocabulary Workshop* plus the new knowledge he was acquiring about the world and combined them to answer a question in Chapter 1 of the history text.

Teach Your Students to Become Word Wizards

Beck et al. (2002) describe an activity called *Word Wizard* that was developed for a vocabulary research study in the upper grades (pp. 118–199). In a campaign to motivate students to pay more attention to words in their environment, they created several categories of word knowledge (e.g., Word Whirlwind and Word Watcher), with the most prestigious category being Word Wizard. Students were awarded points for noticing words in their environment that were first introduced in school.

First-grade teachers Candace Darling, Michelle Judware, and Darlene Carino (Ilion Central School District in upstate New York) have come up with a primary-level twist on the word wizard concept. Their morning routine includes a read-aloud that is related to the current theme in their reading series, a recent holiday, or a topic from another curricular area; both fiction and nonfiction are used. After choosing the read-aloud for the day, the teachers share the responsibility of identifying three vocabulary

Figure 5.4 Student Writing Using Advanced Vocabulary

Student Background

Sixth-grader Brady Gross has attended Lincoln Elementary School in Gering, Nebraska, since kindergarten. He was placed in *Reading Mastery III* and *Reasoning and Writing* C as a second-grade student in 2004–2005. He has completed four years of the Direct Instruction programs: *Reasoning and Writing, Reading Mastery,* and *Spelling.* He was placed in the advanced language arts block for the first time in the fall of 2008–2009. Brady is a very conscientious student who loves to play solitaire and enjoys challenging puzzles and mysteries.

Textbook

Understanding U.S. History: Through 1914 (Carnine et al., 1996) is used as one part of the Reading Curriculum for Grades 4-5-6 Advanced Students when they have completed *Reading Mastery VI.*

Students engage in reading and writing together as they take notes or prepare one of several graphic organizers suggested to help them organize their thoughts. After reading and taking notes, they write in response to their reading by summarizing, analyzing, and synthesizing what they have read to answer various test questions. In addition to U.S. history through 1914, the program teaches a variety of higher-order thinking and problem-solving skills that are subsequently applied to the historical content as well as to modern problems through written response.

Assignment

Students were asked to write an essay answering the following Core Test Question in Chapter 1: *List the two general types of problems, the five types of solutions, and the three types of effects.* On his own, Brady decided to incorporate new vocabulary he had acquired in *Vocabulary Workshop* (Shostak, 2005). These words are shown in bold type. This assignment was completed in the first week of October 2008–2009 after two units of *Vocabulary Workshop* had been completed.

Peer Editing Process

When students complete their essay answers for a test, the work is to be their best work. Essay test questions are first written in draft form. Then students work with a peer editor and complete their final study copy. When students complete their test essays, they have written several final drafts. Following is Brady's final draft of Question 1 in which he voluntarily decided to use newly acquired vocabulary.

Two general types of problems are economic and rights of people. When someone has an economic problem, they can't get and keep the things they need and want. Rights of people are protection under the law, freedom of speech and freedom of religion. Protection under the law is being protected and having a fair trial. Freedom of speech is being able to say what you want without harm of jailing. Freedom of religion is the ability to worship any god or gods without misery. All these rights help from misery and jailing instantaneously. The five solutions [to these problems] are Dominate, Move, Tolerate, Invent, and Accommodate. An easy way to remember these are A.D.M.I.T. Accommodate is to compromise. The British used to **confront** and **manipulate** the Indian tribes to sign a treaty. Dominate is to control. Some people could dominate by **besieging** the enemy's camp. Move is what immigrants do or to try to leave behind the problems. Some people could move **globally.** Invent is to create something new. Some **sage**-like people create **ingenious** inventions. Tolerate is to ignore a problem.

Three effects [of using one of the five methods to solve a problem] are new problem, problem ends, or problem continues. When there is a new problem, the first problem would end, but another problem will be created from the solution. Sometime new problems would **ruffle** people real good. When a problem ends, the problem is over. When the problem continues, the solution does not work and maybe makes it worse like a **barrage** of problems.

Source: Farrell Becking, Teacher, Lincoln Elementary School, Gering Public Schools (NE). Reprinted with permission of Brad E. Gross and Brady Gross.

words, describing how they are used in the text, and writing a child-friendly definition of each word. Once the story has been read and the words have been discussed, a Wizard for the day is chosen. Wizards become human word walls for the day, wearing their word cards with definitions on a necklace and carrying a sign indicating they would like to be asked about the word they are wearing. Wizards must provide definitions of their words to anyone who asks.

If you are short of word wall space in your classroom, put your students to work. The human word wall idea could also be used to review vocabulary related to any classroom theme, test, or unit. Once worn, the words are hung on the vocabulary wall, and points are awarded to students who are caught being a Word Wizard (using the word in writing or conversation in the classroom). See Figure 5.5 for a sample set of words and definitions from a Dr. Seuss story (1990), *Oh, the Places You'll Go!*

Use Nonfiction Read-Alouds to Teach Word and World Knowledge

Linda Gibb, a Reading First (RF) coach in the Omaha Public Schools, undertook a project to encourage Grades 2–3 RF teachers to directly teach more word and world knowledge to students. Teachers are using read-aloud trade books that enrich a basal story theme as a framework for teaching word and world knowledge to their students. RF funds enabled the schools to purchase a wide variety of read-aloud books on various levels that support each of the anthology's weekly selections.

Figure 5.5   Word Wizard

Source: Adapted and reprinted by permission of Darlene Carino, Candace Darling, and Michelle Perry. Copyright © 2006 by Corwin. All rights reserved. Reprinted from *How to Survive and Thrive in the First Three Weeks of School* by Elaine K. McEwan.

Linda explains what motivated the project: "After reviewing the research and hearing from experts in [the] vocabulary development, we selected trade books (as much nonfiction as possible to build content knowledge) from a recommended list provided by our core program's publisher, Macmillan/McGraw-Hill (Flood et al., 2001). Then we chose three high-frequency Tier 2 words (Beck et al., 2002) that occur across a variety of knowledge domains in the upper grades and created posters using a photocopy of the book cover and the three Tier 2 words." See Figure 5.6, Sample Poster for *Benjamin Franklin: American Inventor* (Adams, 1991) and Figure 5.7, a sample lesson for teaching three words from the story.

Figure 5.6   Poster for Third-Grade Read-Aloud to Teach Vocabulary

Benjamin Franklin

American Inventor

Colleen Adams

articles

disagreements

peacemaker

Source: Linda Gibb, Reading First Coach, Omaha (NE) Public Schools.

Reproduction of material from this book is authorized only for the local school site or nonprofit organization that has purchased *Teach Them ALL to Read: Catching Kids Before They Fall Through the Cracks, Second Edition,* by Elaine K. McEwan. Thousand Oaks, CA: Corwin, www.corwinpress.com.

Figure 5.7 Sample Lesson for Teaching Vocabulary From *Benjamin Franklin: American Inventor* (Adams, 2001)

Teacher	One of the words in our story is *articles.* What's the word?
All Students	Articles.
Teacher	Listen to the sentence from the story: *He wrote newspaper articles for his brother James's newspaper.* An article is a story written on a special subject for a magazine, newspaper, or book. What's our word?
All Students	Articles.
Teacher	Tell about a time that you might have written an article. Try to use the word *article* when you tell about it. Give an example sentence. You could start by saying: "The article I wrote was . . ." Turn to your partner and share your sentence. What's our word?
All Students	Articles.

Teacher places the word in the word chart on the poster.

Teacher	Another word in our story is *disagreements.* What's the word?
All Students	Disagreements.
Teacher	Listen to the sentence from the story: *Ben went to England to try to solve disagreements between the colonies and England.* Disagreements are failures to agree or differences of opinion. What's our word?
All Students	Disagreements.
Teacher	Tell about a time you might have had a disagreement. Try to use the word *disagreement* when you tell about it. Give an example sentence. You could start by saying, "We had a disagreement because . . ." Turn to your partner and share your sentence. What's our word?
All Students	Disagreements

Teacher places the word in the word chart on the poster.

Teacher	The last word from our story is *peacemaker.* What's the word?
All Students	Peacemaker.
Teacher	Listen to the sentence from the story: *He was an important inventor, leader, and peacemaker in the history of the United States.* A peacemaker is a person who helps people find answers to their disagreements. What's our word?
All Students	Peacemaker.
Teacher	Tell about a time when you might have been a peacemaker. Try to use *peacemaker* when you tell about it. Give an example sentence: You could start by saying, "I was a peacemaker when I . . ." Turn to your partner and share your sentence. What's our word?
All Students	Peacemaker.

Teacher places the word in word chart and reads the story aloud.

Teacher	We have talked about three words: *articles, disagreement,* and *peacemaker.* Review each word quickly, giving its definition. I am going to try to use our new words as often as I can today. Let's see if I can catch you using our words today.

Source: Linda Gibb, Reading First Coach, Omaha (NE) Public Schools.

In Beck and colleagues' (2002) three-tier model, Tier 1 words are familiar words that most students would know. They require little if any instruction. Tier 3 words are low-frequency words limited to very specific knowledge domains. Tier 2 words have the following attributes: (1) they are characteristic of mature language users and appear frequently across a variety of contexts, (2) they can be taught in various ways to help students build in-depth knowledge and make connections to other words and concepts, and (3) they provide precision and specificity in describing a concept for which the students already have a general understanding (Beck et al., 2002, pp. 8–9).

Linda explains how the instructional materials in Figures 5.6 and 5.7 are used: "The script for introducing the selected words to students is placed on the back of the poster so the teacher can be ready with (1) the pronunciation of the word, (2) a student-friendly definition, (3) a sentence from the story that uses the word, and (4) a sentence starter to be used during the first few weeks or until students are able to start sentences on their own.

"When students bring in evidence of hearing, seeing, or using the target words outside the classroom, their names are written on a flag sticky note and placed next to the word on the book poster. The posters hang in the classrooms all year as a resource for students and teacher to use whenever they have opportunities in their daily language and written work."

SUMMARIZING CHAPTER 5 ■

There is no one best way or any one program guaranteed to work for teaching word and world knowledge. Effective word and world knowledge instruction is highly dependent on the intellect, skill, and motivation of teachers who are committed to giving the gift of words to their students. Effective teachers use multiple methods and vary their approaches. However, effective vocabulary instruction must occur in every classroom on a daily basis, providing students with various opportunities to hear, read, spell, discuss, write, and use the following kinds of words: (1) words needed to understand text that will be read; (2) academic vocabulary the teacher uses in the course of instruction, such as *analyze, illustrate, predict, infer, summarize, compare, classify,* and *explain;* (3) content words from mathematics, science, and social studies; and (4) words that just pop up in daily discussions, current events, and during instruction. Although we do not know as much about teaching vocabulary as we would like to know, Nagy (2005) reminds us that *"we already know enough to do better than we are often doing, especially for our youngest and our most vulnerable students"* (p. 42).

6

Comprehension

Comprehension is the extraction or construction of meaning from text using the seven cognitive strategies of highly skilled readers as appropriate.

Comprehension is difficult to teach. One frustrated literacy coach observed, "Teaching decoding is a snap compared to teaching comprehension skills and strategies." As a beginning middle-grade teacher, I was baffled by comprehension. I found a well-worn Science Research Associates Reading Kit in my classroom containing hundreds of leveled color-coded cards (olive and brown were my favorites), each containing a short reading selection and several multiple-choice questions to check for comprehension. Naive as I was, I thought if my students were reading and answering the questions correctly, I was teaching comprehension. No matter that I had no solutions for the students who dutifully muddled through the selection and got all of the answers wrong.

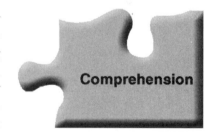

PA, phonics, and fluency are essential pieces of the reading puzzle. However, they are insufficient skills for the comprehension of grade-level text. Once words have been identified automatically and accurately, the reader's working memory is free to comprehend. But what if the reader has looked at all of the words and identified them fluently, but still doesn't get it? I have that problem with texts in Spanish and French. I can fluently decode them, having studied the languages long enough to master their spelling–sound correspondences. My problem is that I cannot comprehend what I have read. Comprehension of text, while certainly dependent on fluency, is also related to another set of variables: (1) familiarity with the text structure, (2) word and world knowledge, and (3) an age-appropriate understanding of how to apply the seven strategies of highly effective readers—variables that rarely remain constant from day to day. Each new text brings its own unique set of challenges, especially for struggling readers.

To understand the complexity of comprehension, think for a moment about your own experiences as a reader. The most difficult text you are expected to read for professional advancement is likely found in educational research studies. The prospect of summarizing multiple research studies has created sleepless nights for more than a few teachers and principals attending graduate school. Consider for example this excerpt from a peer-reviewed journal, *Scientific Studies of Reading:*

> In sum, this study took a multilevel and multivariate latent variable modeling perspective to investigate different potential sources of influences at the classroom level. This approach had several advantages over univariate regression. First, it shifted the focus of research from simplistic prediction to understanding the structure of literacy. Second, a multivariate approach allowed us to empirically evaluate competing but theoretically specified models of literacy in a confirmatory fashion. Third, the multilevel approach made a conceptual and empirical distinction between the construct of literacy at the levels of individual students and classrooms. Finally, it provided a much more parsimonious and substantively appealing account of the phenomenon and moves the discourse in literacy research from a discussion of specific observed measures to the construct of literacy. (Mehta et al., 2005, p. 90)

Unless you have more than a superficial knowledge of several knowledge domains, many of the terms and concepts are unfamiliar. In addition, the writing style is formal and the vocabulary is multisyllabic: *parsimonious, construct, confirmatory, empirical, multivariate, regression.* A single reading of the study would likely result in a disappointing reading comprehension score for many readers, including me. However, if the text were scaffolded by a skilled teacher through preteaching difficult vocabulary and modeling strategic reading, your comprehension would go up dramatically since you are familiar with the concept of literacy and could gather from reading between the lines (inferring) that the researchers were investigating what variables impacted students' literacy levels in the classroom.

If your professor directed you to first read the abstract and then immediately thereafter the Method section, your comprehension would no doubt improve even more. Once you discover that the participants were 1,342 students in 127 classrooms in a longitudinal study from kindergarten through Grade 4 in 17 elementary schools in Houston, Texas, and Washington, DC, you could begin to connect your own knowledge and experiences to the text you were reading. If your teacher suggested that you read the study more than once, possibly three times, so as to become more familiar with the new words, the text would become far more accessible.

Attempting to make sense of difficult text for which you have no specific strategies is frustrating. This is what happens to vast numbers of students daily, and therein lies the challenge of teaching comprehension. Rather than a discrete skill, it is a complex cognitive process requiring readers to draw on word and world knowledge, past experiences, and previously read texts.

In this chapter, I consider how teachers at all grade levels can directly and explicitly teach students how to extract and construct meaning from what they read (or in the case of primary or English language learners, what they hear read aloud). Explaining and demonstrating precisely *how* skilled readers make sense of what they read is the essence of teaching comprehension.

WHAT IS COMPREHENSION AND HOW DO ■ STUDENTS BECOME SKILLED COMPREHENDERS?

Every book has a skeleton hidden between its covers. Your job as an analytical reader is to find it. A book comes to you with flesh on its bare bones and clothes over its flesh. It is all dressed up. You do not have to undress it or tear the flesh off its limbs to get at the firm structure that underlies the soft surface. But you must read the book with X-ray eyes, for it is an essential part of your apprehension of any book to grasp its structure.

—Adler and Van Doren (1972, p. 75)

Comprehension is understanding what one reads. As Adler and Van Doren describe it, it is "reading with X-ray eyes." Extracting meaning from text involves enumerating the key facts, opinions, or ideas in expository text or retelling the story of a narrative. Students must extract meaning to answer questions or summarize. However, comprehension is also about constructing meaning, a process whereby the reader brings a unique set of experiences and knowledge to the text and during reading and interaction with peers and the teacher comes up with new (to the reader) insights and ideas that help to affix the reading experience in long-term memory.

How can teachers know that students actually understand what they have read? Readers can give or write brief summaries of the text. They can construct graphic organizers or draw pictures. They can also think aloud about questions that the text raised for them or explain how they disagree with the author's point of view. They can relate how the text made them think of an experience they have had or gave them insight about a problem they had that was similar to one in the story. Reading can move one to tears, laughing out loud, or anger. Comprehension doesn't always require coming up with one correct answer, although that is the way most teachers and tests assess it.

Students can only become skilled comprehenders by engaging in the following activities on a daily basis, both at school and at home: (1) silently reading a lot of different kinds of texts at a gradually increasing level of difficulty and with accountability; (2) learning lots of new words and constructing a variety of knowledge bases in their long-term memories; (3) listening to skilled readers, especially their teachers but often their peers, think aloud about how they are making sense of the text; (4) thinking aloud for others about what is going on in their minds while they read; (5) receiving explicit and direct instruction in how to use the seven strategies of highly effective readers as appropriate to the grade level and text difficulty; (6) acquiring a personal set of tools (cognitive strategies) and a

Review pages 102–103 in Chapter 5 for a variety of suggestions about how to use and teach content vocabulary daily in a systematic way.

Be sure to look for information in Chapter 8 about the importance of writing during reading (taking notes or preparing graphic organizers) and after reading (writing summaries or short answer essays) as ways to increase comprehension and retention.

repertoire of habits to use whenever the reading gets tough; and (7) talking and writing about reading in both informal and formal ways.

I selected the seven strategies shown in Figure 6.1 for the following reasons: (1) they are used by skilled readers and shown by research to be essential to proficient adult reading, (2) instruction in these strategies results in higher achievement on both teacher-made and standardized tests, and (3) the majority of state standards and assessments expect students to demonstrate proficiency in the use of these strategies. Each of the strategies is multifaceted; using them involves multiple thoughts and behaviors that depend on the reader's purpose for reading as well as the degree of success the reader has in constructing meaning from the text. They can all be explicitly taught to and modeled for students from kindergarten through high school.

These strategies were identified by Pressley and Afflerbach (1995) in a fascinating qualitative study that asked expert readers to think aloud regarding what was happening in their minds while they were reading. The lengthy scripts recording these spoken thoughts of skilled readers regarding their cognitive processing are called *verbal protocols*. These protocols were then categorized and analyzed to answer specific questions, such as, "What is the influence of prior knowledge on expert readers' strategies as they determine the main idea of a text?" (Afflerbach, 1990).

The protocols provide accurate snapshots and even videos of the ever-changing mental landscape that expert readers construct during reading. Researchers have concluded that reading is "constructively responsive—that is, good readers are always

Figure 6.1 Seven Strategies of Highly Effective Readers

Strategy	Definition
1. Activating	Priming the cognitive pump in order to recall relevant prior knowledge and experiences from long-term memory in order to extract and construct meaning from text
2. Inferring	Bringing together what is spoken (written) in the text, what is unspoken (unwritten) in the text, and what is already known by the reader in order to extract and construct meaning from the text
3. Monitoring–Clarifying	Thinking about how and what one is reading both during and after the act of reading for purposes of determining if one is comprehending the text, combined with the ability to clarify and fix up any mix-ups, if necessary
4. Questioning	Engaging in learning dialogues with text (authors), peers, and teachers through self-questioning, question generation, and question answering
5. Searching–Selecting	Searching a variety of sources in order to select appropriate information to answer questions, define words and terms, clarify misunderstandings, solve problems, or gather information
6. Summarizing	Restating the meaning of text in one's own words—different words from those used in the original text
7. Visualizing–Organizing	Constructing a mental image or graphic organizer for the purpose of extracting and constructing meaning from text

Source: Copyright © 2007 by Corwin. All rights reserved. Reprinted from *40 Ways to Support Struggling Readers in Content Classrooms, Grades 6–12,* by Elaine K. McEwan.

changing their processing in response to the text they are reading" (Pressley & Afflerbach, 1995, p. 2). Readers who are reading this way are strategic readers. In order for students, whether struggling or gifted, to benefit from strategy instruction, teachers must daily and intentionally teach and model the seven strategies.

Cognitive strategies are seen by some as mental tools, tricks, or shortcuts to gaining meaning, understanding, and knowledge. Duffy and Roehler (1987) call them "plans [that] readers use flexibly and adaptively depending on the situation" (p. 415). Cognitive strategies are also defined as "behaviors and thoughts that a learner engages in during learning that are intended to influence the learner's encoding process" (Weinstein & Mayer, 1986, p. 315). Such behaviors could include actions— note taking, constructing a graphic organizer, previewing the text, looking back to check on an answer, writing a summary, retelling a story—or thinking out loud, rehearsing the steps or the ideas that are unclear or need to be remembered. The thoughts referred to might include processes such as activating prior knowledge, monitoring comprehension, or inferring meaning.

Strategies have the power to enhance and enlarge the scope of learning by making it more efficient. Strategic students learn and remember more in shorter periods of time with far less frustration. They are able to tackle assignments with a higher level of organizational skill, and more important, they can face challenging assignments and tests with confidence.

Cognitive Strategy 1: Activating

At the root of our ability to learn is our ability to find the experience we have in our memory that is most like the experience we are currently processing.

—Schank (1999, p. 41)

The activation of prior knowledge, both before *and during* reading, is a way that readers prime their cognitive pumps, so to speak. Whether the knowledge stored in long-term memory is factual, conceptual, or experiential, recalling what is already known about a subject and then connecting it to what is being read greatly increases the likelihood, if not the certainty, that readers will understand and remember what is read while also generating increased levels of motivation and attention. Schank (1999) calls this process *reminding* and explains, "Far from being an irrelevant aspect of memory, reminding is at the heart of how we understand and how we learn" (p. 21).

Activating and retrieving what is known about a specific subject or knowledge domain from the long-term memory system for use in working memory gives readers more information with which to make predictions and generate hypotheses. Activating prior knowledge is about asking students what they already know about a specific subject and also involves helping them figure out the connections between what they know and what they are reading.

Cognitive Strategy 2: Inferring

A fully explicit text would not only be very long and boring, but it would destroy the reader's pleasure in imposing meaning on the text—making it their own.

—Oakhill, Cain, and Yuill (1998, p. 347)

I vividly remember my introduction to the intimidating world of writing fiction. I was working on the first book in a series for reluctant readers aged 10–12. My biggest problem as an author: talking too much. Or in this case, making my characters talk too much. My initial attempts at creating believable dialogue were clumsy and boring. "Leave something to the reader's imagination," my editor advised. She could well have said, "Let your readers infer."

Figuring out what an author has left *unsaid* in the text is usually thought to be the essence of inferring. I call it reading the author's mind. Some call it reading between the lines. But inferring is actually putting together and reconciling three different sources of information or knowledge: (1) what is written in the text, (2) what is unwritten in the text, and (3) what is already known by the reader in the form of either background knowledge or prior experiences for the purpose of extracting and constructing meaning from the text. An inference can pop into the minds of readers in several different forms: (a) as a prediction of what might happen later on in the text, based on what they have read so far; (b) as a conclusion regarding a concept, proposition, or principle in expository text; or (c) as a brand-new idea created by combining the readers' prior knowledge with the meaning they have extracted from the text (Anderson & Pearson, 1984).

Inference is defined by van Den Broek (1994) as "information that is activated during reading yet not explicitly stated in the text" (p. 556). Many teachers describe inferring to their students as a combination of reading between the lines (what is unwritten) and reading outside the lines (what is known *only* by the reader). While these phrases are certainly among the most popular definitions of inferring, the expressions are far too figurative to use with students unless the lesson also includes ample amounts of teacher modeling (thinking aloud) *and* direct explanation. Most students need help to see the invisible writing between the lines that their teachers (or other skilled readers) see in their minds' eyes as they read. They also need to hear what kind of prior knowledge and experiences their teachers are combining with the text to construct meaning.

Inferring is one of the most essential cognitive strategies that skilled readers use. It is frequently employed in combination with other strategies, but its complexity and sophistication, as well as its heavy dependence on background knowledge and vocabulary, often make it a challenge to teach to students (Hirsch, 2003). The secret to teaching this strategy is to show students how much inferring they already do in their everyday lives. Once they understand that making inferences is easy when you have background knowledge and experience, teaching them to infer will seem less daunting.

Cognitive Strategy 3: Monitoring–Clarifying

Readers can interpret and evaluate an author's message from the print on the page only to the extent that they possess and call forth the vocabulary, syntactic, rhetorical, topical, analytic, and social knowledge and sensitivities on which the meaning of the text depend.

—Adams (1998, p. 73)

Monitoring is thinking about how and what one is reading both during and after the act of reading for purposes of determining if one comprehends the text. Monitoring is the only thing that stands between mindful and mindless reading. Its cognitive partner, clarifying, consists of fixing up the mix-ups that interfere with comprehension. Monitoring and clarifying function as a team. Monitoring is evaluative; clarifying is regulatory (Baker, 2002). Readers who are monitoring "address text ideas immediately while they are reading . . . try to develop and grapple with ideas, and try to construct meaning" (Beck, McKeown, Hamilton, & Kucan, 1997, p. 6).

Clarifying (clearing up confusion) consists of figuring out what is wrong and fixing it. Highly effective readers fix up their mix-ups in routine and automatic ways, much like skilled drivers adapt to changes in road conditions, detours, or the sudden feeling that they are lost.

Cognitive Strategy 4: Questioning

Asking one's own questions is a form of making predictions and is essential to comprehension—it forces one to construct meaning rather than passively accept text as it is encountered.

—Cecil (1995, p. 3)

Questioning is as common in schools as homework and tests, and often it is just as ineffective in promoting meaningful learning. That's because the wrong individuals, in my opinion, are asking the questions: the teachers. Students are supposed to come up with correct answers as evidence of their comprehension, but more often then not, teachers end up answering their own questions. Beck et al. (1997) suggest that the typical initiate, respond, and evaluate (IRE) questioning model (Dillon, 1988; Mehan, 1979) leaves much to be desired when it comes to uncovering students' comprehension breakdowns. Furthermore, hearing classmates give *correct* answers to questions usually does nothing for students who may have no clue as to why the given answer is an appropriate one. It is the generation and answering of higher-level questions by students themselves that "encourage[s] deeper processing and more thorough organization" (Just & Carpenter, 1987, p. 422).

Questioning, whether in the asking or answering mode, is a powerful strategy for processing text, but students need explicit instruction regarding all types of questions combined with daily opportunities for hearing teachers think aloud about how they self-question, generate questions, and find answers to questions asked by others. The cognitive benefits of teaching a variety of questioning approaches to students include improved memory for text, the ability to answer questions with more accuracy, and the ability to more easily find answers to questions as well as to discriminate between types of questions and how to access answers to them (Trabasso & Bouchard, 2002, pp. 180–181).

The questioning strategy is multifaceted and is generally used in tandem with the inferring, summarizing, and searching–selecting strategies. Teaching your students how to use the questioning strategy in all of its combinations and permutations goes far beyond just asking higher-level questions after students have read a text selection. It includes teaching your students how to ask and answer specific types of questions and how to use questioning in independent study and reading.

Cognitive Strategy 5: Searching–Selecting

While the literacy needs of the adult center primarily on obtaining information from nonfictional texts, literacy instruction in the schools concentrates almost exclusively on fictional texts and literary appreciation.

—Venezky (2000, p. 22)

The foregoing statement highlights a critical problem in many elementary schools: an overly rich diet of fiction. Expository or informational text is not widely used in elementary classrooms (Hirsch, 2003; Hoffman et al., 1994; Kamberelis, 1998;

Pressley, Rankin, & Yokoi, 1996). Expository text is seldom read aloud in primary grades, despite the fact that students engage in more meaning-seeking and meaning-making efforts during informational book read-alouds then when hearing fiction read aloud (Smolkin & Donovan, 2000).

Although the searching–selecting strategy is not mentioned widely in the major reviews of the literature that helped to inform my choice of the other six strategies included in this chapter (NICHD, 2000; Pressley, Johnson, Symons, McGoldrick, & Kurita, 1989; Trabasso & Bouchard, 2000), I believe that it is an essential strategy for all readers to have, given the glut of information on the Internet, not all of it accurate. Guthrie and Kirsch (1987) describe searching and selecting as "the finding of text, browsing through information, or collecting resources for the purposes of answering questions, solving problems, or gathering information" (p. 220). Although searching–selecting is widely cited as both an essential workplace skill (Dreher, 1993; Mikulecky, 1982; Secretary's Commission on Achieving Necessary Skills, 1992; Venezky, 2000) and a vital academic strategy, most teachers do not feel a responsibility to teach it. They defer to the librarian or media specialist and believe that students *must* certainly have adequate searching and selecting skills since they spend so much time surfing the Internet. See the upcoming case study titled "New Literacies," which describes the need for students to be able to search and select.

We cannot, however, expect students to pick up the searching–selecting strategy by osmosis, nor does instruction designed to teach the other cognitive strategies contribute specifically to the ability of students to search and select (Guthrie & Kirsch, 1987). Students need explicit instruction in how to search for and then select the information they need to accomplish an academic task or a personal information quest. Dreher (1993) suggests a model of locating information that includes the following steps: (1) formulate a goal or plan of action, (2) select appropriate categories of a document or text for inspection, (3) extract relevant information from the inspected categories, (4) integrate extracted information with prior knowledge, and (5) monitor the completeness of the answer and recycle through the component processes until the task is complete (p. 295).

Case Study

New Literacies

Debra Berlin

Our world is changing quickly, and so is literacy. The Internet is defining new types of literacy. From wikis to blogs, to search engines and new online communities, the Internet is changing the way we research, read, and communicate. Our students' future success will depend on their ability to read well and critically, both online and offline. Although reports like *Put Reading First* (Armbruster et al., 2001) and *Reading Next* (Biancarosa & Snow, 2004) have helped to establish best practices for teaching reading and comprehending text, there is little research available on the nature of reading online (Coiro & Dobler, 2007). A recent study by the Institute of Education Sciences (2007) found no significant effect on reading ability when technology is employed.

However, it is well known that any discussion of literacy must include the use of technology, both as reinforcement of classroom practices and the effective use of online tools to communicate and research. Online literacy, sometimes referred to as the new literacies, requires the teaching of new strategies that will be essential to our students. Leu, Kinzer, Coiro, & Cammack (2004) reveal five types of reading skills needed to survive in a technological age. These include (1) identifying the essential questions, (2) locating information, (3) analyzing information, (4) synthesizing information, and (5) communicating information. In addition to these skills, students must learn how to effectively and efficiently navigate through search engines and Web pages. Perhaps most critical, they must be taught how to evaluate information found on Web sites to determine its validity, reliability, and potential author bias.

With more than one-third of all children aged 6 to 10 owning iPods (Rayworth, 2008) and 87% of students between the ages of 12 and 17 using the Internet every day (Pew Internet & American Life Project, 2006), clearly the Internet is and will continue to be the predominant source for all of our information. Therefore, it is essential for schools to explicitly and systematically teach children how to effectively research, comprehend, and communicate using online tools, engines, and resources. Their future depends on it.

Source: Reprinted by permission of Debra Berlin.

Cognitive Strategy 6: Summarizing

Summarizing, the ability to recursively work on information to render it as succinctly as possible, requires judgment and effort, knowledge and strategies.

—Brown and Day (1983, p. 1)

Summarizing is one of the more challenging cognitive processes that readers and writers are called upon to execute. The clue to just how challenging can be found in the words *recursively* and *work* in Brown and Day's definition. Summarizing is only possible when the reader rereads and reworks and does some cognitive cud chewing on a piece of text. Summarizing can rarely be done after one reading of a challenging text, or even two.

When eminent historians Doris Kearns Goodwin (1987) and Stephen Ambrose (1994) were taken to task by their literary peers for failing to summarize the ideas of others in their own words and then forgetting to cite the sources from which they inadvertently borrowed the information verbatim (Goldstein, 2002; Kirkpatrick, 2002), I thought of many of my former students. Despite my seemingly clear instructions and warnings, they persistently copied paragraphs from the *World Book Encyclopedia* onto their note cards and then diligently copied the same paragraphs into their final research reports. Even more disheartening was my inability to show them how to do it differently. Today's students are still cutting and pasting, only now it's from the Internet.

Summarizing has its roots in a time-honored tradition of reading comprehension instruction: finding the main idea. In days gone by, main-idea instruction consisted of little more than reading short selections and circling the best title for the selection. That was then. This is now. Today's high-stakes assessments demand that students engage in strategic reading—retelling important events in a story, writing short summaries of text selections, determining the main idea of a selection and supporting it with details—paraphrasing, summarizing, organizing, and recalling ideas.

One of the most difficult assignments for students, whether in kindergarten or college, is writing or orally giving summaries of what they have read. That is, unless they have seen the summarization strategy modeled numerous times by their teachers, been carefully taught the various aspects of the strategy, and then had an opportunity to practice it in cooperative groups under the watchful eye of their teacher—all before being expected to summarize on their own (Brown & Day, 1983; Brown, Day, & Jones, 1983). Researchers have found that summarization instruction improves students' recall of what they read compared to students who are taught using traditional reading comprehension instruction (Armbruster, Anderson, & Ostertag, 1987; Berkowitz, 1986; Taylor & Beach, 1984). Summarization training is a powerful intervention, with "many variations of the technique improving long-term memory of text" (Pressley, Burkell, et al., 1995, p. 62). The time to introduce the summarizing strategy is in Grades K–3.

Cognitive Strategy 7: Visualizing–Organizing

Any sort of systematic attention to clues that reveal how authors attempt to relate ideas to one another or any sort of systematic attempt to impose structure upon a text, especially in some sort of visual representation of the relationships among key ideas, facilitates comprehension as well as both short-term and long-term memory for the text.

—Pearson and Fielding (1991, p. 832)

Visualizing–organizing gets my vote for the most misused, underappreciated, and untapped treasure among the seven strategies featured in this chapter. Oh, make no mistake, there are dozens of stunning graphic organizers and hundreds of beautiful illustrations and photos in every textbook and anthology. Pretty pictures and complex organizers do not necessarily contribute to students' understanding and retention of text, however. Visual images and organizers are of little value to students unless they have personally unleashed their own cognitive powers on visualizing and organizing the text. It is only when students develop their own personal concept maps that the structure of a discipline or the complexity of an idea or proposition sticks with them. In fact, one of the biggest pluses of graphic organizers is the way in which they can reduce cognitive overload by keeping concepts more visible.

A graphic organizer or graphic representation is a visual illustration of a verbal statement (Jones, Pierce, & Hunter, p. 20) and involves the following tasks or abilities: (1) reading text, (2) determining which type of graphic organizer would best be suited for constructing a personal schema in order to better understand and remember large bodies of information, (3) choosing the frames or labels for the parts of the organizer, and (4) constructing the organizer by drawing it either manually or using a software program designed for that purpose.

A second way to tap into the visual aspects of processing is through representational mental imagery (Borduin, Borduin, & Manley, 1994; Pressley, 1976), in which readers paint a picture, take a snapshot, or make a video in their minds of the scene or action taking place in the story. Students who have difficulty with mental images should be encouraged to act out scenes or make a story board to help them understand exactly what is happening in the story. The process of mental imaging can take place while reading is going on, but most students should be encouraged to stop after they have read a particularly well-described scene, action, or location and envision exactly what happened, before they continue reading.

WHEN SHOULD COMPREHENSION BE TAUGHT? ■

Reading to learn doesn't wait until students have learned to read.

—Hiebert (2006b)

Recall from Figure I.5 in the Introduction that there are only three pieces of the reading puzzle that span Grades preK through 12: word and world knowledge, comprehension, and reading a lot. Students must know from their earliest experiences with print that the point of reading is to learn and understand about the world, to explore and know the meanings of lots of interesting words, and to constantly be engaged in constructing meaning for themselves out of everything that is read aloud to them. Skilled teachers think aloud, explain, directly teach, and encourage the exploration and mastery of various disciplines and knowledge domains. These experiences need to happen in every classroom, at every level, and in every discipline from preschool through high school graduation. When educators conclude that students need to learn to read

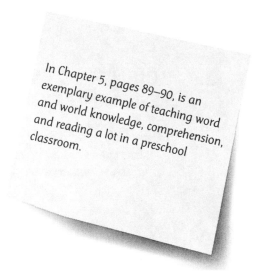

In Chapter 5, pages 89–90, is an exemplary example of teaching word and world knowledge, comprehension, and reading a lot in a preschool classroom.

before they can read to learn, they are short-changing their students. When secondary educators conclude that their students already know how to read and need no scaffolding or direct instruction to comprehend, they are also short-changing their students.

THE ROLE OF COMPREHENSION IN SKILLED READING ■

The process of reading is not a half-sleep, but in the highest sense, an exercise, a gymnast's struggle; that the reader is to do something for himself, must be on the alert, must himself construct indeed the poem, argument, history, metaphysical essay—the text furnishing the things, the clue, the start of the framework.

—Walt Whitman (as quoted in Gilbar, 1990, p. 39)

The role of comprehension in becoming a skilled reader boils down to just six words: Comprehension is the point of reading. If you read it and don't get it, then, guess what, you didn't really read it. All of the instruction in PA, phonics, and fluency only serves to get students ready to read. Only when they can sit down with a book and silently read it *and* get it can we call students readers. As they progress into the upper grades, students must become increasingly aware that comprehension often requires sustained effort and concentration—mindful reading. As Walt Whitman suggests in the foregoing epigraph, reading can be a struggle. Comprehension doesn't always happen immediately as one is reading. Suggesting otherwise to students is to trick them. We cannot afford to wait until students have mastered all of the beginning reading skills before addressing comprehension. Comprehension instruction must be integrated into reading instruction from the first day of preschool or kindergarten. Older students often mistakenly believe they are reading when they are actually engaged in what researchers call "mindless reading" (Schooler, Reichle, & Halpern, 2004), zoning out while staring at the printed page. The opposite of mindless reading is the mindful processing of text by highly effective readers using cognitive strategies. Our goal is to teach the mindful processing of text from the very beginning. For of what value is fluent decoding if students are not able to visualize, organize, summarize, and question what they read?

■ SCIENTIFIC EVIDENCE FOR TEACHING COMPREHENSION

Despite a significant body of research in the 1980s suggesting the effectiveness of strategy instruction, especially for lower-achieving readers, strategy instruction has not been implemented in many American classrooms.

—Dole (2000, p. 62)

There is only one way to teach comprehension, and that is through the direct and explicit teaching and modeling of cognitive strategies. Skilled readers routinely use these "mindtools" (Jonassen, 2000) to process what they read or what they hear (in the case of listening comprehension), similar to the ways that master tradespersons or artisans use their specialized tools. This analogy is an apt one and can be further extended to consider teachers as cognitive masters and students as their cognitive apprentices (Collins, Brown, & Holum, 1991; Collins, Brown, & Newman, 1990). Just as novices in any field observe and learn from the experts, novice academics (students) learn from mind mentors (teachers). When teachers articulate their thinking about academic tasks and explain, model, and scaffold the use of cognitive strategies for students, these novice learners gain confidence and expertise, gradually reaching a point where, when they are confronted with a piece of challenging text, they are able to readily select the appropriate tool (cognitive strategy) from their personal cognitive tool belts or boxes (long-term memory) and apply it when they are confronted with a piece of challenging text.

The seven cognitive strategies of skilled readers as described earlier in the chapter should be part of every teacher's daily lesson plans and classroom conversations. Details about precisely how to do this can be found in a vast body of research on cognitive strategy instruction derived from the discipline of cognitive science (NICHD, 2000; Pressley, 2000; Pressley, Woloshyn, et al., 1995; RAND Reading Study Group, 2002; Rosenshine, 1997; Rosenshine & Meister, 1994; Trabasso & Bouchard, 2000, 2002). Based on more than 200 scientific research studies and meta-analyses, here is what we currently know about the power that cognitive strategies, taught well and consistently, have to increase students' abilities to understand and retain what they read:

- Skilled or expert readers routinely draw from a repertoire of cognitive strategies while they are reading challenging text.
- Students of all ability levels benefit from strategy instruction, both as evidenced in increased understanding and retention and also in higher standardized test scores.

- The effectiveness of a variety of individual cognitive strategies in boosting student achievement is well supported by experimental research.
- The effectiveness of several multiple-strategy instructional approaches is well supported by experimental research.
- There are specific instructional methods to teach cognitive strategies to students that produce results.

Strategies have the power to enhance and enlarge the scope of learning by making it more efficient. Strategic students learn and remember more in shorter periods of time with far less frustration. They are able to tackle assignments with a higher level of organizational skill, and more important, they face challenging assignments with confidence.

EFFECTIVE INSTRUCTIONAL PRACTICES FOR TEACHING COMPREHENSION ■

Teaching comprehension through the use of cognitive strategies is a vastly different undertaking from teaching the discrete skills of beginning reading, like segmenting and blending. Cognitive strategy instruction also differs from teaching study skills, like note taking or test preparation. *Skills* are "procedures readers over-learn through repetition so that speed and accuracy are assured every time the response is called for" (Duffy & Roehler, 1987, p. 415), whereas *strategies* tap higher-order thinking skills in response to the demands of unique reading tasks. Strategies are used situationally, and teaching students how and when to use cognitive strategies is a higher-level teaching skill.

Collins et al. (1991) observed that the practice of strategic reading is not at all obvious in most classrooms, where "the processes of thinking are often invisible to both the students and the teacher" (p. 6). That may have more to do with the difficulty of becoming a strategic teacher than with any difficulty students might have learning how to comprehend, if only they were well taught. Teaching comprehension is hard work. It is much easier to *talk* about the importance of comprehension or to *test* comprehension than it is to actually *teach* it. In a year-long series of observations in 10 fourth- and fifth-grade classrooms, Pressley, Burkell, et al. (1995) found a disturbing lack of comprehension instruction, despite over two decades of research on how to do it and the benefits that students derive from it (p. 198). Pressley further notes that "we are living in a country with a lot of assessment of comprehension and not enough instruction" (M. Pressley, personal communication, September 8, 2001). With the heavy emphasis in low-performing schools on teaching beginning reading skills, little has changed since Pressley's observation in 2001. However, teaching them all to read is not just about decoding and fluency. Once again, the whole point of decoding and fluency is to be able to understand what is read.

There are seven research-based teaching moves that are essential to cognitive strategy instruction: (1) direct instructing and explaining, (2) modeling, (3) giving directions, (4) scaffolding, (5) coaching, (6) attributing, and (7) constructing meaning. Five complementary teaching moves enhance and support these major teaching moves: (1) motivating–connecting, (2) recapping, (3) annotating, (4) assessing–evaluating, and (5) facilitating. Figure 6.2 lists and defines the 12 moves. Following the figure are more detailed descriptions of the seven major moves.

Figure 6.2   Teaching Moves for Teaching Cognitive Strategies

Direct Instructing and Explaining	Verbal input about what will happen in a lesson, what the goals are, why it's being done, how it will help students, and what the roles of teachers and students will be during the lesson
Modeling	The act of thinking aloud regarding cognitive processing as well as engaging in observable behaviors like note taking, producing a graphic organizer, writing a summary, or looking up something in a book or on the Internet
Giving Directions	Unambiguous and concise verbal input that seeks to give students a way to get from where they are at the beginning of a lesson, task, or unit to the achievement of a specific task or outcome; provides wait time for students to process directions, time for students to respond, and opportunities to ask clarifying questions
Scaffolding	A process that enables students to solve problems, carry out tasks, or achieve goals that would otherwise be impossible without teacher modeling, prompting, and support
Coaching	Asking students to think aloud, cueing them to choose a strategy that has been taught thus far to solve a reading problem, delivering mini-lessons where needed, and giving feedback to students
Attributing	Communicating to students that their accomplishments are the result of their strategic approach to reading rather than their intelligence or ability
Constructing Meaning	Working collaboratively with students to extract and construct multiple meanings from text
Motivating–Connecting	The component of instruction that seeks to generate interest, activate prior knowledge, and connect instruction to the real world or the solution of real problems
Recapping	The act of summarizing what has been concluded, learned, or constructed during a given discussion or class period as well as a statement of why it is important and where it can be applied or connected in the future
Annotating	The act of adding additional information during the course of reading or discussion—information that students do not have but need in order to make sense of the text
Assessing–Evaluating	Determining what students have learned and where instruction needs to be adjusted and adapted by assessing, both formally and informally
Facilitating	Thinking along with students and helping them develop their own ideas, rather than managing their thinking, explaining ideas, and telling them what and how to do something

Direct Instructing and Explaining

The first and most essential aspect of effective strategy instruction is *direct instructing and explaining* (Duffy, 2002; Duffy et al., 1987). Direct instructing is explicit in nature. Nothing is left for the student to infer. Explaining conveys the sense of making clear or intelligible something that is not known or understood. The kind of explaining needed for explicit cognitive strategy instruction involves telling students precisely what strategy they will be learning, why learning it is valuable, under what circumstances they will find it to be useful, and showing them what its critical attributes look like in both thought and word.

Direct instructing involves helping students to understand a complex task one step at a time (e.g., writing a summary, making an inference). Students should never have to guess regarding the objectives, tasks, or rationale of strategy lessons. A variety of experimental research studies have investigated and shown the efficacy of direct explanations by teachers to students regarding the exact nature of the strategy, reasons for using cognitive strategies, and the kinds of situations in which different cognitive strategies are most effective (Rosenshine, 1979). Figure 6.3 is a lesson template for teaching any of the cognitive strategies for the first time, while Figure 6.4 is a sample lesson for teaching summarization in the upper grades.

Figure 6.3   A Lesson Template for Teaching Cognitive Strategies

Lesson Steps	Lesson Notes
1. Provide direct instruction regarding the strategy.	
a. Define and explain the cognitive strategy.	
b. Describe the purpose the cognitive strategy serves during the act of reading.	
c. Enumerate and describe the critical attributes of the cognitive strategy.	
d. Provide concrete examples and nonexamples of the cognitive strategy.	
2. Model the strategy by thinking aloud.	
3. Facilitate guided practice with students.	

Figure 6.4   Sample Lesson for Teaching Summarizing

Lesson Steps	Lesson Notes
1. Provide direct instruction regarding the strategy.	
a. Define and explain the cognitive strategy.	Summarizing is restating the meaning of what you have read in your own words—different words from those used in the original text, either in written form or a graphic representation (picture or graphic organizer).
b. Describe the purpose the cognitive strategy serves during the act of reading.	Summarizing enables a reader to determine what is most important to remember once the reading is completed. Many things we read have only one or two "big ideas," and it's important to identify them and restate them for purposes of retention.
c. Enumerate and describe the critical attributes of the cognitive strategy.	A summary has the following characteristics: • Short • To the point, containing the "big idea" of the text • Omits trivial information and collapses lists into a word or phrase • Is not a "retelling" or a "photocopy" of the text
d. Provide concrete examples and nonexamples of the strategy.	Examples of good summaries might include the one-sentence book summaries from the *New York Times* Best Sellers List, an obituary of a famous person, or a report of a basketball or football game that captures the highlights. The mistakes that students commonly make when writing summaries can be more readily avoided by showing students excellent nonexamples (e.g., a paragraph that is too long, has far too many details, or is a complete retelling of the text rather than a statement of the main idea).
2. Model the strategy by thinking aloud.	Thinking aloud is a metacognitive activity in which the teachers reflect on their behaviors, thoughts, and attitudes regarding what they have read and then speak their thoughts aloud for students. Choose a section of relatively easy text from your discipline and think aloud as you read it and then also think aloud about how you would go about summarizing it; then model writing a summary.
3. Facilitate guided practice with students.	Using easy-to-read content text, read aloud and generate a summary together with the whole class. Using easy-to-read content text, ask students to partner-read and create a summary together. Once students are writing good summaries as partners, assign text and expect students to read it and generate summaries independently.

Modeling

Modeling cognitive strategy usage for students requires thinking aloud by teachers—"showing students exactly how a good reader would apply [a particular] strategy" (Pressley, El-Dinary, & Brown, 1992, p. 112). If you have never engaged in thinking aloud for students, your initial attempts may seem awkward and artificial to you, but with practice, you can become a strategic teacher who routinely thinks aloud (Davey, 1983). The challenge of thinking aloud is doing three things at the same time: comprehending the text, figuring out in your mind just what you did to understand it (since the cognitive processing happens in split seconds), and then articulating for students what was going on in your mind. Thinking aloud refers to the "artificial representation[s] of a real experience; a contrived series of activities which, when taken together, approximate the experience of the process that ultimately is to be applied independently" (Herber & Nelson as quoted in Herber & Herber, 1993, p. 140). Here are some brief examples of a teacher thinking aloud using each of the seven strategies:

- *Activating.* What I just read reminds me of something I learned when I was in high school. I can connect those two things to help me remember the new information.
- *Inferring.* I'm sure I know what's going to happen next because the same thing happened to me several years ago.
- *Monitoring–Clarifying.* I got confused at this point because I've never seen this word before, so I used the context to figure it out. It helped that I knew a related word in a foreign language.
- *Questioning.* I wonder why the author chose this word to describe the Civil War. It seems to me that another word would have made more sense.
- *Searching–Selecting.* I had a question when I read this section; I'm either going to ask my friend John who knows a lot about this topic or I'll Google it later.
- *Summarizing.* If I jot down key words in the margins during my reading, it helps me to figure out the main idea and write a summary sentence when I finish reading. The word that came to my mind immediately after I finished this sentence was *unjust.* The treatment of the Indians by the explorers in the West doesn't seem fair to me.
- *Visualizing–Organizing.* I pictured what was happening here, and it helped me understand how the crime was committed. To help me remember the order in which these events happened, I'm going to construct a time line in my notes.

Although skilled readers employ cognitive strategies in a synergistic and interactive way, rather than in the step-by-step fashion necessitated by this somewhat artificial example of thinking aloud, your students will get the point: there's a lot going on in the brains of skilled readers. They will be fascinated when they hear the multiplicity and variety of your thoughts and they will soon begin to follow your lead. Your goal is to have all of your students thinking aloud with you and each other before long.

Some teachers pair up with a colleague, combine their classes, and alternate reading and thinking aloud from the same text to show students that different readers process text in unique ways based on their backgrounds, experience, and strategy usage.

The biggest pitfall for teachers (especially upper-grade and content teachers) during the initial stages of thinking aloud is slipping out of the metacognitive mode and sliding into the teaching mode. Be careful not to let these *nonexamples* of thinking aloud creep into your thinking aloud:

- Explaining what the text means
- Giving a short synopsis of the text
- Teaching what a concept or idea in the text means
- Giving the impression that students should be getting the same meaning from the text as you are
- Lecturing to students about the importance of cognitive strategy usage (save that for another time)
- Giving the impression that you never have any comprehension problems when you read

The purpose of thinking aloud is to show students how *you* personally process and respond to what you read. In so doing, you become the master reader and your students serve as cognitive apprentices.

Giving Directions

You might think it unusual to find a section on giving directions in a discussion of the components of cognitive strategy instruction, but this essential aspect of cognitive strategy instruction is frequently given short shrift in the interests of time. Giving directions to students is one of the more important teaching moves; in the absence of clear and precise directions from their teachers, many students (especially those at risk of academic failure) shut down and tune out.

Scaffolding

The educational concept of scaffolding is analogous to the scaffolds that workers install to keep themselves from falling when they are washing windows, painting, or framing. In the instructional realm, scaffolding is in place when the tasks that students are asked to complete or master are graduated in difficulty, with each new one being only slightly more difficult than the last. Scaffolded instruction ensures success and keeps students confident and motivated to learn.

Scaffolding can support students by any of the following means: (a) people, (b) text, (c) tasks, and (d) materials (Dickson, Collins, Simmons, & Kame'enui, 1998). Teachers or instructional aides usually provide the *people* scaffolds, but peers can also provide instructional support for their classmates if they are taught to do so and then affirmed by adults for their encouraging attitudes. This process also coincidentally aids the understanding, retention, and achievement of more able students (Johnson & Johnson, 1989). The most common kind of teacher scaffolding takes place through the modeling of specific cognitive strategies. Less common, although extremely important, is metacognitive modeling that articulates the rationale for why and how a certain strategy is chosen for a specific reading task. As teachers fade out thinking aloud (modeling) during cognitive strategy usage, they should always be ready to step in as needed when students are having difficulty with a piece of text or are struggling with finding a key word to use in a summary. Students need encouragement, instruction, and ongoing opportunities to model their own thinking for one another. Then as teachers reduce the amount of modeling, responsibility can gradually be released to students for this task.

Content (i.e., the text to be read or the subject to learned) can also be scaffolded to make cognitive strategy instruction less threatening and confusing for students. To scaffold text, use easy, high-interest reading material during the initial phases of cognitive strategy instruction. Students will have more of their working memory available for processing if they are not struggling with text at their instructional level or higher.

A third kind of scaffolding involves the *tasks* that students are expected to master. For example, in order to write or give a summary, students first need to know how to chunk text (i.e., divide it up into smaller manageable pieces). They also need to know how to collapse lists and delete trivial and unimportant information. The ultimate cognitive challenge of summarizing is conceptualizing key words for each chunk and connecting them into a summary sentence. Only when students have reasonably mastered the preliminary cognitive processes of summarizing will they be able to produce a summary in writing or orally. A fourth kind of scaffolding is provided by a variety of *instructional activities* (i.e., the procedures, prompts, and props) that support students throughout initial cognitive strategy instruction.

Coaching

In the context of strategy instruction, *coaching* refers to the things that teachers do to foster students' independence in learning. Coaching occurs in the context of a cognitive apprenticeship (Collins, 1991; Collins et al., 1990; Collins et al., 1991; Schoenbach, Greenleaf, Cziko, & Hurwitz, 1999). In a cognitive apprenticeship relationship, students observe and emulate their master teachers who regularly think aloud regarding their thought processes, not only during reading and writing but also during other classroom activities. This running commentary by teachers helps students to gradually become self-regulated and cognitively competent. In the meantime, however, strategic teachers are engaging in coaching by way of encouraging, cueing, and prompting (Pressley et al., 2001; Taylor, Pearson, Clark, & Walpole, 1999).

Coaching includes the concept of stretching students a bit farther during each succeeding guided practice while still maintaining the instructional level within their zones of proximal development (Mason, Roehler, & Duffy, 1984; Vygotsky, 1934/1986), where expectations are higher than students can handle independently but not so high as to frustrate their efforts. The following behaviors are just a few of the ways that teachers engage in coaching during strategy instruction:

- Asking students to think aloud as they use cognitive strategies to extract and construct meaning from text
- Cueing students to choose one of the strategies that have been taught thus far to solve a reading problem
- Delivering mini-lessons whenever appropriate during the reading of text to demonstrate for students how they knew which strategy to use and how they were using it
- Giving feedback to their students regarding their progress
- Modeling thinking or offering prompts to remind students of possible thoughts or actions they might take

Coaching usually occurs during the portion of the reading lesson designated as guided practice, in which students are in various stages of assuming increasing responsibility for independent strategy usage and the teacher is gradually releasing responsibility to students as they gain expertise. Pearson and Gallagher (1983) refer to this as a model of planned obsolescence, in which teachers work themselves out of their explicit instruction and detailed modeling roles and into the following instructional components of attributing and constructing.

Attributing

Reading for meaning is hard work. Effective teachers are constantly promoting the worth of complex cognition to students. They take every opportunity to point out to students that their success in understanding and remembering difficult concepts and ideas is directly related to their cognitive strategy usage. When teachers receive excellent written summaries from their students or overhear a student making a spectacular inference, they are quick to attribute the quality of written work and cognitive processing to their students' resourceful use of cognitive strategies. Effective strategy teachers communicate to students that their thinking is not the result of how smart they are or aren't, but rather the result of their successful application of cognitive strategies. Strategic teachers continually emphasize the importance of the process (cognition), as opposed to the product (the assignment).

Constructing Meaning

Constructing meaning is the most energizing and rewarding aspect of strategy instruction. It is tempting for educators to bypass the more mundane teaching moves, like explaining and giving directions, preferring to fast-forward to the construction of meaning. That is not to say that strategic teachers do not emphasize extracting and constructing meaning whenever students are processing real text (Brown & Campione, 1994). However, strategic teachers know that they will be unable to enjoy the delights of constructing meaning at increasingly more challenging levels of text with their students if they have not laid an instructional foundation of explaining, modeling, and coaching during their instruction. As individual group members (students with their teacher) discuss their reactions to their reading, they are in turn influenced by the opinions, experiences, and feelings of other group members. The final meaning of the text that emerges is the product of the group's interaction (Pressley, Woloshyn, et al., 1995). This more inclusive definition of comprehension not only permits more diverse individual response and interpretation, but allows for the consideration of multiple avenues of meaning (Borokowski & Muthukrishna, 1992; Fielding & Pearson, 1994).

■ TAKE COMPREHENSION INSTRUCTION TO THE NEXT LEVEL

The single most important summary measure of reading skill in third grade and later is performance on a well-constructed test of reading comprehension.

—Torgesen and Hayes (2003, p. 1)

When students perform poorly on state assessments at the third-grade level or above but yet perform above the 39th percentile on tests of PA, word reading accuracy, and fluency, retesting with a group test of reading comprehension and vocabulary, such as the *Stanford Diagnostic Reading Test* (Karlsen & Gardner, 1995), is suggested. Below-grade-level performance on this test indicates the need for intensive instruction to build vocabulary and fundamental reading comprehension strategies. A more informal reading inventory, such as the *Qualitative Reading Inventory-4* (Leslie & Caldwell, 2005), might provide additional information regarding precisely how to focus instruction.

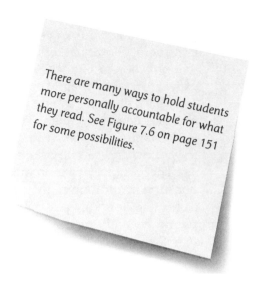

There are many ways to hold students more personally accountable for what they read. See Figure 7.6 on page 151 for some possibilities.

In addition to notching up the direct instruction of word and world knowledge as described in Chapter 5, there are four primary ways to increase the intensity of comprehension instruction: (1) Spend more time teaching comprehension (cognitive strategies); (2) increase the amount of direct teaching, explaining, and thinking aloud; (3) use only nonfiction text related to grade-level content standards; and (4) decrease the number of students in your instructional group so that the below-level student cannot hide in a larger instructional group. Struggling students tend to avoid eye contact and generally drift off during comprehension discussions. Accountability is key.

Increase the Time

When it comes to comprehension instruction, many educators are stuck in the late 1970s. Durkin (1978–1979) found that teachers devoted only 2% of the classroom time designated for reading instruction to actually teaching students how to comprehend what they read. Updates of Durkin's study found that little had changed in 20 years, even in schools where reading achievement in the lower grades exceeded what one would have predicted, given the school's demographics (Pressley, 2000; Taylor et al., 1999). Only 16% of the teachers who responded to surveys in these studies emphasized comprehension. *Therefore, if you want your students' comprehension to improve, spend more time teaching comprehension.*

Increase the Amount of Direct Teaching and Thinking Aloud

We know that children with average to low-average comprehension skills make gains when their teachers directly and explicitly teach strategies to them. They do not become better readers with long periods of sustained silent reading, student-managed comprehension activities in cooperative groups, or independent work with a comprehension activity or worksheet (Connor, Morrison, & Petrella, 2004). We also know that among general education teachers, modeling and describing a skill or strategy are among the lowest in frequency of observed teacher behaviors (Lenz, 2004). *Therefore, if you want your students' comprehension scores to improve, increase your thinking aloud and direct instructing and explaining of the seven strategies of skilled readers.*

Use Predominantly Nonfiction Text to Teach Comprehension

A third way to improve comprehension is to change what your students are reading. There is evidence that primary students not only prefer to read informational text (Pappas & Barry, 1997), but also as noted earlier in the chapter, engage in more meaning-seeking and meaning-making efforts during informational book read-alouds then when hearing fiction read aloud (Smolkin & Donovan, 2000).

In many classrooms, students are fed an exclusive diet of fiction. In addition, there are few attractive nonfiction texts on students' independent reading level available in classrooms. Book baskets are usually filled with fiction. Then suddenly, after a steady diet of fiction in Grades K–3, students find themselves in fourth grade where they are expected to read mainly expository text in math, science, and social studies textbooks. They have difficulty coping with new text structures and a heavy load of difficult content and academic vocabulary. Furthermore, there are expectations that students will both understand what they read and be able to take end-of-unit tests to demonstrate what they know and can do by answering short-answer and essay questions.

These expectations require the abilities to summarize, visualize, organize, and question in addition to the other three cognitive strategies. Absent explicit instruction in how to apply these strategies to expository text, their comprehension scores will plummet. Without the ability to read strategically, the "fourth-grade slump" sets in (Chall et al., 1990). No matter that your students learned to read and were fluent readers in third grade, capable of reading *Charlotte's Web* (White, 1980) and *The Mouse and the Motorcycle* (Cleary, 1965). The reading landscape changes dramatically in fourth grade and gets harder every year thereafter. *Therefore, if you want your students' comprehension scores to improve, change the kind of texts you regularly expect them to read and comprehend and scaffold their reading of such texts as long as necessary for them to achieve success.*

Change the Student–Teacher Ratio During Comprehension Instruction

Struggling students need either a 30-minute scaffolded comprehension tutorial, after the Reading Recovery model that is so popular in first grade, or the opportunity to learn reading comprehension in a group of students on the same instructional reading level for 30–45 minutes per day. If you are serious about notching up reading comprehension in the upper grades, more personalized and intensive instruction is essential for struggling older readers (Allington, 2001, 2006a). Although one-to-one tutoring is clearly an effective intervention when provided by skilled, trained teachers (Shanahan, 1998; Wasik & Slavin, 1993), small-group interventions work as well, when students are strategically grouped for reading levels (Mathes et al., 2005).

■ SUMMARIZING CHAPTER 6

The challenge of teaching comprehension to students can be met by organizing instruction around the seven strategies of highly effective readers and becoming metacognitive in your approach to teaching comprehension. The most effective teaching moves for strategy instruction are direct instructing, explaining, and modeling (thinking aloud). Become a cognitive mentor or master for your students by thinking aloud for them daily about how to extract and construct meaning from text.

7

Reading a Lot

> *Reading a lot* is characterized by the mindful and engaged reading of a large volume of text both in and out of school, at increasing levels of difficulty, with personalized accountability.

I firmly believe in the power of reading a lot to improve the word and world knowledge of students as well as their comprehension. Between 1983 and 1991, when the students in my K–6 elementary school increased the amount of time they spent reading every year, our library's circulation figures *and* our school's standardized test scores went up in tandem every year except one. Of course, I cannot say with certainty what percentage of our achievement gains was due to increased voluntary reading by our students and what percentage was attributable to any or all of the other research-based instructional and environmental interventions that we employed:

Reading a Lot

- More time spent on reading instruction in all Grades K–6 (Berliner, 1981; Fisher & Berliner, 1985)
- More direct instruction by teachers using programs like *Reading Mastery* (Becker & Engelmann, 1983) and *Cooperative Integrated Reading and Composition* (Slavin & Madden, 1983)
- More cooperative learning schoolwide (Johnson & Johnson, 1989)
- A faculty-developed set of language arts learning outcomes (English, 1992)
- Increased professional development in cognitive strategy instruction and schoolwide implementation of cognitive strategy instruction (Pressley, Burkell, et al., 1995).
- Higher expectations and accountability for students, teachers, *and* parents (Goddard, Hoy, & Hoy, 2004)
- Increased faculty collaboration around issues like developing interventions for students at risk and curricular alignment (Schlechty, 2005)

- Increased participation by staff members in decision making (Hord, 1997)
- Regular RIF (Reading Is Fundamental) special events and book giveaways (McLloyd, 1979)
- Afterschool tutoring programs, summer school, and school–business partnership enrichment programs (Berliner, 1986)
- Proactive program by the media specialist to foster independent reading of 100 books per year by upper-grade students (Stanovich & Cunningham, 1993)

I must give some of the credit for our improved reading achievement (from the 20th to 70th percentile on standardized tests in Grades 2–6) to reading a lot, because it was a major emphasis every year. Therefore, I was more than a little distressed when I received my copy of the National Reading Panel's report in the summer of 2000 (NICHD, 2000) and read their conclusion that there was no experimental research to demonstrate that when we motivate students to do more silent reading, their abilities to read more fluently as well as to better understand what they read improve. In fact, the panel's search for experimental studies to verify our long-standing belief in the efficacy of a daily period of sustained silent reading turned up only slightly more than a dozen studies, none of which enabled panel members to conclude that schools should adopt programs to encourage more reading. The panel reported, "Despite widespread acceptance of the idea that schools can successfully encourage students to read more and that these increases in reading practice will be translated into better fluency and higher reading achievement, there is not adequate evidence to sustain this claim" (NICHD, 2000, sec. 3, p. 28).

Unfortunately their conclusion confused many educators who proceeded to totally eliminate silent reading from the school day, especially in the primary grades. Clearly, panel members did not intend that educators abolish silent reading in their classrooms. As Hiebert (2006b) points out, "Silent reading is the primary mode for proficient readers. If primary-level students only read aloud during instruction, it is doubtful that their reading rate and comprehension in silent reading will progress at the level required to be proficient. That is, their rate of thinking about text will be limited to their rate of oral reading fluency."

Hiebert (2006b) goes on to explain that if the only time students get to read silently in school is when other students are reading orally, their silent reading experiences will be impoverished. In addition, although Hiebert does not make this assertion, students will be unprepared to silently read the state assessment.

I do not recommend that teachers and principals stop motivating students to read or stop transitioning from mostly oral to mostly silent reading when they are ready. In fact, I suggest that you notch up reading a lot in your school in as many ways as you possibly can.

■ WHAT IS READING A LOT AND HOW DO STUDENTS BECOME VORACIOUS READERS?

Before we examine the definition of *reading a lot* more closely, we need to clarify what reading a lot is not. Reading a lot is not sending everyone to the library for a book and devoting 30 minutes to sustained silent reading, with no regard for whether all students can independently read the books they have chosen. Although much has been made of how teachers can motivate students to read by modeling the act of silent reading, sitting at one's desk reading a newspaper while struggling readers are staring at an unintelligible page of print is a waste of instructional time. A more

productive and powerful way to use the time might be to think aloud for students about how you approach reading the newspaper and how that differs from how you read the science and social studies textbooks of your grade level. Scaffolded instruction in how to read silently would also be an excellent use of time.

In the first edition, reading a lot was defined as *reading a lot of text at increasing levels of difficulty with some measure of accountability.* I suggested that the intersection of these three conditions would result in a more productive reading experience called "reading in the zone," as illustrated in Figure 7.1.

After several years of working with this definition and explaining it to groups of teachers, I find it to be too vague. It doesn't specify what kind of reading (oral or silent, assisted or independent). It doesn't describe the state of the reader's mind while reading (engaged or disengaged, mindful or mindless, in the zone or zoned out) or the reader's level of commitment (engaged or disengaged) and desire (motivated or apathetic). Furthermore, the definition doesn't specify where the reading is taking place (at school, home, or elsewhere) nor does it describe the type of accountability (personalized or depersonalized) that is required. Last, the definition offers no information as to how much reading students should be doing. The following definition fills in some of the gaps: *Reading a lot is characterized by mindful, silent reading of a large volume of text both in and out of school, at gradually increasing levels of*

Figure 7.1 Reading in the Zone

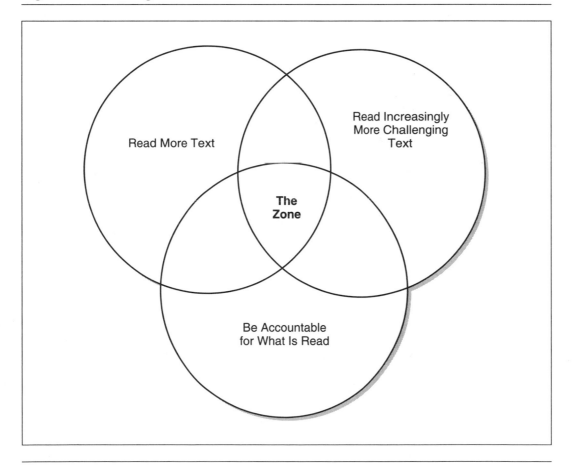

difficulty, with personalized accountability. I address a proposed definition of reading volume later in the chapter. Figure 7.2 defines the wide variety of terms that come into play when discussing reading a lot, while Figure 7.3 illustrates the improved model of reading a lot—mindful reading.

Figure 7.2   Words to Know About Reading a Lot

Term	Definition
Engaged reading	The extent to which a reader has a positive regard toward reading, seeks out texts, and makes time to read. Engagement is known to be a critical variable in reading achievement (Brozo, 2008)
Mindful reading	All of the reader's cognitive resources are focused on extracting and constructing meaning from the text. The reader is aware of the state of attentiveness and is able to pull back from mindless reading and refocus attention (Schooler et al., 2004)
Mindless reading	Similar to being zoned out (definition follows). The reader is going through the motions but is not cognitively processing the text
Zoned-out reading	The reader's eyes continue to move across the page while the mind is elsewhere, the literary equivalent of driving for miles without remembering how you got there (Feller, 2006)
Silent reading	Unvocalized reading of text
Self-selected reading	Books or materials that the reader has chosen independently without being asked to read the text for a class assignment
Assigned reading	Books or materials that the teacher has selected and assigned to be read
Personalized accountability	Accountability that involves a personal contact or relationship with a teacher or librarian, as compared to answering questions on a computer with no feedback or monitoring by a teacher or librarian
Accessible reading	Text that the reader can read independently without scaffolded assistance from the teacher
Reading volume	The number of pages or words that a student reads in a given period of time or the amount of time a student spends reading
Individual motivational programs	Programs that offer individualized extrinsic rewards, prizes—recognition for reading a lot
Schoolwide motivational programs	Programs that encourage students to meet a schoolwide reading volume goal, with all students receiving the same reward at the end if all students meet the goal
Scaffolded silent reading	Silent reading that is done with a tutor or teacher who thinks aloud for students, offers periodic comprehension checks to refocus readers' attention, and continually coaches them in the use of cognitive strategies
Assisted reading	Oral reading done with a tutor or teacher
Independent reading	Unassisted oral or silent reading

Figure 7.3   Mindful Reading

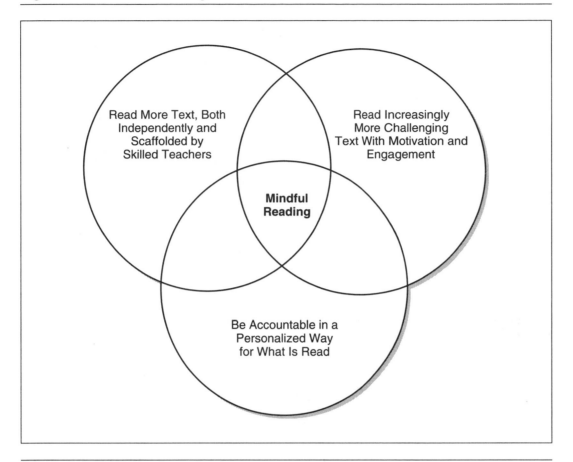

Although the Mindful Reading model serves to describe the reading done by average and above-average students who have the skills and desire to read, it fails to address two problems that impact our students most at risk: (a) they *can't* read well, and therefore (b) they *won't* try. In order to increase the reading volume of students at risk, teachers must do far more than schedule time for silent reading and publish a new set of expectations for reading volume. They must (1) provide daily scaffolded silent reading instruction and (2) provide materials and reading opportunities that are known to intrinsically motivate disengaged students.

During the years that I was a media specialist, I worked with dozens of disengaged readers, developing personal relationships with them and finding accessible books that motivated them to keep reading. My efforts were focused on the most reluctant readers, and I worked with them personally one-on-one. However, when I transitioned to the principalship, I experienced a more comprehensive and exciting example of engaged reading. For five years, the Battle of the Books program motivated our Grades 4–6 students and teachers to become totally engaged in reading (Cook & Page, 1994). The building virtually hummed with excitement over books. Reading engagement is the extent to which students (a) have a positive regard toward reading, (b) seek out texts, and (c) make time to read (Brozo, 2008). We had all three of these conditions to the max.

The program, which ran from October to March of each school year, involved the strategic reading of large quantities of challenging, well-written, and varied text; reciprocal teaching and cooperative learning; group and individual accountability; and healthy team competition. All of this was in addition to what students gained from their regular 60-minute reading class. Although we did not gather many statistics during the years we participated in the project, during five of the eight years we focused on raising reading achievement, the Battle of the Books was specifically responsible for the engagement and empowerment of large numbers of students, especially those who typically did not read a great deal or get good grades in school.

Every student participated in a cooperative team made up of five students with varying reading abilities. This was not a voluntary or negotiable activity. It was part of every student's reading grade. Each team was jointly responsible for reading a list of 40 books chosen by our town's youth services librarian. The books ranged in reading level from third to ninth grade. Students reached consensus in their teams regarding which books would be read by each team member, with eight books being the *minimum* number to be read by an individual. Some team members chose to read all 40 books, but each student was accountable for reading his or her assigned eight books and knowing them inside out. Team competitions were organized at the building level to prepare for the library-sponsored competition, and students made up questions for other teams to answer. Teams met during lunch and after school to talk about the books they had read and to anticipate what types of questions the library staff would select to stump them during the semifinal and final rounds. Our librarian ordered multiple copies of all of the titles so that no one would have to wait to read a chosen book. Teachers read some of the more challenging titles aloud in class and discussed complex themes and difficult vocabulary with students. Some teachers personally read all of the titles themselves and discussed the books with their students, not only during reading class but also at odd moments on the playground, while waiting in line for music or art classes, or before being called to the gym for an assembly. Every spare moment of the school day was spent talking about books.

As the date for the library competition to select the team that would represent our school drew near, our teams began to meet on their own initiative in the evenings and on weekends. During the initial year of competition, one of our sixth-grade teams took first place in the city. One of the team members had only attended our school since fourth grade and could scarcely read a word when she enrolled—a student who had definitely fallen through the cracks. She learned to read almost overnight, it seemed, under the tutelage of our special education teacher, and she became one of our most avid readers. Although our school was the acknowledged underdog, we soundly defeated all of the other teams from the private and more privileged schools in our district.

What was responsible for our stellar showing? Our students were engaged in mindful reading for a purpose. They were focused on gaining meaning from what they read as opposed to putting in time. After our first-year success, students were motivated to read with even more intensity and focus in successive years. We managed to capture two more titles during a five-year period, until other schools discovered our secret strategy—mindful and engaged reading.

■ WHEN SHOULD READING A LOT BE TAUGHT?

We should begin teaching students to read a lot on the very first day of preschool or kindergarten. I developed a methodology to do that as a media specialist in two different schools and took it with me when I became a principal. It raised the eyebrows of my kindergarten teacher and media specialist when I first suggested it. They were of the opinion that a visit to the library once a week was enough, but I convinced them that to teach students to read a lot, you had to get them in the habit. Here's how the system worked. On the first day of school, every kindergarten student went to the library for the first time. There they were assisted in checking out a picture book. There were plenty of volunteers to help them select their books and sign their names on the checkout cards. When they got back to the classroom, they put their books in their new backpacks. Their parents were notified at the parent orientation about the books that would be coming home and had received instructions about how to read the book aloud to their child just before bedtime. As soon as the book is read, it goes right back into the backpack where it is returned to school the next day.

The teacher carefully teaches students the routine for returning their books to school, getting a star on the chart for the story they "read" before bedtime, "writing" their name on the easel using a scribble or symbol that is meaningful to them, and then going to the library to return their book and check out a new one at the appointed time. Oh, there are always a few glitches, like the child who returns his book with the alarming news that nobody read a story to him. The teacher does some checking to find out if the parent understood the directions, if the parent reads English (we had a large selection of picture books in Spanish), or if the parent would prefer that we send a tape player home with the book so the child can listen to his book on tape multiple times. By the end of the first week, all of the children are telling the teacher and other adults about their stories, getting their stars, and checking out another book. This program was powerful because it built a habit of reading before bedtime that we would reinforce for the rest of the child's elementary school career. We trained the parents to read. When they didn't, their children reminded them over and over. We then planned to transition the children from having stories read aloud to reading stories aloud to their parents.

During the years when the district preschool was located at Lincoln School, we used the same routine with the preschool class. In the schools where I served as the media specialist, I did a story hour once a week for three- and four-year-olds to encourage their familiarity with our library. Students checked out books and brought them back to the next story hour.

THE ROLE OF READING A LOT ■
IN SKILLED READING

Do students become skilled readers because they read a lot or do they read a lot because they are skilled readers? Actually, the answer is yes—to both questions. Cunningham (2005) uses the Matthew effect described earlier to explain how good readers get more proficient while poor readers fall farther behind. Students who begin second grade with strong reading skills read increasingly more books, which results in fluency and increased vocabulary. The combination of fluent reading and knowing the meaning of lots of words leads to increased reading comprehension. When students understand what they read, reading is a more rewarding experience. This sense of enjoyment and fulfillment quite naturally leads to a desire to read more. As students' reading volume increases, their skills become stronger. And so it goes. The good readers soar to the top of the charts. Of course, most all of the reading that is done by proficient readers is silent, except for some oral reading in school at the beginning of second grade.

In contrast, students who begin second grade with weak reading skills have fewer opportunities to read accessible text and generally spend much less time reading in school than their stronger counterparts (Allington, 1984; Cunningham & Stanovich, 1998; Nagy & Anderson, 1984). Their phonemic decoding skills are often labored, and they have far fewer sight words available in their long-term memories for instant retrieval. Therefore, their fluency is marginal and they know the meanings of fewer words. This sad state of affairs leads to diminished comprehension. For struggling readers, reading is a frustrating and unrewarding experience to be avoided at all costs. They have almost no motivation to read, thus depressing their reading volume, and so it goes. The poor readers are left at the end of the school year with seemingly fewer reading skills than they had at the beginning, and the gap between them and their reading-rich peers grows ever wider.

In order to break this depressing cycle for struggling readers, something needs to happen to turn them on to reading. Sometimes a teacher is able to help students break through some instructional barrier and begin to experience success. Sometimes the librarian provides the just-right books that make interesting reading accessible for the first time. Sometimes it's a strong interest in a topic that students want to learn about. But above all, there must be success. Success in any field of endeavor, whether basketball, ballet, or reading, engenders more success. Struggling readers of any age need high-success reading experiences to keep them practicing until they get better. How long does anyone fail before giving up? Variables like a strong interest in a subject, an opportunity to have a choice about what to read, or a growing sense of self-efficacy engendered by effective instruction are essential components for engaging upper-grade struggling readers.

■ THE LACK OF SCIENTIFIC EVIDENCE FOR READING A LOT

We noted earlier the lack of experimental research regarding the effectiveness of reading a lot in raising student achievement. I would like to propose a hypothetical experimental research study to test the hypothesis that motivating students to read a lot plays a significant role in students becoming skilled readers. Our null hypothesis is that *reading a lot has no impact on reading achievement,* and our goal is to disprove our null hypothesis. In order for our research to be considered experimental, we must have two conditions: a randomized sample and a control group. I propose three different treatments for our sample groups: (1) an accessible text treatment, in which all of the classrooms in the school are stocked with hundreds of books on every topic and reading level imaginable; (2) a reading volume treatment, in which students sign contracts promising to read a certain amount of time or a certain amount of text; and (3) a combined treatment of accessible text and reading volume. Our control school will maintain the usual instructional reading program with no additional materials or motivational reading programs.

The unit of randomization in our study will be K–8 schools in three large urban districts. All of the schools are of similar size, have similar student demographics, and are low performing overall. In order to control for variables of instructional effectiveness on the part of teachers or instructional leadership of the principal, we ask schools from the total number of K–8 schools to volunteer to be part of the study. We then randomly select schools from the total pool of volunteer schools to be part of the study.

Eight schools from each city will be randomly chosen from those schools that volunteered. From those 24 schools, 4 will be randomly assigned to a control group,

4 to the Accessible Text (AT) treatment, 4 to the Reading Volume (RV) treatment, and 4 to a combined Accessible Text and Reading Volume treatment (ATRV).

The AT treatment will consist of buying hundreds of books on every topic and reading level imaginable. These books will be distributed in equal amounts to all of the classrooms in the participating schools, offering a range of topics and reading levels for each classroom. They will be available for checkout by the students. All schools will receive the same selection of books.

In schools receiving the RV treatment, each student in Grades 2–8 will sign a simple contract and commit to reading a certain number of words during the school year, both in and out of school. Reading can be either oral or silent depending on the grade and fluency levels of students. A third group of four schools will receive both the accessible texts and the reading volume treatments (ATRV). Absent experiments like this imaginary one, we have only correlational research to show us the effect of reading volume on reading achievement. Figure 7.4 summarizes it.

Figure 7.4   Correlational Research Support for Reading a Lot

Type of Research	Research Findings
Differences in the amount of reading done by high- and low-achieving students	Higher-achieving students do more reading in school than their lower-achieving counterparts (Allington, 1977, 1980, 1983, 1984; Allington & McGill-Franzen, 1989).
	Higher-achieving students read more outside of school (Anderson, Wilson, & Fielding, 1988; Nagy & Anderson, 1984). Anderson and his colleagues found that students achieving at the 90th percentile read 40 minutes per day, which amounted to well over 2 million words per year, while students achieving at the 50th percentile read only 12.9 minutes per day for a total of 601,000 words per year; students achieving at the 10th percentile read a scant 1.6 minutes per day for an appallingly low 51,000 words per year.
Correlational research showing a relationship between amount of reading both in and out of school and reading achievement	The most persuasive, contemporary, and extensive correlational study showing a relationship between reading a lot and achievement is the 1998 National Assessment of Educational Progress (Donahue, Voelkl, Campbell, & Mazzeo, 1999). At all grades (4, 8, and 12), students who reported reading more pages daily in school and for homework had higher average scale scores than students who reported reading fewer pages daily.
Acquisition of second languages through reading a lot	Reading a lot makes a huge impact on the acquisition of a second language when the learners are beyond the beginning reading level. There is a wide body of literature that makes one wonder why we aren't more proactive about motivating our ELLs to read a lot in English (Pilgreen & Krashen, 1993). Language and literacy development around the world has been stimulated by reading a lot: United States (Krashen, 1993), England (Haifiz & Tudor, 1989), Japan (Mason & Krashen, 1997), South Africa (Elley, 1999), Sri Lanka (Elley, 1999), and Hong Kong (Tsang, 1996).
Relationship of academic learning time and student achievement	When students are actually engaged in learning tasks with a high level of success, their achievement goes up (Berliner, 1981; Fisher & Berliner, 1985). A logical conclusion one can draw from this literature is that time spent reading at a high level of success will result in reading achievement.

■ EFFECTIVE INSTRUCTIONAL PRACTICES FOR TEACHING READING A LOT

There is no program that can teach students to read a lot. There are, however, a variety of instructional practices that can provide students with more rewarding and successful reading experiences, thereby increasing reading volume—a condition that is highly correlated with reading achievement. To list them all in one place, these practices include (1) stop ignoring the students who can't read grade-level texts, (2) make accessible reading available to all students in their classrooms, (3) enlist students in personal goal-setting for reading improvement, (4) increase the amount of time spent reading, (5) increase the number of pages or words read, (6) use instructional approaches known to be intrinsically motivating to students, (7) read more nonfiction to build world and word knowledge, (8) scaffold mindful silent reading, and (9) create personalized accountability systems.

Stop Ignoring the Students Who Can't Read Grade-Level Texts

I have told the story of Robert Uber at many workshops and in earlier books (McEwan, 2001, 2007). However, his story illustrates what can happen when teachers ignore students who can't read. By the time Robert entered high school in 1997, he had been in and out of a variety of self-contained classes for students with behavior difficulties. He was on course to become a dropout statistic when his academic trajectory took a sharp turn upward. What was behind this dramatic turnaround?

A gifted special education teacher in a small northern Michigan high school learned the source of Robert's frustration when his older brother shared this remarkable insight: "All Robert wants is to learn to read." It seemed that when former teachers ignored Robert's inability to read, focusing instead on controlling his behavior, he became aggressive and unmanageable. On the auspicious day that Robert met his new teacher, she offered him a way out: if he would stick with her, she would teach him to read. In addition, he would get a high school diploma. First of all, Robert was given a choice. He could choose to stay in the class or he could choose to become the behavior problem there that he had been in every other class since first grade. He was interested enough in the teacher's offer that he returned to school the very next day. Robert believed the teacher and committed himself to a four-year goal. His teacher's honesty combined with her ability to give Robert the gift of success every single day he attended school motivated and engaged him. During his high school career, Robert not only reached his reading goal, he also received a citizenship award, worked in the media center, went to the prom with an honor student, and attended vocational school. His teacher reported that Robert was so engaged in learning to read that he never once, in four years, exhibited any of his former behavioral disorders.

Since his high school graduation in 2001, Robert has married his prom date, fathered a son, and realized his dream of owning his own business, a truck and automobile repair shop. A high school diploma, combined with the ability to read and write, changed Robert's life forever. His story is still being written, but the first chapter has a very happy ending—thanks to a gifted teacher using a research-based methodology (McEwan, 2007, pp. 1–2).

Robert was taught to read using the Spalding Method, a multi-sensory, direct instruction approach (Spalding & Spalding, 1957/1990). To view a video showing a Spalding classroom in action, go online to www.spalding.org.

Make Accessible Reading Available to All Students in Their Classrooms

Accessible reading consists of books or other materials (Web sites, graphic novels, magazines, or fanzines for upper grades) at students' independent reading levels. Whenever I present a workshop to intermediate through high school teachers, I ask them if they are provided with information about their students' reading levels at the beginning of each school year. Some are surprised by my question. "Why would I need to know that?" one Language Arts teacher asked. "I don't teach reading." Teachers at every level and in every content area should know the reading levels of their students so they can make accessible reading available and provide scaffolded silent reading experiences in their classrooms.

I was once a media specialist and I love libraries. That led to my mistaken notion that all of the books in a school should be housed in the library. However, the depth and breadth of reading difficulties in classrooms today requires a different approach. Libraries are daunting places for struggling readers. Library skills lessons rarely take into account struggling readers. Reluctant readers are not likely to seek out the librarian to ask for an easy book to read. If forced to choose a book, they pick the first available thin one and pretend to read it or choose a book they have looked at in an earlier grade and look at it again. This is a waste of valuable instructional time.

Note: When asked to read a book for a book report, my granddaughter Abigail regularly chose *Pick of the Litter* (Wallace, 2005) or other titles by Wallace. I purchased the book for her, and her mother told me, "That's the book she always reads for her book reports."

I have come to believe that every classroom needs lots of books on many different reading levels. At lower levels there should be a mix of fiction and nonfiction. In Grades 4–8, all of the books should support the content standards. If there is a range of books from easy to difficult on content topics like the rainforest or World War II, the teacher can readily remove the stigma attached to reading easy books by pointing out how much information on the topic is available in a very quick read and then encouraging everyone to choose at least one or two easy books to read for immediate concept development.

May I remind you that if you are looking for information on a topic about which you know nothing, you do not find a book written by an expert, or locate a 20-page article in *Encyclopedia Britannica*. You find the easiest reading source. Absent online access, you will likely choose *The World Book*. If we want our students to read a lot, we must make accessible reading available. The books must be interesting, varied, and help students build knowledge on topics related to the content standards of their grade level. The logistics, both financial and otherwise, of making a wide range of books on relevant topics available in specific classrooms a reality in every school may seem mind-boggling, especially for teachers who teach in three or four different classrooms every day. However, I do not think we can merely pay lip service to the goal of teaching them all to read if students cannot read anything in their classrooms, including the textbook.

There are educators who prefer to buy *Accelerated Reader* (*AR;* Advantage Learning Systems, 2001), believing that everyone can find accessible reading in that collection. And most likely they could, if they only would. But they won't. There are two reasons why *AR* doesn't work for the most at risk readers. The books are too far away from the classroom for the neediest readers. They need books right there in front of them, with enticing covers and exciting titles. The *AR* books are graded by points. The minute struggling readers discover that a book on their level is only worth .5 points, they don't want to read it. When you're behind before you begin, why begin at all?

Enlist Students in Personal Goal Setting for Reading Improvement

Talk honestly with upper-grade students about their reading deficiencies and explain to them what they can do to improve. Show them their test scores. Let them know where they should be and exactly what they need to do to reach those goals. Depending on their age and grade, students can set personal reading goals for the week, month, or year. Relate the goals to their deficiencies (phonemic decoding, fluency, silent reading comprehension), and then provide high-success experiences every day that help them reach those goals. The following case study of Jason, once a highly dysfluent reader, is illustrative of what can happen when students set their own reading goals.

Case Study

The Case of the Highly Motivated Dysfluent Reader

It's not often that reading specialist Jan Price works one on one with students anymore. Her current job description now includes consultative work and professional development on top of teaching classes all day. So she was surprised when a fourth grader knocked on her office door at recess time asking for help. "He had sort of a hangdog look," she says, "and I couldn't refuse to see him." It was March, and Jason told Jan he was worried about his reading. He didn't have a label and he hadn't been referred, but he knew where he stood. "I felt so sorry for him that I squeezed him in between all of my other commitments that day," Jan related. She checked on his status before the appointment and discovered that in October, Jason's oral reading fluency was abysmally low—27 words per minute (85 words correct per minute is the minimum for comprehending text). Now it was March, and although his fluency had improved somewhat, it was still very low (50 words per minute).

Jan was intrigued by a student who was motivated enough to seek her out, and she couldn't refuse his plea for help. She talked at length with Jason about exactly what he would have to do. She explained that it would take a lot of oral reading to improve his fluency, but that he could definitely get better before June. She suggested that he set a goal and agreed to give him passages to read at home and to test him every other day. Then she asked him what his goal would be. After reviewing Jan's chart for district standards, Jason boldly ventured a goal of 118 words per minute by June. Jan was a bit dubious about what she perceived to be a highly unrealistic goal, but Jason was resolute. It was 118 words per minute, and that was that.

During the warm spring months when other students were enjoying the lengthening evening hours out of doors, Jason was inside doing a lot of repeated oral reading. In the beginning, Jan provided Jason with short passages on which to practice. He stopped by without fail every other day to be tested and to have his new rate posted on a graph that Jan hung on her office wall. He decided his progress would be even faster if he started reading book chapters aloud repeatedly and began stopping by the library to find things to read. The increase in his oral reading fluency was gradual, but it moved steadily upward. Jason's mother contacted his teacher; she couldn't believe the change in her son. He was bringing home books to read every afternoon and reading voraciously every evening. She had never seen him so motivated to read and wondered what was behind this frenzy of reading activity. Jan explained Jason's goal and how committed he was to reaching it. His mother got in the act, offering her support and encouragement every day. By June, Jason was reading over 130 correct words per minute. His oral reading rate shot off the charts. Jason not only exceeded the seemingly impossible goal he set for himself but in the process, also discovered the pleasure and enjoyment that comes from reading.

Increase the Amount of Time Spent Reading

Although most educators agree that students should read more, there is no agreed-on standard for exactly *how much* they should be reading—either at the elementary or secondary levels. Many educators think in terms of words, pages, or books (Honig, 1996, p. 103), but Allington (2001) recommends that reading volume should be measured in *time.* I concur. To expect beginning or slower readers to read the same number of pages or books as a more skilled reader can easily lead to frustration and discouragement. I call this "the accelerated reader syndrome." As soon as struggling readers determine that they will never achieve enough points by reading books on their level, they quit. The only students left reading are those that can race through dozens of high-point-value books and win the coveted prizes.

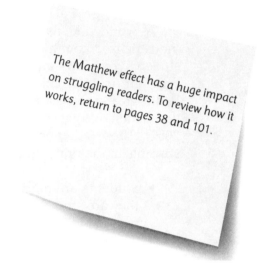

The Matthew effect has a huge impact on struggling readers. To review how it works, return to pages 38 and 101.

Although time is a more equitable metric by which to measure reading volume, since all readers have equal amounts of it at their disposal, we will always have the problem of struggling readers who, when the Matthew effect kicks in, can't catch up with their reading-rich peers. In order to catch up, struggling readers need to spend more time reading than their peers who are reading fluently.

Allington (2001) asserts that the volume of daily *in-school* reading that most elementary school children experience is far below an optimum level and suggests that students should be doing an absolutely mind-boggling 90 minutes of *actual* reading *in school* every day. This 90 minutes would include any and all kinds of reading during the school day—content area reading, reading done during reading instruction, silent reading, voluntary reading, assigned reading for which the student is held accountable, oral reading, repeated reading, guided reading, and buddy reading. Allington (2001) further recommends that teachers at each grade level jointly develop reading volume standards that are zealously adhered to by *every* staff member.

I would also recommend that *out-of-school* reading volume standards be established. At Lincoln, we developed reading homework standards and expected every student to read for a certain period of time nightly (or weekly, depending on the grade level). This reading could include a read-aloud by an adult or older sibling to a student, listening to a commercially taped read-aloud, reading aloud by the student to an adult or sibling, repeated oral reading, or silent reading.

Increase the Number of Pages or Words Read

Some researchers study reading a lot using the variable of words. There are recommendations out there that students in the primary grades should read at least 1,000,000 words in school by the end of third grade and another million outside of school. Hiebert (2006b) suggests one way to make this happen. Add increasingly more minutes of scaffolded silent reading to the school day as students move from Grade 1 to Grade 3. By third grade, she suggests that students be reading 20 minutes daily during reading instruction at 100 words per minute for a total of 360,000 words and 20 minutes daily in scaffolded silent reading for the same amount of time for another 360,000 words, bringing the third-grade total of in-school reading to 720,000. These are reading goals that can appropriately be shared with second- and third-grade students. If they know that reading a million words is important to be successful in school, they will climb aboard the Million Word Express (or whatever you want to call it in your classroom). We must remember to give students reasons for reading every day.

Use Instructional Approaches Known to Be Intrinsically Motivating

A worldwide reading assessment and survey of 15-year-old students in 32 industrialized countries including the United States offers a fascinating snapshot of students' opinions and feelings about what motivates them to read. Called the Program for International Students Assessment, it found that reading engagement had a greater impact on achievement than either socioeconomic status or parental occupation (Organization for Economic Cooperation and Development [OECD], 2002). These additional findings are helpful when considering how to motivate students in the upper grades:

- Students are more motivated to read when the reading is related to content they are studying and when they are given reasons to read that connect with real-world purposes for reading (Greenleaf, Jimenez, & Roller, 2002; OECD, 2002).
- Students are more motivated to read when they set personal goals regarding what and how much they want to read and then get regular feedback from the teacher regarding their progress (Ryan & Deci, 2000).
- Students are more motivated to read when they are expected to explain the meaning of the text to other students (OECD, 2002).
- Students are more motivated to read when they can choose materials to read that are related to a content goal in the classroom—preparing a report, giving a brief talk, or making a poster (OECD, 2002).
- Students are more motivated to read when the goal is mastery of specific content rather than performance goals in which students are measured against each other and ranked (OECD, 2002).
- Students are more motivated to read when they can choose what to read (Guthrie & Davis, 2003; McLloyd, 1979; Turner, 1995).
- Students are more motivated to read when the material is related to new media, like song lyrics, cheat sheets for computer games, comic books and graphic novels, fashion magazines, motorcycle and car magazines, and maintenance manuals (Alvermann, 2003).
- Students will expend the effort needed to read if they are interested in the material (Eccles, Wigfield, & Schiefele, 1998; Guthrie & Humenick, 2004).
- Students are more motivated to read when they can learn something they did not know before from reading the text (Harp & Mayer, 1997).
- Students are more motivated to read when social collaboration is involved. In addition, collaborating during reading increase students' ability to comprehend the reading material (Ng, Guthrie, Van Meter, McCann, & Alao, 1998).

Read More Nonfiction to Build Word and World Knowledge

Students must read more expository text at every grade level. The early childhood emphasis on picture books and fairy tales plus the literature-based instruction that has dominated the reading lists of many early elementary students has not prepared most upper-grade, middle, and high school students for reading expository text. They can deal with plots, settings, and characters. But they are baffled by comparing and contrasting, cause and effect, or a sequence of historical events. With the advent of the Readers' Workshop (Atwell, 1998) and literature-based instruction (Peterson & Eeds, 1990), nonfiction has fallen on hard times.

ACT, the nation's largest provider of tests for college-bound students, periodically surveys middle-school, high school, and college teachers regarding the types of skills thought to be needed by students to succeed in college as well as the type of reading that should consume the majority of students' reading time. Teachers across the levels were in agreement about the skills needed for success in college, with drawing conclusions and making inferences from the text rated as the top two skills. They differed, however, on the most important type of reading needed for college success (ACT, 2000).

Middle school and high school teachers ranked prose fiction as the most important type of reading, ahead of text from the social sciences, humanities, and sciences. College teachers, on the other hand, ranked social science reading as being most important, with the humanities second and prose fiction third (ACT, 2000, p. 10). "There should be greater use of multiple texts in reading instruction, and most especially, the texts studied should not only be narrative, but also expository" (Kibby, 1993, p. 48).

Scaffold Mindful Silent Reading

One way to scaffold mindful silent reading is by teaching students a set of prompts or procedures to use as they read. This type of scaffolding helps students to engage in mindful reading but gradually releases to them the responsibility for using a variety of cognitive strategies, such as activating prior knowledge and questioning the author. A sample lesson is shown in Figure 7.5.

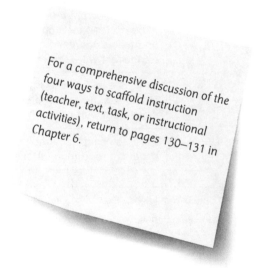

For a comprehensive discussion of the four ways to scaffold instruction (teacher, text, task, or instructional activities), return to pages 130–131 in Chapter 6.

Another way to scaffold silent reading for comprehension is to teach six signals that indicate a need for comprehension repair (Tovani, 2000, p. 38). These signals function as prompts for struggling readers to help them internalize and routinize comprehension monitoring:

- The inner voice inside the reader's head stops its conversation with the text and only the reader's voice is heard pronouncing the words.
- The camera inside the reader's head shuts off, and the reader can no longer visualize what is happening.
- The reader's mind begins to wander, and the reader becomes aware of thinking about something far removed from the text.
- The reader cannot remember or retell what has been read.
- The reader is not getting clarifying questions answered.
- Characters are reappearing in the text and the reader doesn't recall who they are.

Figure 7.5   Sample Lesson for Scaffolding Silent Reading (15–20 Minutes)

Step	Teacher Script	Student Actions
First read	Before you read, think about what you already know about the topic. Also look for two words that might be challenging. Underline those words or put a sticky arrow on them.	Students skim through the text looking for challenging words. They underline them or put down a sticky arrow.
	Now read the passage silently. If you finish reading before others, please write a sentence telling the main idea of the passage on your whiteboard.	Students take as much time as they need to read the passage silently.
	Now that you have read the passage, write down a few words or phrases that will help you remember what is important about the topic.	Students jot down their key words or phrases or construct or complete a simple graphic organizer.
Second read	Now I'm going to read the selection aloud as you read along silently. Follow along with me. (Teacher reads the passage aloud at the target rate per minute.)	Students follow along as the teacher reads orally.
	What is one thing the author wants you to remember from this selection? Write it on your whiteboard.	Students write down what they think the author wants them to remember on a whiteboard or in their reading journal.
Third read	Now read the selection one more time. Your goal is to read as much of the passage as you can in one minute. (Teacher stops the reading after one minute and tells students to circle or put down a sticky arrow on the last word they read before time was called.)	Students read the passage silently. Students circle or put down a sticky arrow on the last word read.
	Write a question on your white board that you would like to ask the author if he or she were here in the classroom with us.	Students write their questions.
	Let's ask each other some of these questions and see if we can read the author's mind.	

Source: Adapted from Hiebert (2003) and Hiebert and Fisher (2002).

One caveat before you are tempted to give your struggling students a handout with these six signals listed and announce that whenever these things happen, they need to refocus their attention. Struggling readers won't know what you are talking about. They hear no inner voices. They see no cameras or video recorders. Start from scratch and think aloud for students about one signal at a time. Explain very clearly what your inner voice is saying to you at various times. Tell them precisely where you zoned out and started thinking about what you were going to have for lunch. Then as you work with them in scaffolded silent reading groups, stop the reading every five minutes to talk about what their inner voices were saying when you called time. After spending a week or two with the inner-voice prompt, try the camera prompt. These will be new insights for your students and perhaps even for you as a reader.

Create Personalized Accountability

The recent trend toward computer-based motivational reading programs, such as *Accelerated Reader* (Advantage Learning Systems, 2001), has left the mistaken impression with some teachers that they no longer need to be concerned about either what or how well their students are reading because the computer will handle that. In reality, answering a few relatively easy factual questions about a book that may or may not be at an appropriate level of difficulty is not the kind of accountability that engaged reading demands. Meaningful accountability demands the flexing of cognitive muscles. Teachers must also be aware that students, eager to earn points and prizes, are often expending more energy beating the computer's scoring system than in reading books. There are dozens of ways to encourage students' creativity, personal response, and interpretation while still ensuring a more personalized and rigorous form of reading accountability. Figure 7.6 displays just a few of them.

Figure 7.6 Personalized Ways to Hold Students Accountable for Their Reading

Type	Description
Portfolios	A portfolio is "a collection of student work, connected to what has been read and studied, that reveals student progress. It might include items such as personal responses to reading assignments; self-assessments, teacher observations, attitude and interest surveys; writing samples (both complete and in progress); evidence that the student reads for enjoyment and information; and summaries" (Educational Research Service, 1998, p. 5). It might also include a list of books read by the student; a summary of several books read during the school year; a listing of books read categorized by genre to illustrate the breadth of reading during a school year; a description of a favorite book, a list of books read at home or a list read at school; a brief description of the five latest books read; or a list or descriptions of favorite authors. Portfolios can be adapted to any grade level from second grade through high school.
Reading journals	Reading journals contain daily written responses to what has been read during a silent reading period or for an assignment. There are many ways to approach journal writing in response to reading, depending on the grade level or the type of text (narrative or expository).
Reading logs	Learning logs serve as a running record of students' perceptions of how and what they are learning. The paper is divided into three columns: "What I Did," "How I Worked and Learned," and "What I Learned" (Alvermann & Phelps, 1998).
Every-pupil response activities	After reading a portion of text, either in class or for a homework assignment, every student completes a brief written response to the text. Students then participate in a discussion with a partner. The writing assignment might include a brief explanation of a specific situation, problem, or question as a way of assessing their understanding of the concepts about which they were reading. These self-assessments are collected sporadically and never graded. The goal is to reach consensus with their partners regarding the question that was posed, by supporting their responses with text evidence and good reasoning as well as by considering the evidence and rationale presented by their partners (Gaskins, Satlow, Hyson, Ostertag, & Six, 1994, pp. 559–560).

■ **SUMMARIZING CHAPTER 7**

Although reading a lot is almost the last of the instructional–curricular pieces of the reading puzzle we are putting in place, it could well have been the first one. From the first simple three-letter words that students independently read, motivating them to become voracious readers ought to be our goal. Unless students practice those simple beginning reading skills by devouring dozens of little books and easy readers, they are unlikely to develop the fluency they need to become skilled readers. Unless upper grade readers continue to build their word and world knowledge through reading a lot, they will encounter frustrating comprehension challenges in the upper grades. Reading a lot not only enhances students' academic options and career choices for the future, it also provides a lifetime supply of learning, escape, comfort, consolation, pleasure, and beauty.

8
Writing

Writing is the ability to communicate through various written formats, such as graphic organizers, short answers, essays or reports. Writing employs the skills of handwriting or keyboarding, spelling, and punctuation. It draws on the writer's knowledge of vocabulary, syntax, and textual conventions and requires an understanding of the audience and purpose for writing.

Writing, although undeniably a part of a comprehensive literacy curriculum, was not a piece of the reading puzzle in the first edition of *Teach Them ALL to Read*. When the National Reading Panel (NICHD) released its report in 2000, educators were still figuring out how to teach phonemic awareness and build fluency. Some mistakenly thought that writing instruction could wait until after students had mastered reading; others believed that if reading ability was sufficiently  developed, writing proficiency would follow. Still others did not see how writing instruction would fit into an already overloaded reading block. These views are not surprising since reading and writing have been considered and taught as separate subjects since colonial times (Nelson & Calfee, 1998).

Educators can no longer afford to exclude writing from the reading puzzle. One of the most pressing reasons for the inclusion of writing is that many high-stakes standards-based reading assessments include a constructed response section, thereby making students' reading proficiency scores somewhat dependent on their writing abilities (Jenkins, Johnson, & Hileman, 2004). However, there are additional reasons for paying more attention to writing:

- Of students in Grades 4–12, 70% rank as low-achieving writers on the most recent National Assessment of Educational Performance (Persky, Daane, & Jin, 2003).

- Referrals of students with written expression problems sharply increase around Grade 4 when the amount and complexity of written assignments typically increase (Levine, Oberklaid, & Meltzer, 1981).
- Although students at risk in high-poverty schools can achieve grade-level reading proficiencies with early reading interventions, their spelling and writing achievement generally falls behind (Moats, 2006).
- Serious deficits in the ability to use writing to make sense of reading have contributed to the achievement gap in schools (Collins, Lee, et al., 2008).

When I decided to make writing a part of the reading puzzle in this second edition, I originally called it *writing in response to reading,* or as Collins (1998) calls it, *writing about reading.* However, as I reflected on my own experiences as a writer, I realized that writing about reading was too limited in scope. For example, in preparation for this chapter, I began writing in advance of reading. I wrote to determine what I already knew from my personal experiences as an upper-grade teacher and principal, as well as a published author of both fiction and nonfiction.

The exercise of *writing before reading* focused my thinking, generated questions I needed to answer, and improved my comprehension when I eventually began to read the books and journals I had collected for my research. This is a technique I perfected in preparation for tests in high school, college, and graduate school. I would regularly generate a number of possible questions a teacher might ask; do my note taking, rereading, and studying to answer those questions; and then write essays in response, checking my notes and the textbook from time to time for details I had not yet stored in either my short- or long-term memories.

Levenger's Catalog for Readers sells this marvelous reading tool. You can see it on their Web site at www.levenger.com. Search for book weights or reading tools. I have several of them in various colors and weights.

When my background knowledge is insufficient, I read widely in a variety of disciplines to determine the latest research findings, sometimes taking notes and jotting down key words or questions as I go. Sometimes I read from cover to cover to get the big picture. However, when I wrestle with a subject in earnest, I do what Collins, Lee, and colleagues (2008) call "two-handed reading:" *reading and writing at the same time.* I write with one hand on a book (or article) and the other on my pen or computer keyboard. Sometimes, if the book weighs too much or I'm reading from a number of books simultaneously, I use my leather book weights to hold them open, thereby giving myself extra hands.

In this stage I am doing what Scardamalia (1981) calls "knowledge telling," using writing in a straightforward manner to report and summarize what I have read. Later, I will transition to "knowledge transforming," writing to analyze, synthesize, and evaluate what I have read for the practitioners who will read my books. Frequently my reading and writing includes practices like marking up the text, putting sticky notes or flags on big ideas, or making notes in PDF files using my Adobe Acrobat software. I am incessantly reading and writing simultaneously. Often, when my husband Ray and I run errands together, he drives while I read and write; then I take time out from my work to run into the cleaners or the grocery store while Ray takes a crossword puzzle break in the car.

Unlike university academics, I do not have colleagues in nearby offices with whom to talk about my writing. Instead, I use my telephone and e-mail to *talk and write about my reading and writing during the process of writing.* Writing can be a social, interactive, and collaborative process. I ask teachers and administrators to read what I have written. They pose questions and make comments that drive me back to my keyboard to rewrite or back to my materials to read. I question experts in various disciplines and talk with them about their work and how it might inform mine. I interview teachers and principals about what they are doing and why. And I write during these conversations. When Ray and I take our daily walk in the Santa Catalina foothills, I talk about my writing as well. He gives me the best kind of advice: wordless.

Before I begin the formal writing of a book, I have already engaged in multiple kinds of writing: (1) writing before reading; (2) reading and writing at the same time; (3) talking about reading and writing; and (4) writing in response to reading. Writing includes all of the combinations of writing *and* reading that take place in classrooms. I do not believe it is possible to write (even fiction) without also reading. Even if writers are not reading what others have written during the writing process, they are surely reading their own writing during the revision process, one of the most important kinds of reading when writing for publication.

WHAT IS WRITING AND HOW DO STUDENTS LEARN TO WRITE? ■

To pay conscious attention to handwriting, spelling, punctuation, word choice, syntax, textual conventions, purpose, organization, clarity, rhythm, euphony, and reader characteristics would seemingly overload the information processing capacity of the best intellects.

—Scardamalia (1981, p. 81)

Writing is a tool kit that serves two purposes for students: (1) It enables them to eventually accomplish a variety of academic goals, such as writing reports, essays, short stories, opinion pieces, or short answers on tests; and (2) it enables them to more readily and fully process, understand, and retain subject matter, whether literature, science, history, or mathematics (Collins, Lee et al., 2008; Graham & Perin, 2007). Writing is a complex skill involving multiple tasks as noted in the epigraph. It is also a recursive process, one in which all writers, not just struggling ones, cycle back and forth between knowledge telling and knowledge transforming as they deal with the challenges inherent in reading difficult text and completing specific assignments.

Some students become proficient writers rather effortlessly, while others need intense instruction. But all students benefit from direct, systematic, and scaffolded instruction coupled with assignments that are challenging enough to create some frustration but manageable enough that they can prevail and complete the task (Collins, 1998, p. 136).

In spite of the complexity of the writing process, some theorize that writing is simple. Berninger and her colleagues (2002) hypothesize a model represented by a triangle in which the area represents working memory, similar to the way a computer desktop functions, holding all of the bits and pieces one needs ready access to while writing. The working memory activates long-term memory during composing and short-term memory during reviewing, rewriting, and editing. The vertex of the triangle is labeled *text generation* (the words and sentences the writer uses to communicate), the triangle's left angle is labeled *transcription* (handwriting or keyboarding and spelling), and the right angle represents *the executive functions* that take place in the short-term, working, and long-term memories (conscious attention, planning, reviewing, revising, and strategies for self-regulation). I have adapted their simple model to a graphic organizer shown in Figure 8.1. It illustrates the various areas of the brain needed to plan and execute the composition of a paragraph, either in response to a prompt from the teacher in advance of reading or in response to reading a piece of text.

■ WHEN SHOULD WRITING BE TAUGHT?

Reading comprehension and writing are two symbolically mediated and complementary aspects of language use. Language structure is processed to gain (comprehend) or convey (write) intended meanings. Reading comprehension entails input processing (decoding) while writing entails output processing (encoding).

—Moats and Sedita (2006, p. 23)

Students' writing fluency depends to a great extent on their mastery of graphomotor skills, letter formation, alphabet production, word knowledge, grammar, and spelling. Many students are poor writers because of their early difficulties with handwriting and spelling, most probably because of their lack of early instruction. Poor handwriting and spelling interfere with writing fluency and hence writing quality (Berninger et al., 1997), and based on more than a decade of research on the prevention of writing problems, Berninger and Amtman (2003) recommend the direct and explicit teaching of handwriting and spelling early to students at risk, which may well eliminate the large numbers of students who experience writing difficulties in upper grades.

■ THE RELATIONSHIP BETWEEN READING AND WRITING

Moving from reading to writing or from writing to reading is not like reversing directions on the same road. The difference in functional starting points can be enough to require different roads altogether. Consequently, reading is a somewhat easier task than writing, and reliance on identical memories would be insufficient to make reading and writing identical processes.

—Fitzgerald and Shanahan (2000, p. 43)

To this point in putting together the reading puzzle, each of the pieces has been shown to play a key role in students becoming proficient readers. However, reading isn't dependent on knowing how to write in the same way that it is dependent on phonemic decoding and fluency. Unless your state assessment requires students to write in response to reading, you may have decided to focus on reading and hope for the best. In support of this decision, one can point to the many individuals who speak foreign languages but are not able to write them well or at all or to the many skilled readers who cannot write at all and others whose writing is substandard (Stotsky, 2001). On the flip side of the writing–reading connection, there are some excellent writers with less than stellar reading comprehension. Recall my granddaughter,

Figure 8.1 The Writing Process

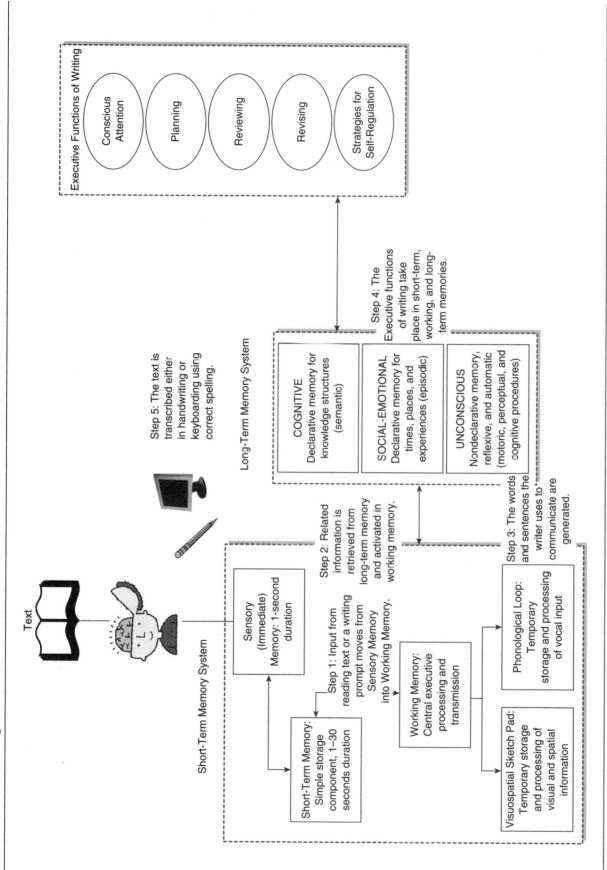

Source: This figure was developed using Inspiration® Software and is based on the author's interpretation of the discussions, theories, and research found in Baddeley (1997), Baddeley and Logie (1999), Beatty (2001), Berninger et al. (2002), Engle, Cantor, and Carullo (1992), Engle, Kane, and Tuholski (1999), Engle, Tuholski, Laughlin, and Conway (1999), Miyake and Shah (1999), Novak (1998), Pressley and Afflerbach (1995), Squire and Kandel (1999), van den Broek, Young, Tzeng, and Houston–Price (1999), van Someren, Barnard, and Sandberg (1994), and Weinstein and Hume (1998).

Abigail, in Chapter 2. Her writing skills were sufficiently skilled to offset her reading comprehension difficulties.

To be fully literate in a language, however, requires the abilities to speak, read, and write it proficiently. We know, however, that second language learners in any language seldom attain the reading and writing proficiencies in their second language as they have in the first *unless* they have received excellent instruction in both languages.

Moats and Sedita (2006) call writing "the road to reading comprehension," while Stotsky (2001) refers to writing as "the royal road to reading comprehension" (p. 276). Although I agree that writing is a powerful way to deepen comprehension and aid in the retention of important content, I do not completely agree with the road metaphor. These authors make writing sound like a stroll down memory lane or a relaxed drive up a winding road to a four-bedroom Tudor with six baths. In order for the writing road to lead to reading comprehension, it must be paved with explicit, systematic, strategic, and scaffolded instruction, especially for those students who struggle with both reading and writing. I prefer Collins's (1998) description of the relationship: Writing about what they have read helps students move from knowledge telling to knowledge transforming (p. 109), a process that writers must master anew each time they tackle a new topic in their writing (Bereiter & Scardamalia, 1987).

Writing and reading, while certainly not flip sides of a coin, *are* closely related: (1) They are both acts of communication through which students gain knowledge about how communication works by acting as both sender (writer) and receiver (reader); (2) they can be used in tandem to accomplish specific academic goals, such as taking notes while reading, summarizing a text that has been read, or answering questions from the text; (3) they employ many of the same cognitive processes and access similar knowledge sources (Fitzgerald & Shanahan, 2000); and (4) they are both essential for success in mastering content subjects.

The reading–writing connection has critical implications for instruction. Reading and writing must be taught in concert with one another—not necessarily simultaneously or even at the same level of difficulty, but instruction in writing must be ongoing at the same time that reading is being taught because eventually all students must learn how to write before, during, and after their reading. Unless reading and writing are connected on a daily basis, students will be less mindful about what they read, and teachers will miss golden opportunities to teach content as well as thinking and problem-solving skills.

Having made the decision to teach writing, educators must determine the instructional approach that best serves all students, but especially those at risk and gifted. As in the field of reading instruction, there exists a tension between the group of educators who view writing as a set of skills to be learned and those who view writing as a process to be acquired (Collins, 1998, p. 13). This unfortunate dichotomy does little to help students at risk who require direct and systematic writing instruction and flourish in settings where teachers both directly teach *and* facilitate the acquisition of both reading and writing abilities (Delpit, 1995; Dunn, 1995).

Don't make the mistake of delegating thinking and solving problems to your Accelerated Reader program. Reread the section on page 151 about ways to hold students personally responsible for their thinking and pay special attention to the example from the Gering School District on pages 167–168. Students in their advanced language arts program are held accountable for writing essay responses to sample test questions.

SCIENTIFIC EVIDENCE FOR ◼
THE WRITING–READING CONNECTION

Although reading and writing are complementary skills whose development runs a roughly parallel course, they do not necessarily go hand in hand.

—Graham and Perin (2007, p. 7)

Scientific research about how best to teach writing is difficult to find, whether the writing is in response to reading, in advance of reading, or just plain writing. And once found, it is even more difficult to interpret. Some studies measure the effectiveness of a given treatment by looking at the quality of students' writing output, others by measuring the amount of content learning, and still others on the basis of students' reading comprehension.

Hefflin and Hartman (2002) reviewed a substantial number of studies related to the reading–writing connection and lamented that most of the research as well as instructional practice focused solely on the effect of *writing in response to reading* (Durkin, 1978–1979; Farr, 1993; Goodlad, 1984; Olson, 1996). Hefflin and Hartman (2002), however, wanted to know if writing could be used in the service of reading comprehension as asserted by Stotsky (2001) and Moats and Sedita (2006) and subsequently undertook a second review of the literature to determine if there was any evidence in that regard.

Hefflin and Hartman (2002) assembled a comprehensive collection of writing-to-reading practices that included well-known instructional activities, like Story Impressions (McGinley & Denner, 1987), K-W-L (Ogle, 1986a, 1986b), and Probable Passages (Wood, 1984), as well as many other lesser-known approaches for facilitating reading comprehension with writing in advance of reading. They eventually concluded that although the aforementioned practices and the many others they described were widely used, there was no experimental research showing whether writing-to-reading practices improved either students' writing *or* reading skills.

In 2004, Bangert-Drowns, Hurley, and Wilkinson conducted a meta-analysis of school-based writing-to-learn interventions on academic achievement and concluded that the research was ambiguous. They found only two factors worked in favor of increased achievement: the use of metacognitive prompts (teaching students a set of prompts to use before and during writing) and increased treatment length. Two factors worked against increased achievement: implementation in Grades 6–8 and longer writing assignments.

In 2007, the Carnegie Foundation commissioned a report titled *Writing Next: Effective Strategies to Improve Writing of Adolescents in Middle and High School* (Graham & Perin, 2007). Although the review focused on middle and high school writing, the grade span included in the analysis was 4–12, making the findings pertinent to upper-grade teachers (e.g., Grades 4–6). On the basis of effect size, 11 elements of effective instruction were identified: writing strategies, summarization, collaborative writing, specific product goals, word processing, sentence combining, prewriting, inquiry activities, process writing approach, study of models, and writing for content learning. They further concluded that no single approach to writing instruction meets the needs of all students and cautioned educators that these elements do not constitute a curriculum.

NOTCHING UP READING AND WRITING INSTRUCTION

Two instructional approaches that connect reading and writing have produced results with students at risk, albeit in different ways: (1) Writing Intensive Reading Comprehension (WIRC), a recently developed intervention for upper-grade students at risk; and (2) *Reasoning and Writing* (RW), a comprehensive K–12 Direct Instruction curriculum for students at any level with decades of research and development behind it (Engelmann, 1993).

Although WIRC and RW differ in the ways they approach the reading–writing connection, they have the following characteristics in common:

- The materials and methods of both programs have been field tested and refined with students.
- Both have experimental research showing their effectiveness.
- Both require extensive teacher training, supervision, and monitoring to ensure fidelity of implementation.

WIRC and RW are quite different in their theoretical foundations as well as their research depth:

- Teacher talk and teaching moves during WIRC are open-ended and situational, with teachers making decisions on the spot about how to respond to students, while RW is scripted, providing consistency of wording within and across grade levels and lessons.
- WIRC is relatively new, with only a three-year implementation track record (Collins, Lee, Fox, & Madigan, 2008; Collins, Madigan, & Lee, 2008), while RW and other Direct Instruction curricula have multiple large-scale studies and meta-analyses to support their effectiveness (Adams & Engelmann, 1996; Swanson, Hoskyn, & Lee, 1999).
- WIRC is based on constructivist theory and research, while RW is based on behaviorist theory and research.

Writing Intensive Reading Comprehension: A Classroom Intervention

The WIRC study was funded by the Institute of Education Sciences, U.S. Department of Education, and conducted in the fourth and fifth grades of the lowest-performing urban elementary schools in Buffalo, New York (Collins, Lee, et al., 2008; Collins, Madigan, et al., 2008). The study tested the hypothesis that scaffolded writing during reading improves reading comprehension. Its methodology combined randomized experiments to determine the effectiveness of the approach in improving reading comprehension on a high-stakes test combined with qualitative case studies and observations to determine precisely how and why the approach worked or in some cases didn't.

WIRC integrates reading and writing instruction through the use of cognitive scaffolding tools called *thinksheets.* Although thinksheets have been used in prior studies (Englert, 1995; Raphael, Kirschner, & Englert, 1986, 1988) to assist struggling writers, in the WIRC method, the thinksheets guide students through the cognitive steps to comprehension via their writing. The researchers define a thinksheet as a "customized guide to writing about a literary selection," and they define an interactive thinksheet as "one writers use discursively with teachers and with other students" (Collins, Lee, et al., 2008, p. 8). The researchers concluded from their study that

- Students using thinksheets to write about their reading improved more than students receiving traditional instruction.
- Fourth-grade students in the experimental group showed statistically significant gains on multiple-choice items [on the New York English–Language Arts Test] but not on constructed response items. Once researchers controlled for teacher fidelity of implementation, fourth-grade experimental students showed greater gains than students in control groups for both multiple-choice and constructed-response items.
- Fifth-grade students in the experimental group outperformed students in control groups on both multiple-choice and constructed-response items even before controlling for teacher fidelity of implementation; gains became larger once controls for teacher fidelity were calculated.
- Students using thinksheets in the experimental condition for two years, that is, in both fourth and fifth grades, outperformed all other groups (Collins, Madigan, et al., 2008, pp. 3–4).

The scaffolded thinksheets at first glance look like reading workbook pages that once accompanied all basal readers—questions about a story with blanks for students to fill in the answers. However, the researchers were very specific in their training and observation of teachers during the preliminary design and extensive piloting of the thinksheets: "We did not want teachers to hand thinksheets to students and then walk away. From the beginning of our work, we envisioned teachers using thinksheets interactively and discursively with students in focused reading-writing workshops where discussions and individual conferences and teacher modeling guide the use of thinksheets for students, including students who struggle with literacy" (Collins, Madigan, et al., 2008, p. 11).

The difficulty that the researchers encountered in training teachers to use their carefully constructed thinksheets illuminates the difficulty of training teachers to use any kind of prompts or templates during reading and writing instruction. In order for teachers to think aloud, ask probing questions, and motivate students to assume some responsibility for thinking, they must be willing to release responsibility for the final product into the hands of students whose writing is still immature. The process involves short periods of cooperative or individual work, followed by mini-lessons or explanations from the teacher. The pace of instruction is left to the teacher's discretion.

The WIRC research team designed their thinksheets to accompany the fourth- and fifth-grade selections in the Harcourt *Trophies* Series (Beck, Farr, & Strickland, 2003). They usually chose a question from the teacher's manual as the big question for a thinksheet. The thinksheets scaffolded the reading and writing processes by providing students with certain passages reproduced on the sheets or by giving page numbers to help students locate answers. Prior to producing the final written product, students were either given a specific graphic organizer or provided with a choice of organizers to help them visualize their writing project. The thinksheets were typically five to seven pages in length but sometimes were as long as 12 pages.

The thinksheet is not magical. In fact, as one member of the teacher observation team discovered, it was possible for teachers, despite their training, to miss the whole point (Phelps, 2007). Phelps had identified one teacher in particular, Mrs. Carpenter, as her favorite, believing that she was implementing the thinksheet intervention with extraordinary fidelity. She wrote this statement about Mrs. C. in a paper highlighting outstanding teachers: "It was truly remarkable to observe the progress of Mrs. Carpenter's students over the year as their knowledge transformational thinksheet experience took them from struggling emergent writers to confident authors eager to share their writing with anyone remotely interested" (Phelps, 2007, p. 3).

When the posttest results arrived, Phelps was astonished to discover that with the exception of two students, Mrs. Carpenter's class had failed to show improvement. She immediately concluded that there was something wrong with the test. However, when she objectively examined the data by conducting a case study to investigate the teacher's practices more thoroughly, such was not the case.

She chose two students, one from Mrs. Carpenter's unsuccessful class and a second student from the more successful classroom of another teacher, Mrs. Lesswing. Both subjects were African American boys in the lowest scoring group of their grade level: the *intensive group*. Both had attention difficulties and scored at Level 1 on the pretest. On the posttest reading comprehension test, Bobby (from Mrs. Lesswing's class) improved to a Level 2, while Devan (from Mrs. Carpenter's class) dropped from Level 1 to a 0.

After reviewing audio tapes, video tapes, observation notes, and all of the thinksheets completed by both students during the entire year of the study, Phelps found the root cause of the achievement problem in Mrs. Carpenter's classroom: Mrs. Carpenter was doing all of the work. The teacher had faithfully written out the correct answers on the board, and her students copied her answers on to their thinksheets word for word. When Phelps compared Bobby's thinksheets (Mrs. Lesswing's student) with Devan's (Mrs. Carpenter's student), she found that Bobby's work revealed the kind of work one would expect from an intensive student—simple vocabulary, many partial sentences, and many incomplete thinksheets. In comparison, Devan's thinksheets contained complete sentences with sophisticated vocabulary.

Phelps (2007) examined the thinksheets from all of Mrs. Carpenter's students, and they revealed a pattern of uniform copying. Phelps concluded that "the teacher bypassed the positive effect of the intervention because the teacher did all of the work" (p. 12). In order for thinksheets to be effective, teachers had to think aloud, coach, encourage, and affirm students, but then ultimately release responsibility for the work to students, even if the work products did not yet meet the teacher's standards. In the case of integrated reading and writing instruction using thinksheets, the process is far more important than the product.

Reasoning and Writing: A Direct Instruction Core Program for Writing

Intervention programs that seek to teach students how to read and write after they have fallen through the cracks have limitations. The most effective way to build strong writers and readers is to teach all of the skills and knowledge needed for proficient writing simultaneously with reading instruction, beginning in preschool with language development and adding other components in kindergarten and first grade as appropriate: handwriting, spelling, language usage, grammar, syntax, and vocabulary. The ideal way to teach them all to read and write is to catch them before they experience failure.

Direct Instruction (DI) provides a comprehensive and field-tested Grades K–12 writing curriculum—*Reasoning and Writing: Levels A-F* (Engelmann, various)—along with reading, language, and spelling programs. The scientific evidence for the effectiveness of DI programs for all types of students is extensive and impressive (Adams & Engelmann, 1996); however, there has long been confusion about the difference between direct instruction and Direct Instruction. When the term *direct instruction* (lower case) is used, it refers to the use of certain generic principles or approaches, such as pacing or choral responses in teaching.

Direct Instruction (upper case) is a series of published curricula written by Engelmann and various associates. The unique aspect of these curricula is the extensive field testing with students that DI programs have undergone before publication and during subsequent revisions. Literacy curricula from major publishers are never field tested to determine if the programs get results with students. The program components (too many and varied to test in any one experiment) are generally dictated by the mandates of large states, such as Florida, California, and Texas. They are written by a team of academics and curriculum developers and then heavily marketed directly to teachers. DI curricula are written and revised with a view to their effectiveness in bringing students to mastery in specific curricular areas: reading, writing, and spelling, to name a few.

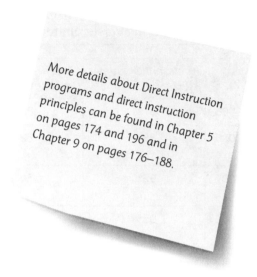

More details about Direct Instruction programs and direct instruction principles can be found in Chapter 5 on pages 174 and 196 and in Chapter 9 on pages 176–188.

While DI undeniably gets results, teachers who have enjoyed complete autonomy in their choice of programs and instructional methodologies for years often have a difficult time adjusting to the scripted lessons and the pace of instruction. Adams and Carnine (2003) describe the nature of this controversy:

> On a purely scientific basis, it would be expected that Direct Instruction programs would be highly accepted based on probable achievement scores. Instead they are highly scorned. A major reason is one of the main features of Direct Instruction programs—the use of scripts. It is apparent that many teachers have never been told the rationale behind the use of scripts (e.g., consistency of wording within and across lessons). Other teachers believe that following a script makes them less of a teacher because it is not their wording; it is the program's. (p. 412)

However, in communities and schools where large numbers of students at risk as well as average students are failing to thrive academically, DI provides the curricula and instructional support that students and teachers need. In the Gering Public Schools (NE) where 43% of the students receive free and reduced-fee lunch and the number of Hispanic students has nearly doubled since 1993 to 26%, the challenges of teaching them all to read *and* write might seem insurmountable. But the staff at Gering's four elementary schools are using research-based curricula (DI programs) and implementing those curricula with fidelity.

Reasoning and Writing (RW; Engelmann, various) is one component of Gering's reading–language arts program. The complete range of DI programs and an account of their implementation are found in Chapter 9. Implementing these programs with fidelity, educators have closed the achievement gap between Hispanic and white students and reduced their special education population to 5% below the state average. Gering educators and parents have watched their fourth-grade writing scores on the Nebraska State Writing Test soar from nearly last place in 2004 among the 25 largest school districts in Nebraska to third place on the list in 2008, beating out more affluent and suburban districts in eastern Nebraska with far smaller percentages of low-income students. Figure 8.2 displays the progress of writing achievement in Gering.

Figure 8.2 Nebraska Fourth-Grade Writing Assessment: Percentage of Proficient Students at Gering Versus State of Nebraska

Year	Proficient Students at Gering	Proficient Students in Nebraska	Explanatory Notes
2005	57%	83%	Before DI implementation; 100% students tested
2006	85%	82%	Tested students had received two years of *Reasoning and Writing;* 99% of students tested
2007	92%	86%	Tested students had received three years of *Reasoning and Writing;* 99% of students tested
2008	95%	91%	Tested students had received years of *Reasoning and Writing;* 99% of students tested

Source: Boden (2008).

Reading coach Bev Hague admits, "This has not been an easy road, but most things of value are not easily attained. The more struggles we encounter, the more determined we are to keep doing what is best for students. We have chosen good programs, there's no doubt about that. But no matter how good a program may be, if it is not presented with a high degree of proficiency and with high expectations for teachers, students, and administration, it will not be effective. Our effective implementation is one of the variables that has had the greatest impact on Gering's success."

Teaching them all to read and write starts with language development in Gering's preschool classes, open to eligible students in the district. Preschoolers begin with the preschool *Language for Learning* (Engelmann & Osborn, 1999a) program. Spelling and handwriting are taught beginning in kindergarten. Figures 8.3 and 8.4 show the handwriting and coloring rubrics students use to evaluate their handwriting and coloring performance with the help of a paraprofessional during independent work time. Kindergarten students are given the language and reading placement tests during the first week of school and are then placed in *Language for Learning* and *Reading Mastery* (Engelmann, various).

The following features are built into the DI programs making them highly effective for preK through first-grade students and especially helpful for English language learners, students at risk of reading disabilities, and students with certain speech difficulties.

- A wide range of language concepts and skills are taught.
- Lessons exercises are sequentially organized.
- Students are tested so they are placed precisely at the right level for learning.
- There are opportunities for both group and individual work.
- Students are consistently checked for mastery in daily lessons and also tested for mastery every 10 lessons.

Figure 8.3 Handwriting Rubric

1	2	3	4
• Poor letter formation, size, and alignment • Letters not on baseline	• Fair letter formation • Some letters marked over • Many floaters and sinkers • Letters too close together	• Good letter formation • Most letters on the baseline • Most letters evenly and correctly spaced	• Excellent letter formation • Letters evenly and correctly spaced • All letters on baseline • Consistent slant • Work is self-checked

Source: Used with permission of Beverly Hague.

Reproduction of material from this book is authorized only for the local school site or nonprofit organization that has purchased *Teach Them ALL to Read: Catching Kids Before They Fall Through the Cracks, Second Edition,* by Elaine K. McEwan. Thousand Oaks, CA: Corwin, www.corwinpress.com.

Figure 8.4 Coloring Rubric

1	2	3	4
• Scribbles • Colors outside the lines • Uses one or two colors • Messy paper • Doesn't finish • Wastes paper	• Starts to understand purpose for coloring • Sometimes stays inside lines • Odd choice of color • White lines showing through coloring • Starting to shade	• Knows purpose • Stays in lines • Uses different colors • No white lines • Colors in same direction • Uses time well	• Expands on purpose • Adds detail • Good use of paper • Different from others • Better, creative, uses brain • Self-checks

Source: Used with permission of Beverly Hague.

Reproduction of material from this book is authorized only for the local school site or nonprofit organization that has purchased *Teach Them ALL to Read: Catching Kids Before They Fall Through the Cracks, Second Edition,* by Elaine K. McEwan. Thousand Oaks, CA: Corwin, www.corwinpress.com.

- While new concepts and skills are regularly integrated into daily lessons, there is review of previously taught concepts and skills in every lesson.
- Repetition is an important part of the organization of material.
- Students are introduced to and regularly practice problem solving.
- Teachers are given clear directions for presenting the program.

Reasoning and Writing is unique for the following reasons:

- Built-in distributive practice allows students to focus on several topics for smaller increments of time as opposed to focusing on a single subject for a long period of time.
- Continuous repetition of skills is built into the program so that students learn and apply skills for 20 to 30 lessons, rather than the 5 or 6 lessons found in most programs.
- Skills and concepts are learned and developed in small increments.
- Students have a clear understanding of what is expected for mastery through continuous presentation and practice of skills.
- The focus of the program is writing, but it also teaches the skills that promote writing mastery by giving students ample time to practice them.
- Skills are introduced in small increments, and eventually these skills are used in more complex writing.
- Teachers focus on both excellence in writing skills and writing fluency.

Students must be able to copy 45 words in three minutes before they can move into *Reasoning and Writing* C, which is where more complex writing projects are assigned. The C Level is considered on grade level for second and third graders. Bev Hague is understandably proud of the quality of writing students are producing: "I think if people could see how these kids are writing, they would be dumbstruck. With this program, we don't just teach the top third of our students anymore. Our Hispanic students are writing as well or better than their more advantaged classmates."

As in other DI programs, the pace of instruction during *Reasoning and Writing* (RW) is fast. There is no time for students to gaze out the window or fiddle with pencils. During the typical one-hour RW lesson in Grades 4–6, there are four to five different mini-lessons. Students write daily, and the reasoning aspect of the RW curriculum gives students a cognitive workout. Principals, teachers, and coaches all note how DI programs have virtually eliminated discipline problems. The secret: students are engaged and experiencing high levels of success during every minute of allocated instructional time.

Parents in Nebraska can choose a school in any district if they provide their own transportation. Sixth-grade teacher Becky Michael and her husband, a physician at the regional hospital, live in a nearby town with its own school district but have optioned their two daughters into the Gering system, thrilled with the content and skills they are acquiring on a daily basis. Becky says, "I've done a lot of research about what students need to do well on the ACT and the SAT; vocabulary and writing proficiency are vital." Becky teaches a group of sixth graders that in any other district would undoubtedly be in a remedial program. In Gering, they are working on or very close to grade level.

Becky says, "My students have learned how to take notes, categorize them into broad, widely applicable topics and are able to write 12 sentences on a topic in 10 minutes. The teaching scripts are wonderful because they allow me to be more focused on my students' needs and the degree to which each one is mastering the various strategies and skills. I don't have to worry about what I say because I know the scripts have been tested on students just like mine. I'm convinced most adults couldn't produce the kind of writing that my students are."

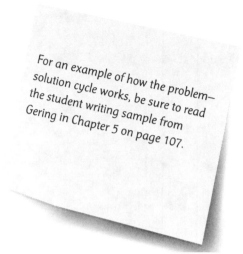

For an example of how the problem–solution cycle works, be sure to read the student writing sample from Gering in Chapter 5 on page 107.

Students learn more than just writing, as the program's name implies. Becky explains, "One of the skills that *Reasoning and Writing* teaches is how to critically read and then critique what others have written. For example, the students will be presented with a group of advertisements, and their challenge is to find the inaccuracies or false statements in the ads. My students have developed a set of higher-order thinking skills that will serve them for the rest of their lives."

In schools where teachers have a heterogeneous group of students for reading and writing, gifted students can become bored and disengaged. In Gering, gifted students are motivated and moved forward in accordance with their achievement. For example, Becky's fifth-grade daughter travels to a sixth-grade classroom for reading and writing where the students have been accelerated above the sixth-grade level. They are reading and writing more like middle and high school students than the usual gifted upper-grade students.

Luanne Cawiezell teaches the group above sixth grade level at Northfield. She explains,

When I started teaching *Reasoning and Writing* three years ago, the expectations and assignments seemed much too difficult for sixth graders. Now that my incoming sixth graders have been in *Reading Mastery* and *Reasoning and Writing* for three years and I've had the benefit of teaching it for three years, I can see how they are able to use their reading, reasoning, and writing skills to process a difficult text like our U.S. History program. They are drawing conclusions, making deductions, and finding problems with arguments. With these skills, they make great debaters. They love to make statements and then back them up with evidence from the text. The thinking skills my students have developed keep me on my toes.

While they are reading our U.S. History text, students are systematically taught to take notes on 4 x 6 cards. Later, they have to write answers to questions about the text, using only the notes they have taken. At the beginning of the year, I model for them how to prepare a note card. At first, we do our note cards together as a class. Now, we have transitioned to the independent phase of writing note cards. In preparation for unit tests, they prepare note cards to help them write their answers to the test questions or present the answers orally, as we frequently do.

Figure 8.5 is an example of note cards prepared by fifth-grade student, Julia Ybarra, a member of the Advanced Language Arts group in Farrell Becking's class at Lincoln School. Figure 8.6 shows the answers Julia wrote using her note cards to help her remember key ideas and concepts.

In addition to well-designed programs using scripted lessons, there are two additional reasons that students excel in RW: (1) they are grouped according to their skills, with more advanced students working above or well above grade level and

Figure 8.5 Note Cards Prepared by Student While Reading History Text

Arctic

Cold—harsh—almost no growing season

Tundra—flat treeless plain

Inuit

Fishing and hunting

Animal furs

Ice and snow igloos

Tent whale bones as poles and animal skins

Seal oil to keep warm

Appalachian Mountains

Temperate

Hilly

Mohawk

Equally fishing, hunting, farming, and gathering

Deerskin

Trees

Great Plains

Temperate

Plains

Pawnee

Bison

Bison hides

Sod houses

Bison's bladder (water)

Northwest Coast

Rainy mild (not too cold,
not too hot)

Shoreline Pacific Ocean

Chinook

Salmon—ritual—coming
back—religious

Cedar bark

Trees

Mountains 200 miles east

Rivers

Breechcloth, deerskin shirt

Whales

Inner bark—clothing

Boat—60–70 feet

Buildings—wood

Southwest

Dry

Desert

Hopi

Farming

Cotton

Rock for pueblos

Canyons

Plateaus

Irrigation

Source: Farrell Becking, Sixth-Grade Teacher, Lincoln Elementary School, Gering Public Schools (NE). Reprinted by permission of Frank Ybarra and Julia Ybarra.

Reproduction of material from this book is authorized only for the local school site or nonprofit organization that has purchased *Teach Them ALL to Read: Catching Kids Before They Fall Through the Cracks, Second Edition*, by Elaine K. McEwan. Thousand Oaks, CA: Corwin. www.corwinpress.com.

Figure 8.6 Short-Answer Responses Using Notes Taken During Reading Text

---

Student

Fifth-grader Julia Ybarra has attended Lincoln Elementary School in Gering, Nebraska, since kindergarten. She has been in DI programs since second grade. Julia entered the Advanced Language Arts Block in fifth grade. The following writing sample was from 2007 at the beginning of fifth grade. Julia is a conscientious student and very competitive athletically, with wrestling being her favorite sport. She is not easily intimidated and loves a challenge. She is currently in sixth grade.

Textbook

Understanding U.S. History: Through 1914 (Carnine et al., 1996) is used as one part of the Reading Curriculum for Grades 4-5-6 Advanced Students when they have completed *Reading Mastery VI.*

Currently, fourth graders participate with fifth and sixth graders in the Advanced Language Arts Block. In the future, advanced students will be paced and enriched at grade level so that students will participate in the advanced block for only two years. Students engage in reading and writing simultaneously as they take notes or prepare one of several graphic organizers suggested to help students organize their thoughts. After taking notes, they write in response to their reading by summarizing, analyzing, and synthesizing what they have read to answer various questions. In addition to U.S. history through 1914, the program teaches a variety of higher-order thinking and problem-solving skills that are subsequently applied through written response to the historical content as well as to modern problems.

Assignment

Students were asked to write short-answer essays to answer core test questions from Chapter 2 of *Understanding U.S. History.* The questions are shown before each of Julia's written responses.

Peer Editing Process

When students complete their essay answers for a test, the work is to be their best work. Essay test questions are first written in draft form. Then, students work with a peer editor and complete their final study copy. When students complete their test essays, the response has been through several final drafts.

Question 31. How did the environment of the Arctic influence the culture of the Native American tribes who lived there? Describe the climate and geography of the Arctic; then describe how one tribe of Native Americans in that region met their three basic needs. Begin with a general statement.

The environment in which a Native American tribe lived influenced their culture. The climate of the Arctic was cold and harsh and had a very short growing season. The geography was tundra, a flat treeless plain with thin soil. One of the Native American tribes that lived there was the Inuit. The Inuit met their need for food by fishing and hunting, which made them excellent fishers and hunters. They met their need for clothing by wearing animal furs that were turned inside out so the fur was on the inside. The Inuit met their need for shelter by making igloo houses made of snow and ice in the winter and by making tents out of whale bones and animal skins in the summer.

Question 32. How did the environment of the Northwest Coast influence the culture of the Native American tribe who lived there? Describe the climate and geography of the Northwest Coast; then describe how one tribe of Native Americans in that region met their basic needs. Begin with a general statement.

The environment in which a Native American tribe lived influenced their culture. The climate of the Northwest coast was rainy and mild. Mild means not too hot and not too cold. The geography was a shoreline that led to the Pacific Ocean. One of the Native American tribes that lived in the Northwest Coast was the Chinook. The Chinook met their need for food by fishing salmon, picking berries and sometimes by hunting game. They met their need for clothing by wearing the inner bark of cedar trees to keep them cool. The Chinook met their need for shelter by cutting down trees and making houses out of the logs.

(Continued)

Figure 8.6 (Continued)

Question 33. How did the environment of the Southwest influence the culture of the Native American tribes who lived there? Describe the climate and geography of the Southwest; then describe how one tribe of Native Americans in that region met their three basic needs. Begin with a general statement.

The environment in which a Native American tribe lived influenced their culture. The climate of the Southwest was very dry and desert-like. The geography was mostly desert. One of the Native American tribes that lived in the Southwest was the Hopi. The Hopi met their need for food by farming corn, squash, and beans. There was very little water so they had to build irrigation ditches. The irrigation ditches would bring water from rivers to the crops. They met their need for clothing by making clothes out of cotton. They met their need for shelter by making pueblos (houses that were connected) out of rock. There were very few natural resources in the Southwest, but the Hopi used what they could.

Question 34. How did the environment of the Great Plains influence the culture of the Native American tribes who lived there? Describe the climate and geography of the Great Plains; then describe how one tribe of Native Americans in that region met their three basic needs. Begin with a general statement.

The environment in which a Native American tribe lived influenced their culture. The climate of the Great Plains was temperate, cold in the winter and hot in the summer. The geography was plains. One of the Native American tribes that lived in the Great Plains was the Pawnee. The Pawnee met their need for food by hunting game. They met their need for clothing by wearing animal furs and skins. The Pawnee met their need for shelter by making tepees (tents) and sod houses (sod is grass with deep roots).

Question 35. How did the environment of the Appalachian Mountains influence the culture of the Native American tribes who lived there? Describe the climate and geography of the Appalachian Mountains, then describe how one tribe met their three basic needs. Begin with a general statement.

The environment in which a Native American tribe lived influenced their culture. The climate of the Northern Appalachian Mountains was temperate, hot in the summer and cold in the winter. The geography was mountains. One of the Native American tribes that lived in the Northern Appalachian Mountains was the Mohawk. The Mohawk met their need for food by fishing, hunting, and farming. They met their need for clothing by wearing deerskin clothes that were sometimes decorated with porcupine quills. They met their need for shelter by making longhouses out of logs. The longhouses would usually be about 100 feet long.

Question 40. Explain what the connection is between how Native Americans lived and their environment.

Native Americans accommodated with the environment. In the Southwest, the Hopi tribe didn't have enough water to farm crops, so they built irrigation ditches so the water from streams and rivers would come to the crops. In the Arctic, the Inuit burned seal oil to keep warm. In the Northwest Coast, the Chinook wore the inner bark of cedar trees to stay cool. In the Great Plains, the Pawnee built houses out of the plentiful sod. Finally, in the Appalachian Mountains, the Mohawk built houses out of log. The houses were about 100 feet long. That is how Native Americans accommodated with the environment.

Question 41. *Causal.* Causal means to "make something happen." Causal comes from the word "cause." One way of thinking about causal is, "the reasons why people do certain things." An example is the reason why the Pawnee used bison to solve their problem of finding food, clothing, and shelter. One reason was the large numbers of bison in the Great Plains.

Write about how the Pawnee solved their problems of finding food, clothing, and shelter. Begin with a general statement: for example, "There were several reasons why the Pawnee used bison to solve their problems of food, clothing, and shelter." Then give reasons from the environment. You can find reasons by thinking about their climate, geography, and natural resources.

There were several reasons why the Pawnee used bison to solve their problems of food, clothing, and shelter. The Pawnee used the bison's brain to rub on leather to make it soft. They used the bison's bladder to carry water. The Pawnee used the bison's hide for clothing. They used the bison's meat for food. They also used the bison's sinew to string bows. That is how the Pawnee used the plentiful bison.

Source: Farrell Becking, Teacher, Lincoln Elementary School, Gering Public Schools (NE). Reprinted with permission of Frank Ybarra (Parent) and Julia Ybarra (Student).

other students working on grade level or slightly below; and (2) they are expected to master the content and skills before they move on. Safeguards are built into the scripts to make sure there are enough repetitions to ensure mastery. Teachers can fully concentrate on one group of students with the same academic needs during the entire reading block. Their groups may change according to the subject, but they never have to juggle three to four groups at the same time.

SUMMARIZING CHAPTER 8 ■

Reading and writing are inseparable in the classroom. Writing in the service of reading comprehension and content acquisition has been shown to be an effective intervention for older learners at risk as well as a key aspect of raising the achievement bar for all students, with special emphasis on closing the achievement gap. When students are explicitly taught from kindergarten how to use reading and writing to learn, they become more confident learners and proficient writers who better understand and retain what they read.

9

A Reading Culture

A reading culture comprises the collective attitudes, beliefs, and behaviors of all of the stakeholders in a school regarding any and all of the activities associated with enabling all students to read at the highest level of attainment possible for both their academic and personal gain.

We are now ready to put the final piece of the reading puzzle in place: *a pervasive and persuasive reading culture.* Recall that in the Introduction, three steps were recommended for bringing the students in your classroom, school, or district to grade-level reading proficiency, *regardless of their readiness to read or their reading levels when they first enrolled in your school:*

1. Consider the paradigms that impact reading achievement and be prepared to challenge and ultimately change the prevailing beliefs that are interfering with your students learning to read.

2. Become knowledgeable about research regarding the role that each piece of the reading puzzle plays in facilitating high literacy levels as well as what types of instruction are most effective for teaching those literacy skills to all students.

3. Utilize your unique leadership and instructional expertise to raise literacy levels wherever you work.

I hope that you have been thinking about these steps during your reading to this point. Just ahead we see how educators in the Gering, Nebraska, School District followed these steps to create a pervasive and persuasive reading culture. In just five years, they have raised the achievement bar for all students and are well on their way to closing the achievement gap between their Hispanic and white students.

More than 20 years ago, my staff and I had to figure out how to create a reading culture on our own: there were no examples to emulate. Today, *you* can learn how to teach them all to read by *benchmarking*. Benchmarking is a process by which an individual teacher, principal, grade-level team, school, or district undertakes an investigation to determine how a similar counterpart has managed to achieve success and then systematically learns how to replicate that success. The best way to benchmark a successful school or district is to visit, ask questions, observe, and take careful notes on what you see.

Our benchmark district is the Gering School District. It serves 2,100 preK through twelfth-grade students. There are four K–6 elementary schools, a junior high, and a high school. The district's population is 70% Caucasian, 26% Hispanic, and 4% Native American. Of Gering's students, 43% receive free or reduced-price lunches. A fact sheet with data about each of the district's elementary schools is found in Figure 9.1. The district has a 13% mobility rate, and 10% of its students are enrolled in Special Education.

In 2004, Gering received a six-year Reading First (RF) grant of 2.1 million dollars. They subsequently adopted the complete spectrum of Direct Instruction (DI) reading and language arts programs published by SRA/McGraw-Hill and contracted with the National Institute for Direct Instruction (NIFDI) to provide intensive training and on-site implementation management. The district's achievement has been moving steadily and in some instances dramatically upward ever since. Many neighboring Nebraska districts, as well as some from other states, have heard about Gering's success and travelled there to benchmark it.

Information about programs in the Gering School District can also be found on pages 106–107 in Chapter 5 and pages 162–170 in Chapter 8.

A DVD, *Closing the Performance Gap: The Gering Story*, can be viewed on the Web site of the National Institute for Direct Instruction: www.nifdi.org. An article by Gering's superintendent can be found at www.ncsa.org.

Figure 9.1 The Elementary Schools of Gering, Nebraska

School	Principal	Coach	Students	Free or Reduced-Price Lunch
Cedar Canyon	Betty Smith	Jadie Beam	83	45%
Geil	Mary Kay Haun	Bev Hague	352	36%
Lincoln	George Schlothauer	Carol Zier	322	46%
Northfield	Pam Barker	Jadie Beam	351	59%

Source: Andrea Boden, EdS, NCSP, Director of Assessment and Reading Coordinator K–6, Gering Public Schools, Gering, Nebraska.

During the later years of implementation, RF Coordinator Andrea Boden hosted over 300 visitors. Since then, several Nebraska districts have replicated all or part of Gering's model. You won't have to take a hair-raising ride on a prop plane from Denver to the Western Regional Airport in Scottsbluff or drive across the endless, windswept highway I-80 from Omaha to visit Gering. Everything you need to know to teach them all to read can be found in this chapter.

WELCOME TO GERING ■

Once teachers can admit that children are not the problem but that instructional strategies are, then learning is going to happen for every child.

—Datrow, Park, and Wohlstetter (2007, p. 26)

Gering, population 7,751, was founded in 1887 at the base of what is known as Scotts Bluff National Monument. Gering has more in common with its western neighbors—Wyoming, 25 miles away and Colorado, 60 miles away—than it does with Nebraska's capital city, Lincoln, or the state's largest city, Omaha, to the east. Gering and its more populous and affluent neighbor across the North Platte River, Scottsbluff, population 14,732, comprise the seventh largest urban area in Nebraska. However, Gering residents are more like pioneers than city slickers. Nowhere is that pioneering spirit more evident than in the RF grant Gering applied for in 2003. The application received the highest score among Nebraska schools—209 out of a possible 212 points. The next closest application scored 170. Only a handful of schools around the country were as forward thinking as Gering, and no Nebraska schools dared to dream as big.

Although there's a rural feel to Gering, the school district faces the same challenges as urban communities. Superintendent Don Hague was aware of the achievement problem when he took over as superintendent in 2001, but until he noticed the photocopy of a check from the federal government for 23 million dollars on a bulletin board in the Nebraska Department of Education in Lincoln, he didn't have the resources in his budget to do something about the problem. He delegated the job of writing the RF grant application to Andrea Boden, currently Director of Assessment and Reading Coordinator K–6, who chaired the grant-writing committee and served as RF Coordinator during the grant's implementation. Andrea is known as a bit of a renegade at the Nebraska Department of Education, and certainly it took someone who thinks outside the box to draft a plan that not only created some controversy in Gering but also put the district on the map of places to visit if you want to know how to teach them all to read. Andrea is a quiet, self-assured school psychologist who knows her stuff and has a passion for student learning that simply will not be extinguished. Principals and coaches in Gering call her brilliant. Superintendent Hague says that she has meant the world to the success of the program.

At the time the RF grant was awarded, most Gering parents and teachers thought their schools were pretty good. One of the reasons for these positive feelings might have been that Nebraska student achievement data have never been widely collected or disseminated to the public. With an approach to assessment unlike any of the other 49 states (Roschewski, 2003), Nebraskans have only one way to compare their neighborhood schools to others in the state: the Writing assessment given annually to fourth, eighth, and eleventh graders.

Gering's teachers functioned as independent contractors with little or no accountability. Teachers chose the most popular innovations to teach reading, many of them based on the whole-language philosophy: *6 + 1 Traits of Writing* (Culham, 2005); *Accelerated Reader* (Advantage Learning Systems, 2001); *The Four Blocks Literacy Model*® (Cunningham & Hall, 2001); and *Letter People*® (Abrams & Company, 2005). Unfortunately for Gering's students, none of these programs are backed by scientific research. Teachers taught to the top third of students in their classes and the rest fell through the cracks. In 2004, 64% of third-grade students did not meet benchmark on the spring *DIBELS (Dynamic Early Indicators of Basic Early Literacy Skills)*, a test that predicts students' future reading success based on various curriculum-based measures (Good & Kaminski, 2000). In the case of the 2004 third-grade cohort, their oral reading fluency scores were similar to those of late first- or early second-grade students. They would be the last group of Gering third graders to fall through the cracks.

There is no prescription or program that can create a pervasive and persuasive reading culture that refuses to let individual students fail, although research-based programs implemented with fidelity *are* essential to success. Money, although certainly critical for reforming reading instruction, cannot buy a reading culture. A pervasive and persuasive reading culture can only be developed over time as strong instructional leaders at both district and school levels along with highly effective teachers perceive needs and respond to them steadfastly in research-based ways.

To teach them all to read, every individual who works in, attends, or sends children to a school must be focused on literacy. This is the defining quality of a *pervasive* reading culture. In addition, any newcomers to the school community will immediately be made aware of the commitment of all of the stakeholders to literacy for every student and soon find that they have been enlisted in the cause. That is what a *persuasive* reading culture is like.

In the first edition of *Teach Them ALL to Read*, I suggested that pervasive and persuasive reading cultures are characterized by 12 descriptors. Those descriptors are shown in Figure 9.2, and you can see them in action in the schools and classrooms of Gering. Gering's educators use the words of civil rights pioneer, Rosa Parks to describe their implementation:

> We are not where we want to be,
>
> We are not where we are going to be,
>
> But, we are not where we were.

■ THE GERING "NO EXCUSES" MODEL

Of all the things that children have to learn when they get to school, reading and writing are the most basic, the most central, and the most essential. Practically everything else that they do there will be permeated by these two skills. Hardly a lesson can be understood, hardly a project finished, unless the children can read the books in front of them and write about what they have done. They must read and write or their time at school will be largely wasted.

—Bryant and Bradley (1985, p. 1)

Figure 9.2 Indicators of a Pervasive and Persuasive Reading Culture

- ✓ Strong instructional leadership and shared decision making by administrators and teacher leaders
- ✓ High expectations and accountability for students, teachers, and parents—a sense of academic press that is shared and supported by the entire school community, including the school board
- ✓ A relentless commitment to results driven by meaningful and measurable short- and long-term goals
- ✓ Research-based curricula and instruction
- ✓ A coordinated instructional delivery system
- ✓ A comprehensive monitoring and assessment system
- ✓ A dedication to allocating and using time for reading instruction
- ✓ A seamless integration and coordination of special services
- ✓ Teacher collaboration
- ✓ Ongoing and meaningful professional development
- ✓ Support of parents and the community
- ✓ Adequate and sustained resources

In order to get from where Gering was in the spring of 2004 to where they are today, educators have zeroed in with laserlike precision on teaching them all to read, write, spell, think, and speak. They are achieving these goals to a greater degree and with a higher level of consistency than in any other district I have observed.

To bring about a reversal in their downward student achievement trend lines, Gering made a 180-degree turn in practice. Educators didn't change just a few things; they changed everything. Their makeover was not cosmetic but transformational. They call their initiative The Gering "No Excuses" Model, and Figure 9.3 lists its key components.

Figure 9.3 Gering's "No Excuses" Model

- Scientifically research-based reading program
- High expectations for the achievement of all students
- Strong preimplementation and ongoing professional development from National Institute for Direct Instruction (NIFDI) and Reading First (RF)
- High level of accountability for teachers, paraprofessionals, and administrators to ensure fidelity of program implementation
- Adequate amount of protected instructional time in daily schedule to teach reading–language arts
- Technically sound assessment instruments used to ensure that all students are making progress
- Strong leadership team focused on student performance
- Relentless resistance to counterproductive and ineffective practices often promoted in education
- Zero tolerance for blaming students and parents for lack of student achievement

Source: Andrea Boden, EdS, NCSP, Director of Assessment and Reading Coordinator K–6, Gering Public Schools, Gering, Nebraska.

Before we examine the specific ways Gering changed their beliefs and practices, consider how Gering's RF implementation differed from most other RF districts and schools in the state and nation:

- Gering adopted an unconventional core reading program that directly specifies how it must be taught and provides scripted lessons for teachers: DI's *Reading Mastery* (RM).
- In addition to RM, Gering also adopted DI language, spelling, and writing programs.
- Gering students are grouped homogeneously so that all students receive language, reading, spelling, and writing instruction targeted to their specific learning levels, whether below, at, or above benchmark. These flexible groups allow students to be taught to mastery rather than by the typical "teach-test-move on" model used in most reading programs.
- Of Gering's students, 90% have their learning needs met in the DI core programs, thereby reducing special education placements and eliminating the purchase of multiple supplemental programs.
- In addition to their RF training, Gering teachers also received extensive training both prior to and during implementation from NIFDI.
- Although not funded by the RF grant, Gering gradually phased DI into Grades 4–6 over a two-year span, creating a seamless continuum of reading, writing, thinking, spelling, and language programs.

The best way to understand Gering's "No Excuses" model is to examine the myriad things these educators changed in their schools in order to teach them all to read. They have dramatically changed their approach in nine different categories. They have shifted their paradigms, developed an incredibly sharp academic focus, adopted research-based programs, turned the instructional delivery system upside down, and begun assessing students regularly using a variety of technically sound instruments. Gering educators have totally rearranged the school schedule, dramatically increasing the amount of time teachers spend directly teaching reading, writing, spelling, and language and completely dismantled heterogeneous whole-group instruction in reading.

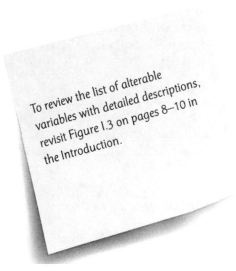

To review the list of alterable variables with detailed descriptions, revisit Figure I.3 on pages 8–10 in the Introduction.

In Gering, professional development is based on formative student data and embedded in classrooms where teachers need focused experiences that will help them improve their teaching and, in turn, student learning. Students, teachers, and administrators are accountable for results, and expectations rise on a yearly basis.

■ PARADIGMS

To increase student learning, approach it directly, and bring the energy of everyone in the school or district to bear on the effort.

—Joyce and Showers (1995, p. 5)

A paradigm, you will recall, is a set of assumptions that govern how people behave. In schools, most of the assumptions that govern teacher behavior relate to students—how and why they learn or don't and what kinds of curriculum and instruction are most effective for teaching students how to read. There are various ways to shift educators' paradigms to include providing information about scientifically based reading instruction, visiting formerly low-performing schools where all students are currently learning to read, or doing a faculty book study.

However, when a once-in-a-lifetime opportunity to apply for more than 2 million dollars in grant money comes across your desk, you apply for the grant first and worry about changing people's paradigms later. Andrea Boden and Don Hague did just that. Many school reformers have learned that it is often easier to change people's behaviors through intensive professional development and then work on shifting their paradigms in the course of a successful implementation. Educators are more apt to change their attitudes when they see the positive effects of a program on their students. Eventually, however, a critical mass of teachers (90%–95%) must demonstrate a willingness to put the needs of their students ahead of personal desires for curricular and instructional autonomy.

Creating a pervasive and persuasive reading culture in Gering has not been easy. Superintendent Hague admits, "I didn't realize how radical this change was going to be. There were definitely some naysayers in the community. They were happy with the way their kids were performing in school and didn't want us to level the playing field, so to speak. But we had a mission statement that said we wanted all kids to learn, but we'd been saying it for years and doing nothing about it."

As RF coordinator, Andrea took some of the heat. However, with remarkable composure and level-headedness, she says, "I just kept my focus on the students. One of our most supportive community members called me after one of our toughest battles and encouraged me with these words: 'You will win when truth and doing the right thing are on your side. Keep fighting for kids.' I greatly appreciated that."

Superintendent Hague credits Andrea with understanding instruction and learning more than any professional with whom he has worked. "She is very hands-on and has been in those classrooms right there with teachers, coaches, and principals. A lot of our success is due to her. There are several districts in Nebraska who have adopted DI because Andrea spent time with them when they visited in Gering and then made presentations to their staff and boards of education."

Teachers and reading coaches were on the front lines of Gering's battle to teach them all to read. Jadie Beam is the reading coach at Northfield and Cedar Canyon schools. She says, "One of our biggest roadblocks to moving ahead was getting everybody to recognize that we needed to change. We *thought* we were effective, but the data said otherwise. Gering wasn't a district that looked at data, but as a special education teacher, I knew we needed to do things differently. Every teacher was doing their own thing. We had a lot of misplaced students. Teachers would have behavior problems with certain students and not want to deal with them. So their solution was to refer them to Title I, even though the students had no documented reading difficulties. Now we only move students to different levels or programs based on data."

Lincoln reading coach Carol Zier found that for some teachers, making the mental shift from total freedom in their classrooms to being accountable for every minute of the school day was very difficult. She says, "Previously, if a teacher decided to do an art project or show a video instead of teaching reading, nobody noticed. Now, everyone is accountable."

There's no question that becoming an effective DI teacher takes expertise and practice. Carol recounts what happened when a group of student teachers from a nearby college observed in Lincoln's classrooms prior to their student-teaching assignments in Gering:

> After a morning spent in various reading classes, they told the principal, "We're not ready for this." It wasn't just the teaching methods. It was the content that scared them off. For example, in *Reasoning and Writing* Levels E and F (upper grades), students are taught how to read and critique text for faulty arguments. That's something that most teachers have never been taught to do."

Carol adds, "Another aspect of DI that has been challenging for teachers is bringing all students to mastery. When we taught heterogeneous classes it was impossible to bring everyone to mastery. So we just taught to the middle with no options for what to do when a child didn't get it or for when students were advanced. Now, every student at every level is experiencing success on a daily basis."

Carol has been teaching for 38 years and observed, "If someone told me today that I had to go back to what we were doing before DI, I'd quit. I'm still amazed when I walk into a kindergarten class in November and see every student reading at least one-page stories." Carol hastened to add, "They haven't just memorized these stories. They are independently reading every word."

Mickie Janecek teaches kindergarten at Northfield and is a member of the district's DI training cadre. When asked how she adapted so readily to DI when some of her colleagues were having a difficult time, she responded, "I had an open mind. I don't think it was easy for anyone in the beginning. It was so different. Especially for primary teachers who were used to all of their 'bells and whistles.' Suddenly they were expected to teach reading for two and a half hours every day [Note: Gering has all-day kindergarten sessions.] But I kept an open mind. I was willing to go to Jadie, our coach, or Pam Barker, the principal, to ask for help. I always got just what I needed."

Teachers weren't the only individuals in Gering who needed to shift their paradigms. Northfield principal Pam Barker confesses, "I was a trainer for High/Scope, a developmentally appropriate early childhood framework in which we waited for children to show us they were ready to learn. At the time High/Scope was going through Nebraska, I trained a lot of the staff in Gering. At one time, we were even a demonstration site for High/Scope. The irony is that I 'highscoped' a lot of my teachers, and now I was asking them to shift their paradigms completely—to begin teaching children to read the minute they arrived in our school."

Pam's staff were naturally apprehensive, but she reassured them. "Let's just give DI a try, trust one another, and be honest with each other. Let's see what the differences in student learning are at the end of the first year."

Pam had read the research and was confident the district was moving in the right direction. She trusted Andrea. And Pam's confidence was not misplaced. She says, "At the end of our first year of implementation (2004–2005), we had awesome data. So the teachers said, 'Let's keep on.' That following year (2005–2006) we added fourth grade to the implementation schedule, and away we went. My staff is great, and we work together as a team. We have grown together as a professional community through this experience."

Students had to change their paradigms as well. Geil principal Mary Kay Haun tells about a student who came to her during the first week of implementation. "This little guy came up to me in the hallway and said, 'What happened to those teachers over the summer?' Of course, I knew what he meant. In the *old* Geil School, there was no sense of academic press or motivation to get work done or learn. Better students didn't have to work hard at all. Overnight, or at least over the summer, we dramatically changed the way we taught and the way we expected students to learn. Suddenly, nobody was ignored. Everybody in the group had to have answers to every question.

Students couldn't slide down in their seats to avoid being called on. There was testing every 5–10 lessons to make sure that everyone was progressing. Our gifted students were being challenged in ways most of us never dreamed possible."

The major paradigm shift that has occurred in Gering is the adoption of a zero-tolerance policy for blaming students and parents for lack of student achievement—"no excuses." There are few, if any, teachers left in Gering who don't believe that their students can learn. You can tell by watching them teach and looking at their students' progress reports. Another shift has been to a relentless resistance on the part of administrators and teacher leaders to the counterproductive and ineffective practices often promoted in education.

Major paradigm shifts like these can only occur when strong instructional leaders raise expectations by allocating substantial amounts of time in their daily schedules to classroom walk-throughs, teaching lessons to various groups of students, and meeting frequently with teachers and coaches to develop interventions for students or teachers who are experiencing difficulties.

There will always be naysayers and yes-butters who challenge change, but Gering leadership has been persistent about addressing the following issues:

- Dealing with some teacher resistance to accountability
- Keeping staff focused on student needs
- Dispelling rumors regarding the program that occasionally get started in the community
- Screening professional development opportunities for staff to make certain that teachers do not lose their instructional focus and that the district stays on message and mission
- Supervising and monitoring some staff members who, despite the incredible success of DI, want to return to their former practices (Boden, 2008)

Building a pervasive and persuasive reading culture takes courage and fortitude as stakeholders with other agendas assert their personal ownership of the schools. These resistant educators have been doing their favorite things for decades and fight strongly against teacher accountability. Geil reading coach. Bev Hague, Superintendent Hague's wife, says, "The people who believed in the program experienced considerable stress. There weren't that many individuals against making the changes, but those who were against them spoke out. The rumors that were spread about the regimentation of DI and how students were being treated like they were in the military were pure propaganda. The reason we have persevered and prevailed is that we've kept our eye on the mission of what's good for kids."

ACADEMIC FOCUS   ■

Knowing the right thing to do is the central problem of school improvement.

—Elmore (2003, p. 9)

The focus in Gering is on bringing all students to the long-term goal of grade-level achievement or above in all subjects and to the short-term goal of meeting the periodic benchmarks in various areas of literacy during the school year.

Cedar Canyon principal Betty Smith is a relative newcomer to Gering. Her former district merged with Gering before the 2006–2007 school year. Betty and her small school of six teachers and 110 students immediately jumped into the middle of the DI implementation. But she is a quick learner and zeroed in on the big ideas of DI. She describes the academic focus in Cedar Canyon's classrooms this way: "When I walk into classrooms, learning is almost tangible. You can touch it and feel it and see it happening every day."

Cedar Canyon's three first-year teachers love the structure of DI. It has enabled them to exclusively focus on student learning as opposed to being distracted by the usual problems of new teachers—discipline and classroom management. Betty explains, "These young people have been able to grow as teachers in so many deeper ways because they haven't had to spend every evening dreaming up lesson plans. Overall, they have received 40 hours of intensive professional development, training that was nothing like what they experienced in college. They had made all of these units to teach, but I told them to put the units away. They wouldn't need them here."

Allison Smith (not related to Betty), a new primary teacher at Cedar Canyon, feels that it is an advantage to be able to put her units away. She confesses, "In college, we had to make lesson plans from scratch out of nothing. There was nothing to guide us, and we had to come up with our own ideas." The district in which she did her student teaching had no organized reading program. She says, "When I asked my supervising teacher what I was supposed to teach, she told me I could do whatever I wanted to. It was kind of stressful. There weren't even any teacher's manuals. I'm a very structured person, and I think kids like knowing what's expected of them also."

Lincoln School principal George Schlothauer is the newest member of the administrative team, having moved from the junior high school. George appreciates the data-driven nature of DI that gives him immediate information about how his students are progressing. He says, "Before DI, we used to have kids incorrectly placed in terms of what they needed, and now we are able to provide instruction right at students' instructional levels and feel certain that we are meeting their needs."

George explains, "When parents have questions about how their children are progressing, it's an easy matter to pull up the data and share it with them. Teachers and students know that if 25% or more of a group fails a mastery test on a particular story, they don't go on. They have to go back and redo the story. The mastery checkouts build on each other in terms of recalling information or skills. Recursive teaching helps us maintain our academic focus."

Gering's academic focus on student learning has resulted in a remarkable reduction in special education placements. For example, in the 2007–2008 school year, Gering had the lowest percentage of K–12 students in special education (10.14%) among the 25 largest school districts in the state. Some of these larger districts have as few as 6% and 7% receiving free and reduced-price lunch as compared to the 43% in Gering.

■ CURRICULUM, INSTRUCTION, AND ASSESSMENT

For too long American teachers were given an overwhelming amount of curriculum to cover and, paradoxically, a great deal of freedom to decide what they taught. This resulted in an unhealthy curriculum anarchy, in which many students graduated with huge gaps in their knowledge and skills and many teachers operated in isolation from their colleagues.

—Marshall (2003)

In most places around the country, the state standards dictate the "what" of instruction (content) as well as the "how" of assessment (high-stakes tests). In

Nebraska, each district develops its own standards, chooses the curricula to teach those standards, and then, with the exception of one curricular area, writing, chooses or creates its own assessments to measure student learning. Gering teachers are very familiar with the standards. They developed them. What they did not have was a research-based curriculum, highly effective instruction, and trustworthy assessments aligned with their standards. Here's how they systematically changed each of those critical variables to create success for all of their students.

Research-Based Curricula

A good school is not a collection of good teachers working independently, but a team of skilled educators working together to implement a coherent instructional plan, to identify the learning needs of every student, and to meet those needs.

—Boudett, City, and Murnane (2005, p. 2)

Many of the mainstream so-called research-based core reading programs approved by RF for adoption were not designed for teaching *all* students to read. Finding a program that had the power to raise achievement for all students would have been a challenge, if not for Andrea's familiarity with the DI research. She had reviewed its comprehensive research base during her graduate studies and thesis writing. She knew that the program, albeit challenging to teach, got results when faithfully implemented.

None of the mainstream reading programs from major publishers are backed by the depth of DI research, which spans more than three decades. For example, when districts or schools adopt a conventionally designed program (i.e., one that includes all of the possible components needed to teach reading), there is much room for multiple interpretations. Each mainstream core program contains dozens of components, many of them philosophically and instructionally at odds with each other in terms of effectiveness. Mainstream basal series are designed to be taught over a 175-day school year to a narrow band of average, on-grade-level students. Students well above or well below this average band do not receive targeted instruction. Students well below average do not get the practice and intense teaching they require, while the well above average students have no opportunities to accelerate their learning. In order for teachers to teach scientifically based reading instruction from a mainstream core reading program, it must be reconfigured on a massive scale, first to identify the essential components of the curriculum that will actually teach them all to read and then to rewrite the lesson plans in the teacher's manual in order to integrate research-based instructional strategies.

For more information about how to adapt your basal reading series to meet the needs of students at risk, read *Reading Instruction for Students Who Are At Risk or Have Disabilities* (Bursuck & Damer, 2007). The Project Pride Model described in the first edition provided the research for this book.

To adopt a new curriculum in any subject matter, no matter the grade level, requires professional development. However, faithful implementation of the comprehensive DI curricula in Grades preK–6, as shown in Figure 9.4, is an achievement that few districts have replicated. Gering educators believe that the following characteristics of the DI curricula have

Figure 9.4   Curricula Used in the Gering, Nebraska, Reading First Implementation (2004–Present)

Direct Instruction Programs	PreK	K	1	2	3	4	5	6
Language Development								
Language for Learning (Engelmann & Osborn, 1999a)	×	×						
Language for Thinking (Engelmann & Osborn, 1999b)		×	×					
Writing								
Reasoning and Writing (Engelmann, various)			×	×	×	×	×	×
Expressive Writing (Engelmann & Silbert, 1993)						×	×	×
Language for Writing (Engelmann & Osborn, 2006)				×	×			
Reading								
Reading Mastery Levels I–VI (Engelmann, various)		×	×	×	×	×	×	×
Horizons (Engelmann, 1993)								
Spelling								
Spelling Mastery A-F (Dixon & Engelmann, 2007)			×	×	×	×	×	×
Non-DI Programs								
The Six-Minute Solution: A Reading Fluency Program (Adams & Brown, 2004)				×	×	×	×	×
Understanding U.S. History (Carnine et al., 1996)							×	×
Vocabulary Workshop (Shostak, 2005)							×	×
Selected Novel Studies (see Chapter 5)							×	×
LitPlans for Teaching Novels (Teachers Pet Publications, 2008)							×	×

Source: Andrea Boden, EdS, NCSP, Director of Assessment and Reading Coordinator K–6, Gering Public Schools. Gering, Nebraska.

been most responsible for their success in both raising achievement overall as well as closing the gap between Hispanic and white students:

- Teachers use scripted lessons to provide direct and explicit instruction.
- Students are homogeneously grouped according to their instructional levels.
- Students are taught to mastery.
- Only 10% of the information presented each day is new.
- Students are highly engaged, giving 12–18 responses per minute.
- Frequent assessments are embedded in the program to check for learning and monitor student progress.
- Large amounts of skill practice and application of those skills on a daily basis are built into the program.

- Skilled reinforcement of desired behaviors with specific praise is used.
- Built-in error correction procedures are used that ensure solid learning. (Boden, 2008)

Research-Based Instruction

While a focus on testing can illuminate potential learning issues, testing alone cannot move learning forward: To improve student performance, classroom instruction needs to improve.

—Ciofalo and Wylie (2006, p. 1)

To change how teachers actually teach once their classroom doors are closed is the most challenging assignment for administrators seeking to teach them all to read. Andrea Boden realized that faithfully implementing the DI delivery model would be extraordinarily difficult in four K–6 elementary schools using at least three and sometimes four brand-new DI curricula (Language, Reading, Spelling, and Writing). That's why the Gering RF grant included four years of training and implementation management from NIFDI.

Geil principal Mary Kay Haun has been part of the Gering district for 31 years, first as a special education teacher, then in regular education, and for the past seven years as principal at Geil Elementary. She has seen it all come and go. "I remember the days when I used *DISTAR* [a precursor to *Reading Mastery*] very successfully with my special education students. I was very uneasy when we decided to go with whole language. I knew that it would never work with students in special education."

Mary Kay decided that the best way to help her teachers manage change was to lead by example and become a master at teaching all six levels of *Reading Mastery*. She says, "I learned all of the programs with all of the levels. I teach them all. I substitute for teachers so they can visit other classrooms to observe. I have taken all of the training with them and that has given me a lot of credibility. I won't ask my teachers to do anything I'm not willing to do myself."

Mary Kay's first challenge was helping her staff change their perceptions of themselves as teachers. She explains, "One of my biggest hurdles was that my teachers thought they were master teachers. Truthfully, I considered them to be excellent teachers. In order to gain their buy-in, I had to show them that although they were effective with some groups of students, readily bringing *them* to grade level, they weren't able to accomplish that for all of their students. I showed them the data regarding what happened to those students who didn't make the grade in their classrooms when they moved on to upper grades."

Addressing the teaching gaps of her staff meant that Mary Kay had to face her own personal teaching gaps. She says, "Even though I had high expectations for my students, there were always those students I didn't reach and teach." With a great deal of humility, Mary Kay stood before the Gering Board of Education and admitted her own inability to teach all kids using reading programs that weren't research based. She says, "I believe my honesty in front of the board gave me a lot of credibility with my staff."

Lincoln fourth-grade teacher and district DI trainer, Tracy Steele, had only been teaching for two years when DI came to Gering. She says, "DI has given me so much confidence as a teacher. During those first two years, I just hoped that what I was doing was the right thing. After the DI training, I understood the rationale of teaching reading and absolutely knew that every move I made was research based and the

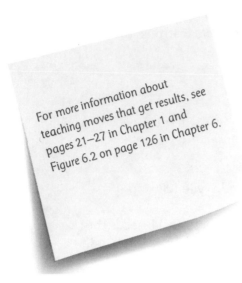

For more information about teaching moves that get results, see pages 21–27 in Chapter 1 and Figure 6.2 on page 126 in Chapter 6.

right thing to do. Tracy has her own unique and exuberant teaching style, one that some might think wouldn't mesh with the structure and scripts of DI. However, Tracy doesn't feel that way at all. She says, "Since I've gained the foundation and skills to teach reading from DI, I can build on that with my own techniques and communicate my own excitement for learning to my students." Tracy is teaching the most challenging group of fifth-grade students this year and has them excited about reading. She said, "One of my students said to me just this week, 'Miss Steele, I really think I like reading.'"

Some of the teaching moves used in delivering the DI curricula are enumerated and described in Figure 9.5. The list doesn't begin to include all of the DI practices, nor are all of them appropriate at every grade level or subject. However, the skillful marriage of field-tested curricula to research-based teaching moves well-trained teachers to raise achievement dramatically. [Note: See Adams & Carnine, 2003, Appendix 24.2, for research on individual aspects of instruction embedded in each DI curriculum, for example, correction procedures, pacing, positive and negative examples, sequences, sound separation, and wording.]

Figure 9.5   Examples of Direct Instruction Teaching Strategies

Teaching Practice	Description
Advance organizer	A verbal road map for students, so they know where they are going and why they are going there. Start each lesson with a predictable routine.
Unison or choral response	All students respond together on teacher's signal. Unison responses are effective for single-word answers. Be sure to allow a few seconds of thinking time between asking the question and requiring a response.
Signaling	A signal can be visual, such as a hand drop, or auditory, such as a clap or a tap on a clipboard or teacher manual. If students are looking down at their stories, signals must be audible.
Ongoing practice	Students at risk need ongoing practice and review. Merely presenting information and moving on to the next skill is insufficient. Never leave critical information in the past. If it is important for students to know, be sure it is repeated, revisited, and rehearsed through the year. Practice must be sufficient, varied, distributed, and integrated.
Explain or model	Teacher names the task for students, clearly explains the task to students, and models the correct response using a signal.
Individual turns	Teacher provides individual turns as a check when it appears that the group is consistently answering all items correctly chorally. Keeping all students tuned in while one student is giving an answer is essential.
Error correction	Teacher provides correction when students make an error or when students answer too early or too late (not with signal). When students are reading in unison, the teacher should make a correction if a student misreads a word. Teacher also provides a correct answer when students answer comprehension questions incorrectly.

Teaching Practice	Description
Eliminating extraneous teacher talk	Teacher refrains from excess talk during instruction or error correction and remains focused on the lesson.
Monitoring	In beginning reading instruction, teachers monitor by watching students' eyes and mouths and by listening to their responses. Teachers should not call on students in a predictable way. Some teachers use tongue depressors with students' names written on them tucked under a rubber band around the teaching manual.
Scripts	There are a variety of scripts to teach various reading skills. An example of such a script adapted for a core reading program can be found in Chapter 5, Figure 5.7.

Source: These examples are meant to be illustrative and not inclusive of all DI teaching strategies. Examples were informed by Bursuck and Damer (2007), Carnine et al. (2004), McEwan and Bresnahan (2008), and McEwan and Damer (2000).

Data-Driven Improvement

When there is no data to show how kids and teachers are doing, you are left with opinions. Data doesn't offer an opinion or an excuse. The data is what the data is. We cannot continue to blame our kids for our inability to teach them. If the "greatest" teachers in the world are failing to teach half of their students, the teachers need to change their instruction.

—Principal Dave Montague (as quoted in McEwan, 2009, p. 183)

Schools that teach them all to read are data driven, using a variety of technically sound assessment instruments for three primary purposes: (1) to make placement decisions about students, (2) to formatively assess how students are progressing in order to adjust instructional groups and pacing, and (3) to summatively assess student progress on a yearly basis so that stakeholders in the school and community have evidence that their students actually know more and are able to do more at the end of each school year. Implementing data-based decision making in a school district where data had never been used to evaluate the quality of teaching and learning has been a major achievement in Gering. The various assessments that Gering has used are listed in Figure 9.6.

Critical to the success of any reading improvement initiative is formative assessment. A powerful component of the DI model is its built-in monitoring system. Teachers cannot keep moving forward if their students fail. The Progress Monitoring Forms must be turned in, and teachers are held accountable for student mastery. DI virtually eliminates teaching to the top third of students and moving on without regard for those who are left behind. The DI progress-monitoring system catches both students and teachers before they fail. Teachers who lack confidence find the Progress Monitoring Forms to be the most intimidating aspect of DI because they shine a bright light on the tiniest glitches in instruction and highlight exactly where students and teachers are having the most difficulty. Teachers who are eager to know how their students are progressing are the first to have their Progress Monitoring Forms turned

Figure 9.6   Gering Public Schools Assessment Calendar, K–12

Assessment	Content	Dates	PreK	K	1	2	3	4	5	6	7	8	9	10	11	12
Preschool child observation record (High/Scope, 1992)	Readiness skills	September and May	×													
Preschool assessment	Language, math	September, January, April	×													
Direct Instruction placement test	Language, reading	First week of school		×	×[1]	×[1]	×[1]	×[1]	×[1]	×[1]						
Kindergarten and first grade	Math	First week of May		×	×											
Second grade	Math	Second week in April				×										
K–6 DIBELS (Dynamic Indicators of Basic Early Literacy Skills) (Good & Kaminski, 2000)	Reading	September, January, April		×	×	×	×	×	×	×						
TerraNova	Reading, math, science, social studies	Last week of March or first week of April					×	×	×	×	×	×	×	×	×	×
STARS Nebraska online	Math	Throughout the year						×				×			×	
STARS Nebraska online	Reading	Throughout the year					×	×	×	×	×	×				
STARS Nebraska online	Science	Throughout the year								×						
STARS Nebraska online	15 questions per learning standard	Throughout the year						×		×	×	×				
EXPLORE (ACT, 2000)	English, math, reading, science	First week of November										×				
PLAN (ACT, 2000)	English, math, reading, science	Second week of October												×		
ACT Practice Test (ACT, 2000)	English, math, reading, science	Second week of October													×	
Nebraska State Writing Test	Writing	January to February						×				×			×	
Gates MacGinitie (MacGinitie, MacGinitie, Maria, Dreyer, & Hughes, 2000)	Reading	Last week of April				×	×									
Gray Oral Reading Test-4 (Weiderhold & Bryant, 2001)	Reading	First week of May				×										

Assessment	Content	Dates	PreK	K	1	2	3	4	5	6	7	8	9	10	11	12
NAEP (National Assessment of Educational Progress) Voluntary	Reading, math, science	Last week of January, first week of April						×			×	×				
AIMSweb Math	Math	September, January, April		×	×	×	×	×	×	×						

Source: Andrea Boden, EdS, NCSP, Director of Assessment and Reading Coordinator K–6, Gering Public Schools, Gering, Nebraska.

Note: [1]Newly enrolled students.

in. When the results are disappointing, they seek out the coach and the principal for a conversation about what else they can be doing.

Progress monitoring is habitual in Gering. Andrea says, "We progress monitor religiously." The DI programs have checkouts every five lessons in *Reading Mastery* based on accuracy and fluency and Mastery Tests every 10 lessons. These scores are recorded, and there are specific criteria that must be met by each child—for example, to read a passage in a minute with fewer than two errors. The school leadership team, comprised of Andrea, the principal, and the reading coach, meets weekly in each building to review every teacher's progress-monitoring data. These data are used to make changes such as moving students to different groups, adding interventions, or having the teacher back up a few lessons and redo them.

Implementation of the DI programs with fidelity has been the paramount goal from the outset. Fidelity is the degree of exactness with which something is reproduced. In Gering, the exactness with which teachers have been able to reproduce the pace, the teaching moves, the subtle shifts back and forth between choral responding when students are learning a brand-new skill to individual responding when a skill is being solidified, and the signaling, among other complex moves in the choreography of DI instruction, can be seen in the upward trajectory of student achievement in Gering. Figure 9.7 shows how the achievement bar in Gering has risen for all students and how the achievement gap between Hispanic and white students is rapidly closing.

GROUPING AND TIME ◼

The primary and immediate strategy for catch-up growth is proportional increases in direct instruction time.

—Fielding et al. (2004, p. 53)

Educators frequently blame insufficient time for their inability to teach all students to read. Remarkably, effective schools with high-achieving students have the same number of school days as low-performing schools. Both kinds of schools have roughly the same number of hours in a school day—allocated learning time. Changing how time is allocated and used for instruction makes a powerful impact on student

Figure 9.7   Raising the Bar and Closing the Gap in Gering: 2004–2008

Nebraska State Writing Test, Fourth Grade: Percentage Proficient

	2004–2005	2007–2008	Explanatory Notes
All fourth-grade students, Nebraska	83%	91%	The percentage proficient on the Nebraska State Writing Test reflects all students at the fourth grade statewide as compared to the percentage proficient in the various demographic groups in Gering. The 2004–2005 scores reflect preimplementation of Reading First and Direct Instruction.
All fourth-grade students, Gering	57%	95%	
White fourth graders, Gering	64%	97%	
Hispanic fourth graders, Gering	39%	93%	
Free or reduced-price lunch fourth graders, Gering	53%	90%	The fourth-grade cohort received Direct Instruction *Reasoning and Writing* for 3 years (2005–2006 through 2007–2008).
Special education fourth graders, Gering	29%	80%	

TerraNova Sixth-Grade Reading: Gering Students At or Above 50th Percentile

	2004–2005 (no DI)	2007–2008 (four years of DI)	Explanatory Notes
All sixth-grade students	49%	64%	The TerraNova Reading Test is administered yearly to students in Grades 3–8. The 2004–2005 sixth-grade scores are *preimplementation* of Direct Instruction.
White sixth graders	53%	70%	
Hispanic sixth graders	22%	62%	The sixth-grade cohort received Direct Instruction in *Reading Mastery, Reasoning and Writing,* and *Spelling Mastery* for four years beginning in third grade (2004–2005 through 2007–2008).
Free or reduced-price lunch sixth graders	31%	44%	
Special education sixth graders	0%	24%	

Source: Andrea Boden, EdS, NCSP, Director of Assessment and Reading Coordinator K–6, Gering Public Schools, Gering, Nebraska.

achievement. In Gering, the school schedule is finely tuned and calibrated to meet the needs of every student.

Here are some of the highlights of the academic schedule at the elementary schools. A visual display of this information can be found in Figure 9.8.

- 8:00–10:00 a.m. and 12:00–1:00 p.m. are reserved for reading–language arts in Grades 1–6 (3 hours)
- 10:00–11:30 a.m. and 1:00–2:00 p.m. are reserved for kindergarten reading (2½ hours)

Figure 9.8 Gering's Direct Instruction Schedule

Sample Two-Group Rotation for Grades 1–2

Time	Name of Group	Subject	Time Allocation
8:00–8:45	Blue (teacher)	*Reading Mastery* II	45 minutes
	Purple (paraprofessional)	*Language for Thinking*	45 minutes
8:45–9:30	Blue (paraprofessional)	*Language for Thinking*	45 minutes
	Purple (teacher)	*Reading Mastery* II	45 minutes
9:30–10:00	Whole class (teacher)	Kit Spelling II	10 minutes
		Independent Work	20 minutes
12:00–1:00	Note: Same rotations as the morning, excluding spelling and independent work; 30-minute rotations for reading and language. In Nebraska, paraprofessionals are able to teach supplementary programs, like *Language for Thinking.* All paraprofessionals have received the same DI training as certified teachers.		

***Reading Mastery* III Through *Reading Mastery* IV Schedule**

Time	Subject
8:00–8:20	*Spelling Mastery*
8:20–10:00	*Reading Mastery*
	Note: Included in the reading time block is daily fluency practice using *The Six-Minute Solution Reading Fluency Program* (Adams & Brown, 2004) and daily check outs on fluency. For reading levels above RM I and II, teachers do not have paraprofessional help since all of the subjects are presented to the teacher's assigned homogeneous group.
12:00–1:00	*Reasoning and Writing* C–F

Source: Bev Hague, Reading Coach.

The scheduling of Grades 1–6 to dovetail with the kindergarten schedule frees up all of the paraprofessionals and specialists to work with smaller kindergarten groups so that the youngest students can get off to the strongest start possible. Paraprofessionals are able to teach supplementary programs, such as *Language for Learning* and *Language for Thinking.* In Levels 3–6 of *Reading Mastery,* students who are below grade level have double sessions of RM. If students are at grade level in RM Levels 3–6, they have RM and *Spelling Mastery* in the morning and *Reasoning and Writing* in the afternoon.

Students in Grades 1–2 have one hour of RM, 15–20 minutes of *Spelling Mastery,* and 30–40 minutes of either *Language for Learning, Language for Thinking,* or *Reasoning*

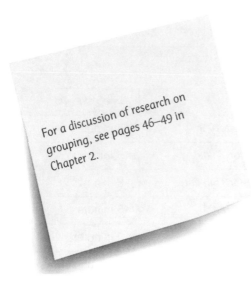

For a discussion of research on grouping, see pages 46–49 in Chapter 2.

and Writing A-B in the morning. Their afternoon block of one hour is typically devoted to about 30 minutes of RM and 30 minutes of some type of language learning in the programs mentioned earlier.

Time allocation within the daily schedule is based on the needs of each group of learners, based on their reading skills achievement levels. For example, the group of kindergarten students most at risk has their reading lesson presentation during the first 30 minutes of the reading block, then has seat work practice with a paraprofessional, and ends the morning with a *Language for Learning* lesson. There are two para-professionals in every kindergarten classroom during the 2½-hour reading block.

Mickie Janecek teaches three different groups in her kindergarten class. She says, "One of my groups is starting the second book of *Reading Mastery I,* and they are already (end of November) reading out of storybooks. Another group is still working on basic sounds and blending, while a third group is on Lesson 120 in Storybook 2 and doing timed checkouts on their reading once a week. Everyone in this class will learn to read and be on grade level by the end of second or third grade, but those who are reading well beyond their grade placement are being challenged and excited by school. I think it would really be sad if my most fluent readers were gluing buttons on cardboard B's during the allotted kindergarten reading time instead of learning to read."

■ PROFESSIONAL DEVELOPMENT

From the beginning we understood that we wanted the highest quality professional development available. . . . We also wanted to build our capacity to maintain the implementation of DI at a high level of fidelity into the future. We knew that we could simply buy the Direct Instruction materials commercially and try to implement them without training and support [but instead] we chose the National Institute for Direct Instruction (NIFDI) to provide support services.

—Hague (2008, p. 13)

Prior to implementation in the fall of 2004, the teachers, coaches, and principals in Gering received intensive training from NIFDI trainers and RF experts. As the responsibility for monitoring and supervising shifted from NIFDI and RF to the district in 2008–2009, Andrea, along with Gering's principals and coaches, developed their internal instructional capacity by training outstanding DI teachers to be trainers of new and struggling staff members in the district.

Andrea has strong feelings about the need to provide embedded and personalized professional development (PD). She explains, "It's hard for me to see how a district or school can improve instruction with 'brochure-based' professional development. A brochure comes in the mail, and its gets passed around to teachers to see who wants to go. In the past, as soon as other schools in the area adopted a program, we would jump on the bandwagon so we could look progressive and forward looking."

The personalized and embedded PD in Gering identifies a teacher's specific instructional needs and then provides an intervention that is prescriptive to the identified problem, in much the same way that students receive interventions if they are struggling academically. Typical teaching challenges include the inability to maintain the perky pace of instruction that is needed to keep students engaged, lack of organization and classroom management that leads to wasted time, and the inability to hit the 100% mark on error corrections. From least restrictive to most restrictive, the teacher interventions include the following: (a) participating in a conference with the coach or principal to talk about the weak area followed by a practice session, (b) watching the coach model a lesson with the teacher's class, (c) pairing up with another teacher and practicing various moves during times scheduled and monitored by the principal, (d) visiting another school to observe a highly proficient teacher with several assignments to complete during the observation, (e) attending a training session given by a member of the district training cadre who is expert in the particular area of instructional delivery with which the teacher is struggling, and (f) participating in a conference with Andrea and the principal to develop a plan that may include repetition of earlier steps.

Andrea notes that repetition with continued feedback on areas of improvement or ongoing problems is the secret to success. She says, "Most teachers improve with this kind of prescriptive PD plan, and it certainly beats sending them to a convention or a one-day training that likely does nothing to impact students' learning."

EXPECTATIONS ■

No amount of good feeling is adequate without that pedagogical dimension, without students actually knowing more and being able to do more at the end of a school year than they could at the beginning.

—Kohl (1998, p. 27)

Raising expectations remains a high priority in Gering. In the beginning, teachers were frightened of the accountability and apprehensive about regular observers in their classrooms. Principals were nervous about monitoring and supervising a program they were learning alongside their teachers and worried about how they were going to find time to be in classrooms as often as required. But as the program was implemented, the principals found that no one has been permitted to fail or lag behind. Everyone has been provided with multiple opportunities to learn. Struggling students have been provided with intensive interventions and so have struggling teachers. Principals have attended RF workshops to help them become stronger instructional leaders.

At the beginning of each school year, all teachers, whether new or successful veterans, are required to practice until multiple observations give evidence of proficiency with all of the critical teaching moves of the program. In Gering all teachers are expected to teach and all students are expected to learn. Teachers are discovering that once they have mastered their particular DI programs, they are far less exhausted at the end of a school day.

Kindergarten teacher Mickie Janecek says, "Before DI, all of my brain power was constantly spent looking for the next clever unit I could put together. Now, my research-based program and instructional methods to teach them all to read are right there on top of my desk. Before DI, I thought I was a wonderful teacher and doing the very best I knew how, but most of the time, my teammates and I weren't really teaching reading during reading time. Now I am explicitly teaching reading during every minute of my allocated reading time. Of course the students and I have time for conversations and dramatic play and other important aspects of kindergarten, but I am also teaching them all to read."

■ SUSTAINABILITY BEYOND NIFDI AND RF

Sustainability is the ability of a program to withstand shocks over time while maintaining core beliefs and values and using them to guide its adaptations to change.

—Century and Levy (2002, p. 4)

The training and implementation monitoring contract with NIFDI ended in the spring of 2008, and the K–3 RF implementation officially ended in the spring of 2009. When the external support frameworks are withdrawn from a massive district reform like the one in Gering, participants feel enormous pride at their accomplishments as well as an almost unconscious letdown. However, the team cannot rest, because each new kindergarten class enters school in the fall with the same challenging demographics as the class that graduated from high school in the spring. In the beginning stages of implementation, everyone is intently focused on fidelity, but in order to sustain a program over time, leaders must maintain that fidelity while making adaptations as unpredicted or unexpected changes occur.

When NIFDI and RF monitoring and supervising ended, Andrea and her team were prepared to take over full responsibility for program implementation. Three frameworks were established to ensure sustainability: (1) the formation of a district leadership team (DLT) that meets regularly on Wednesday afternoons to address implementation issues and make decisions to ensure consistency among buildings, (2) a plan for increased monitoring and supervision at the building level, and (3) the development and training of a district training cadre (DTC) to build instructional capacity in-house.

Formation of a District Leadership Team

To maintain cohesion and collaboratively deal with implementation, Andrea formed a district leadership team comprised of coaches and principals. Each Wednesday afternoon, the DLT meets to deal with issues like how to keep expectations for teachers and students high and how to make adjustments as more and more students reach the junior high at higher achievement levels. A recent activity was called "Rate Your Building." Andrea selected an aspect of DI instruction, and each coach and principal rated their building on a scale of 1 to 10 with 10 being the best. Then they wrote comments for what they felt they could be doing to improve areas of instruction that need work. Examples of items the team has evaluated include (a) how faithfully teachers and paraprofessionals correct 100% of the errors students make, (b) how rigorously the three-hour language arts block is protected and how faithfully teachers start on time and teach to the end of the block, and (c) how well the lessons are paced, with 12–18 responses per minute during word attack portions of lessons.

During another activity, the DLT selected three aspects of instruction to target for the week. Each principal–coach team then sent an e-mail to all teachers explaining that they would be out observing during the week looking for top-notch examples of teaching. At Week 4 of the school year, coaches and principals were asked to work together and develop a list of hot spots—teachers and paraprofessionals that required more frequent observation and possibly even some supervised or assisted practice sessions. Andrea wanted them to be sensitive to the fact that certain teachers require much more observation than others to make sure the program is taught with fidelity but that all teachers need affirmation and encouragement. They then revisited the list later in the fall to see if the list had changed or if improvements had been realized. Andrea said, "Principals sometimes forget that although some teachers require extra monitoring because they need extra help with certain instructional techniques, all teachers need be told specifically what their strengths are and how they are impacting their students! Sustaining an initiative like ours requires high levels of energy and motivation. We have to keep the best teachers affirmed."

Increased Monitoring and Supervision by the Building Leadership Team

Each Wednesday morning, Andrea makes the rounds of the elementary schools, meeting with the coach and principal to review the building data and discuss questions of placement and classroom monitoring and supervision. To ensure that principals and coaches maintain a strong visible presence in classrooms, measures to increase the frequency of classroom observations by members of the leadership have been instituted, and everyone on the DLT has committed to the following observation guidelines:

- *Reading Coaches.* Daily visits for hotspot classrooms (those in which teachers either need help or more intensive supervision) and weekly classroom visits for all other teachers
- *Principals.* Weekly visits for all classrooms and more frequent visits in hotspot classrooms
- *Andrea.* Monthly visits for all classrooms; weekly during the first month of school and more frequently in hotspot classrooms

Formation of a District Training Cadre

After NIFDI and RF, Gering has created its own cadre of trainers. Twelve individuals (11 teachers and one paraprofessional) were selected by the DLT based on their outstanding delivery of DI for a minimum of two years. They attended a weeklong Trainer of Teachers training by NIFDI in Eugene, Oregon, as well as additional training in Lincoln sponsored by RF. Their assignment has been to train new staff members and retrain weak or struggling staff needing improvement in the delivery of their lessons. The team trained its first group of teachers at the beginning of the 2008–2009 school year and was given release time later in the fall to observe the teachers they had trained. They then provided each teacher with written comments regarding their strengths and weaknesses. The team has also provided DI training for other districts in Nebraska.

Superintendent Hague is four years away from retirement. He is committed to staying in Gering until the current seventh-grade class graduates from high school. He explains, "I want to see the ACT scores of that class. They had four years of DI before they went to junior high school, and I'm expecting great things from them— ACT scores at least in the 25–26 range. We're now at the national average of about 20–21. But when this group gets to high school, our secondary teachers will have to ratchet up their expectations and curriculum to keep pace with them. The teachers can't use that old excuse of the kids not being able to read the textbooks anymore." In Gering, they are teaching them *all* to read.

■ SUMMARIZING CHAPTER 9

We need to learn to set our course by the stars, not by the lights of every passing ship.

—Omar Bradley

Anna White Crane Walking, an Oglala Sioux Indian, has three children in the Gering School District—Brandon at the middle school and Brianne (sixth grade) and Laura (third grade) at Northfield. When Brandon enrolled in kindergarten, he hardly spoke a word. He was extremely shy and failed to respond at all to the general education curriculum. No one really knew the potential behind his wide eyes and sober expression. Brandon was tested for special education eligibility and verified with a moderate mental handicap. He was placed into a self-contained special education classroom for all of his academic instruction. His sister, Brianne, enrolled the next year and was as shy and unresponsive as her brother. She followed Brandon into the self-contained classroom.

Jadie Beam, then a special education teacher at Northfield, did not buy the conventional wisdom about Brandon and Brianne's abilities, and so when DI came to Gering, they were placed in *Language for Learning* and *Reading Mastery I.* We cannot know what aspect of DI drew language out of the White Crane Walking children. Perhaps it was the choral responding when their voices were joined with those of their peers. However, Brandon and Brianne bloomed like roses in the summer sunshine. They learned to read and write and spell. They began to talk to their teachers and classmates.

Anna White Crane Walking will be forever grateful to the educators in Gering. In a letter of appreciation to the staff at Northfield School, she wrote, "You have taught my kids to read. You have given them a great gift." Brandon left Northfield Elementary as a sixth grader reading at benchmark, and Brianne is reading at grade level in sixth grade at Northfield Elementary. Younger sister Laura has been diagnosed with autism, but Brandon and Brianne read aloud to her every day, and she is blossoming. Anna said that doctors were very pessimistic about Laura ever learning to walk after she underwent heart surgery as an infant, but today she is an active third grader who enjoys school.

Anna has high praise for the educators at Northfield, especially principal Pam Barker. "Whenever I go into the school, I am greeted with a smile. It makes me feel so relaxed, like I am part of a family. Mrs. Barker is a role model for her staff and students." The educators in Gering have established a pervasive and persuasive reading culture that is also warm, caring, and empathetic.

In Gering, there are no more excuses for why students can't read. Gering's administrators, reading coaches, and teachers are teaching all of their students to read, write, spell, think, and engage in dialogue with their teachers and peers. They are raising the achievement bar and closing the achievement gap. These committed individuals have something to teach us all: *We can, whenever and wherever we choose, successfully teach all children to read. We already know more than we need to do that. Whether or not we do it must finally depend on how we feel about the fact that we haven't so far* (adapted from Edmonds, 1981, p. 53). Use the following questions to reflect on your feelings about the current state of literacy in your classroom, district, or school and plan to take the first step to teach them all to read.

1. Do I have any beliefs that may be standing in the way of my students achieving literacy? Are there any paradigms that I need to shift?

2. Am I doing all that I can in my classroom, school, or district to ensure that all students reach expected or higher levels of literacy?

3. Am I conversant with the critical components of the reading puzzle that need to be in place to achieve the goal of teaching them all to read?

4. In what ways can I enhance my leadership skills to advance the goal of teaching them all to read?

I wish you and your students the greatest success possible as you put all the reading puzzle pieces together, as shown in Figure 9.9.

Figure 9.9   The New Reading Puzzle

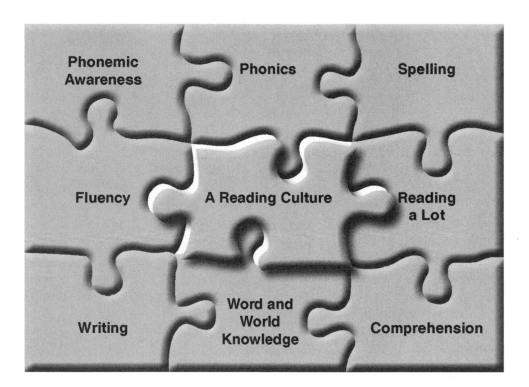

References

Abrams & Company. (2005). *Letter people®*. Waterbury, CT: Author.

ACT. (2000). *What reading and writing skills should college-bound students have? High school and college teachers disagree.* Retrieved April 27, 2009, from http://www.act.org/news/releases/2000/04-12-00.html.

Adams, C. (2001). *Benjamin Franklin: American inventor.* New York: Rosen.

Adams, G., & Brown, S. (2004). *The six-minute solution: A reading fluency program.* Longmont, CO: Sopris West.

Adams, G., & Carnine, D. (2003). Direct instruction. In H. L. Swanson, K. R. Harris, & S. Graham (Eds.), *Handbook of learning disabilities* (pp. 403–416). New York: Guilford.

Adams, G. L., & Engelmann, S. (1996). *Research on Direct Instruction: 25 years beyond DISTAR.* Portland, OR: Educational Achievement Systems.

Adams, M. J. (1990). *Beginning to read.* Cambridge: MIT Press.

Adams, M. J. (1991). A talk with Marilyn Adams. *Language Arts, 68,* 206–212.

Adams, M. J. (1998). The three-cueing system. In F. Lehr & J. Osborn (Eds.), *Literacy for all: Issues in teaching and learning* (pp. 73 –99). New York: Guilford.

Adams, M.J. (2006). The promise of automatic speech recognition for fostering literacy growth in children and adults. In M. McKenna, L. Labbo, R. Kieffer, & D. Reinking (Eds.), *Handbook of literacy and technology* (Vol. 2, pp. 109–128). Hillsdale, NJ: LEA.

Adams, M. J. (2008). The limits of the self-teaching hypothesis. In S. B. Neuman (Ed.), *Educating the other America: Top experts tackle poverty, literacy and achievement in our schools* (pp. 277–300). Baltimore: Paul H. Brookes.

Adams, M. J., & Bereiter, C. (2002). *Open court.* New York: SRA/McGraw-Hill.

Adler, M. A., & Fisher, C. W. (2001). Early reading programs in high poverty schools. *The Reading Teacher, 54*(6), 616–619.

Adler, M. J., & Van Doren, C. (1972). *How to read a book.* New York: Simon & Schuster.

Advantage Learning Systems. (2001). *Accelerated reader.* Wisconsin Rapids, WI: Author.

Afflerbach, P. (1990). The influence of prior knowledge on expert readers' main idea strategies. *Reading Research Quarterly, 25,* 31–46.

Allington, R. L. (1977). If they don't read much, how they ever gonna get good? *Journal of Reading, 21,* 57–61.

Allington, R. L. (1980). Poor readers don't get to read much in reading groups. *Language Arts, 57*(8), 872–876.

Allington, R. L. (1983). Fluency: The neglected goal. *The Reading Teacher, 36,* 556–561.

Allington, R. L. (1984). Content coverage and contextual reading in reading groups. *Journal of Reading Behavior, 16,* 85–96.

Allington, R. L. (1985, February). *What is remedial reading? A descriptive study.* Paper presented at the annual meeting of the Colorado Council of the International Reading Association, Denver, CO.

Allington, R. L. (2001). *What really matters for struggling readers.* New York: Longman.

Allington, R. L. (2006a). Critical factors in designing an effective reading intervention for struggling readers. In C. Cummins (Ed.), *Understanding and implementing Reading First initiatives: The changing role of administrators* (pp. 127–138). Newark, DE: International Reading Association.

Allington, R. L. (2006b). Fluency: Still waiting after all these years. In S. J. Samuels & A. E. Farstrup (Eds.), *What research has to say about fluency instruction* (pp. 94–105). Newark, DE: International Reading Association.

Allington, R. L., & McGill-Franzen, A. (1989). School response to reading failure: Chapter 1 and special education students in grades 2, 4, and 8. *Elementary School Journal, 89,* 529–542.

Allred, R. (1977). *Spelling: The application of research findings.* Washington, DC: National Education Association.

Alvermann, D. E. (2003). *Seeing themselves as capable and engaged readers: Adolescents and re/mediated instruction.* Naperville, IL: North Central Regional Educational Laboratory.

Alvermann, D. E., & Phelps, S. F. (1998). *Content reading and literacy: Succeeding in today's diverse classrooms.* Needham Heights, MA: Allyn & Bacon.

Ambrose, S. (1994). *D-Day: June 6, 1944: The climactic battle of World War II.* New York: Simon & Schuster.

American Institutes for Research. (2008). *Reading First state annual performance report: 2003-2007.* Washington, DC: U.S. Department of Education, Office of Elementary and Secondary Education.

Anderson, B. (1981). The missing ingredient: Fluent oral reading. *The Elementary School Journal, 81,* 173–177.

Anderson, R. C., & Nagy, W. E. (1992). The vocabulary conundrum. *American Educator, 16,* 14–18, 44–47.

Anderson, R. C., & Pearson, P. D. (1984). A schema-theoretic view of basic processes in reading. In P. D. Pearson (Ed.), *Handbook of reading research* (pp. 255–292). White Plains, NY: Longman.

Anderson, R. C., Wilson, P. T., & Fielding, L. G. (1988). Growth in reading and how children spend their time outside of school. *Reading Research Quarterly, 23,* 285–303.

Apel, K. (2007, March 20). *Word study: Using a five-block approach to improving literacy skills.* Presentation to the Texas School Health Association, Austin, TX.

Apel, K. (2008, February). *Word study and the speech-language pathologist: Using a five-block approach to improving literacy skills.* Presentation to the annual conference of the South Carolina Speech-Language-Hearing Association, North Charleston, SC.

Apel, K., & Masterson, J. (2001). Theory-guided spelling assessment and intervention. *Language, Speech and Hearing Services in Schools, 32,* 182–195.

Apel, K., Masterson, J., & Hart, P. (2004). Integration of language components in spelling: Instruction that maximizes students' learning. In L. C. Wilkinson & E. R. Silliman (Eds.), *Language and literacy learning in schools: Collaboration between speech-language pathologists and classroom teachers* (pp. 292–315). New York: Guilford.

Apel, K., Masterson, J. J., & Niessen, N. L. (2004). Spelling assessment frameworks. In A. Stone, E. R. Silliman, & L. C. Wilkinson (Eds.), *Language and literacy learning in schools* (pp. 292–315). New York: Guilford.

Armbruster, B. B., Anderson, T. H., & Ostertag, J. (1987). Does text structure/summarization instruction facilitate learning from expository text? *Reading Research Quarterly, 22,* 331–346.

Armbruster, B., Lehr, F., & Osborn, J. (2001). *Put reading first: The research building blocks for teaching children to read.* Washington, DC: Partnership for Reading.

Atwell, N. (1998). *In the middle: New understandings about writing, reading and learning.* Portsmouth, NH: Heinemann.

Atwood, M. (2003). *Negotiating with the dead: A writer on writing.* New York: Anchor.

Auster, P. (2006). *The Brooklyn follies.* New York: Picador.

Avi. (1992). *The true confessions of Charlotte Doyle.* New York: HarperCollins.

Baddeley, A. (1997). *Human memory: Theory and practice.* East Sussex, UK: Psychology Press.

Baddeley, A., & Logie, R. H. (1999). Working memory: The multiple-component model. In A. Miyake & P. Shah (Eds.), *Models of working memory: Mechanisms of active maintenance and executive control* (pp. 2–61). Cambridge, UK: Cambridge University Press.

Baker, L. (2002). Metacognition in comprehension instruction. In C. C. Block & M. Pressley (Eds.), *Comprehension instruction: Research-based best practices* (pp. 77–95). New York: Guilford.

Ball, E. W., & Blachman, B. A. (1991). Does phoneme awareness training in kindergarten make a difference in early word recognition and developmental spelling? *Reading Research Quarterly, 24*(1), 49–66.

Bangert-Drowns, R. L., Hurley, M. M., & Wilkinson, B. (2004). The effects of school-based writing-to-learn interventions on academic achievement: A meta-analysis. *Review of Educational Research, 74*(1), 29–58.

Bear, D., Invernizzi, M., Templeton, S., & Johnston, F. (2000). *Words their way: Word study for phonics, spelling, and vocabulary development* (2nd ed.). Upper Saddle River, NJ: Merrill/Prentice Hall.

Beatty, J. (2001). *The human brain: Essentials of behavioral neuroscience.* Thousand Oaks, CA: Sage.

Beck, I. L., Farr, R., & Strickland, D. (2003). *Trophies.* New York: Harcourt.

Beck, I. L., McKeown, M. G., Hamilton, R. L., & Kucan, L. (1997). *Questioning the author: An approach for enhancing student engagement with text.* Newark, DE: International Reading Association.

Beck, I. L., McKeown, M. G., & Kucan, L. (2002). *Bringing words to life: Robust vocabulary instruction.* New York: Guilford.

Becker, W. C. (1977). Teaching reading and language to the disadvantaged—what we have learned from field research. *Harvard Educational Review, 47,* 518–543.

Becker, W. C., & Engelmann, S. (1983). *Reading Mastery.* Chicago: SRA/McGraw-Hill.

Bereiter, C., & Scardamalia, M. (1987). *The psychology of written composition.* Hillsdale, NJ: Erlbaum.

Berkowitz, S. J. (1986). Effects of instruction in text organization on sixth-grade students' memory for expository reading. *Reading Research Quarterly, 21,* 161–178.

Berliner, D. C. (1981). Academic learning time and reading achievement. In J. Guthrie (Ed.), *Comprehension and teaching: Research reviews* (pp. 203–225). Newark, DE: International Reading Association.

Berliner, D. C. (1986). In pursuit of the expert pedagogue. *Educational Researcher, 15*(7), 5–13.

Bernard, R. (2000). *The life of a butterfly.* New York: Scholastic.

Berninger, V. W. (1999). Coordinating transcription and text generation in working memory during composing: Automatic and constructive processes. *Learning Disability Quarterly, 22*(2), 99–112.

Berninger, V. W., & Amtman, D. (2003). Preventing written expression disabilities through early and continuing assessment and intervention for handwriting and/or spelling problems: Research into practice. In H. L. Swanson, K. R. Harris, & S. Graham (Eds.), *Handbook of learning disabilities* (pp. 345–363). New York: Guilford.

Berninger, V. W., Vaughan, K., Abbott, R. D., Begay, K., Coleman, K., Byrd, K., Curtin, G., Hawkins, J. M., & Graham, S. (2002). Teaching spelling and composition alone and together. Implications for the simple view of writing. *Journal of Educational Psychology, 94,* 291–304.

Berninger, V. W., Vaughan, K. B., Graham, S., Abbott, R. D., Abbott, S. P., Rogan, L. W., Brooks, A., & Reed, E. (1997). Treatment of handwriting problems in beginning writers: Transfer from handwriting to composition. *Journal of Educational Psychology, 89,* 652–666.

Biancarosa, G., & Snow, C. E. (2004). *Reading next—A vision for action and research in middle and high school literacy: A report to Carnegie Corporation of New York.* Retrieved April 27, 2009, from http://www.all4ed.org/publications/ReadingNext.

Biemiller, A. (1999). *Language and reading success.* Cambridge, MA: Brookline.

Blachowicz, C. L. Z., Fisher, P. J. L., Ogle, D., & Watts-Taffe, S. (2006). Vocabulary: Questions from the classroom. *Reading Research Quarterly, 41*(4), 524–539.

Bloom, B. S. (1980). The new direction in educational research: Alterable variables. *Phi Delta Kappan, 61,* 382–385.

Boden, A. (2008, October 6). *A district's success story: What it takes to improve achievement and close the gap.* Presentation to the Fifth Annual Hispanic/Latino Education Summit, Nebraska Department of Education, and the Mexican-American Commission, Omaha-LaVista, NE.

Borduin, B. J., Borduin, C. M., & Manley, C. M. (1994). The use of imagery training to improve reading comprehension of second graders. *Journal of Genetic Psychology, 155*(1), 115–118.

Borokowski, J. G., & Muthukrishna, N. (1992). Moving metacognition into the classroom: "Working models" and effective strategy teaching. In M. Pressley, K. R. Harris, & J. T. Guthrie (Eds.), *Promoting academic competence and literacy in school* (pp. 477–501). San Diego, CA: Academic Press.

Bosman, A. M. T., & Van Ordern, G. C. (1997). Why spelling is more difficult than reading. In C. A. Perfetti L. Riegen, & M. Fayol (Eds.), *Learning to spell: Research, theory, and practice across languages* (pp. 173–194). Mahwah, NJ: Lawrence Erlbaum.

Boudett, K. P., City, E. A., & Murnane, R. J. (Eds.). (2005). *Data wise: A step-by-step guide to using assessment results to improve teaching and learning.* Cambridge, MA: Harvard Education Press.

Bradley, L., & Bryant, P. (1983). *Rhyme and reason in reading and spelling.* Ann Arbor: University of Michigan Press.

Bransford, J. D., Brown, A. L., & Cocking, R. R. (Eds.). (2000). *How people learn: Brain, mind, experience and school.* Washington, DC: National Academy Press.

Brenner, D., Tompkins, R., Hiebert, E., Riley, M., & Miles, R. (2007, May). *Eyes on the page: A large-scale intervention to increase time spent reading accessible texts.* Paper presented to the 2007 International Reading Association Annual Convention, Toronto, Ontario, Canada.

Brown, A. L., & Campione, J. C. (1994). Guided discovery in a community of learners. In K. McGilly (Ed.), *Classroom lessons: Integrating cognitive theory and classroom practice* (pp. 229–270). Cambridge: MIT Press.

Brown, A. L., & Day, J. D. (1983). Macrorules for summarizing texts: The development of expertise. *Journal of Verbal Learning and Verbal Behavior, 22,* 1–14.

Brown, A. L., Day, J. D., & Jones, R. S. (1983). The development of plans for summarizing texts. *Child Development, 54,* 968–979.

Brown, I. S., & Felton, R. H. (1990). Effects of instruction on beginning reading skills in children at risk for reading disability. *Reading and Writing: An Interdisciplinary Journal, 2,* 223–241.

Brozo, W. G. (2008, May). *Lessons learned about engagement in reading from the Program for International Student Assessment (PISA).* Presentation to the annual convention of the International Reading Association, Atlanta, GA.

Bryant, P., & Bradley, L. (1985). *Children's reading problems: Psychology and education.* Oxford, UK: Basil Blackwell.

Burnett, F. H. (1911/1998). *The secret garden.* New York: HarperTrophy.

Bursuck, W. D., & Damer, M. (2007). *Reading instruction for students who are at risk or have disabilities.* New York: Pearson.

Byrne, B., & Fielding-Barnsley, R. (1989). Phonemic awareness and letter knowledge in the child's acquisition of the alphabetic principle. *Journal of Educational Psychology, 81,* 313–321.

Calfee, R. C., & Piontkowski, D. C. (1981). The reading diary: Acquisition of decoding. *Reading Research Quarterly, 16,* 346–373.

Carbo, M. (1988). Debunking the great phonics myth. *Phi Delta Kappan, 70,* 226–240.

Carbo, M. (1996). Whole language or phonics? Use both. *Education Digest, 61,* 60–64.

Carle, E. (1981). *The very hungry caterpillar.* New York: Philomel.

Carnine, D. W., Crawford, D., Harness, M., & Hollenback, K. (1996). *Understanding U.S. history: Through 1914.* Eugene, OR: Considerate Publishing.

Carnine, D. W., Silbert, J., Kame'enui, E. J., & Tarver, S. G. (2004). *Direct instruction reading* (4th ed.). Upper Saddle River, NJ: Prentice Hall.

Carroll, J. B., Davies, P., & Richman, B. (1971). *Word frequency book.* Boston: Houghton Mifflin.

Cecil, N. L. (1995). *The art of inquiry: Questioning strategies for K–6 classrooms.* Winnipeg, Manitoba, Canada: Peguis.

Century, J. R., & Levy, A. J. (2002, April 3). *Sustaining change: A study of nine school districts with enduring programs.* Paper presented at the annual meeting of the American Educational Research Association, New Orleans, LA.

Chall, J. S. (1983). *Learning to read: The great debate.* New York: McGraw-Hill. (Original work published 1967)

Chall, J. S. (1989). Learning to read: The great debate 20 years later—A response to "Debunking the Great Phonics Myth." *Phi Delta Kappan, 70,* 521–537.

Chall, J. S., & Dale, E. (1995). *Readability revisited: The new Dale-Chall Readability Formula.* Cambridge, MA: Brookline.

Chall, J. S., Jacobs, V. A., & Baldwin, L. E. (1990). *The reading crisis: Why poor children fall behind.* Cambridge, MA: Harvard University Press.

Chenoweth, K. (2007). *It's being done: Academic success in unexpected schools.* Cambridge, MA: Harvard University Press.

Ciofalo, J. F., & Wylie, E. C. (2006, January 10). Using diagnostic assessment: One question at a time. *Teachers College Record.* Retrieved April 4, 2008, from http://www.tcrecord.org. ID Number: 12285.

Cleary, B. (1965). *The mouse and the motorcycle.* New York: William Morrow.

Cohen, J., (1977). *Statistical power analysis for the behavioral sciences* (2nd ed.). Hillsdale, NJ: Erlbaum.

Coiro, J., & Dobler, E. (2007). Exploring the online reading comprehension strategies used by sixth-grade skilled readers to search for and locate information on the Internet. *Reading Research Quarterly, 42*(2), 214–257.

Coleman, J. S., Campbell, E., Hobson, C., McPartland, J., Mood, A., Weinfeld, F., & York, R. (1966). *Equality of educational opportunity.* Washington, DC: National Center for Education Statistics.

Coles, G. S. (1997, April 2). Phonics findings discounted as part of flawed research [Letter to the editor]. *Education Week,* 45.

Coles, G. S. (2000a). *A reply to Louise Spear-Swerling's review of Misreading Reading: The Bad Science That Hurts Children.* Retrieved March 20, 2001, from http://www.educationweek .org.

Coles, G. S. (2000b). *Misreading reading: The bad science that hurts children.* Portsmouth, NH: Heinemann.

Collier, J. L. (1984). *My brother Sam is dead.* New York: Simon & Schuster.

Collins, A. (1991). Cognitive apprenticeship and instructional technology. In L. Idol & B. F. Jones (Eds.), *Educational values and cognitive instruction: Implication for reform* (pp. 121–138). Hillsdale, NJ: Lawrence Erlbaum.

Collins, A., Brown, J. S., & Holum, A. (1991). Cognitive apprenticeship: Making thinking visible. *American Educator, 15,* 6–11, 38–41.

Collins, A., Brown, J. S., & Newman, S. E. (1990). Cognitive apprenticeship: Teaching the crafts of reading, writing, and mathematics. In L. Resnick (Ed.), *Knowing learning and instruction: Essay in honor of Robert Glaser* (pp. 453–494). Hillsdale, NJ: Erlbaum.

Collins, J. (1998). *Strategies for struggling writers.* New York: Guilford.

Collins, J., Lee, J., Fox, J., & Madigan, T. (2008). *When writing serves reading: Randomized trials of writing intensive reading comprehension (WIRC) in low-performing urban elementary schools.* Unpublished manuscript. State University of New York, Buffalo.

Collins, J., Madigan, T., & Lee, J. (2008). *Using thinksheets to improve higher-level literacy.* Unpublished manuscript. State University of New York, Buffalo.

Connor, C. M., Morrison, F. J., Fishman, B. J., Schatschneider, C., & Underwood, P. (2007). Algorithm-guided individualized reading instruction. *Science, 315*(5811), 464–465.

Connor, C. M., Morrison, F. J., & Katch, L. E. (2004). Beyond the reading wars: Exploring the effect of child-instruction interactions on growth in early reading. *Scientific Studies of Reading, 8*(4), 305–336.

Connor, C. M., Morrison, F., & Petrella, J. N. (2004). Effective reading comprehension instruction: Examining child x instruction interactions. *Journal of Educational Psychology, 96*(4), 682–698.

Connor, C. M., Morrison, F., & Slominski, L. (2006). Preschool instruction and children's literacy skill growth. *Journal of Educational Psychology, 98*(4), 665–689.

Connor, C. M., Schatschneider, C., Fishman, B., & Morrison, F. J. (2008, June). *Individualizing student literacy instruction: Exploring causal implications of child x instruction interactions.* Paper presented to the Institute for Education Sciences, Washington, DC.

Cook, S. A., & Page, C. A. (1994). *Books, battles & bees.* Chicago: American Library Association.

Covey, S. R. (2004). *The 8th habit: From effectiveness to greatness.* New York: Free Press.

Coxhead, A. (2000). A new academic word list. *TESOL Quarterly, 34,* 213–238.

Coyne, M. D., Simmons, D. C., & Kame'enui, E. J. (2004). Vocabulary instruction for young children at-risk of experiencing reading difficulties. Teaching word meanings during shared storybook reading. In J. F. Baumann & E. J. Kame'enui (Eds.), *Vocabulary instruction: Research in practice* (pp. 41–58). New York: Guilford.

Craik, F. I. M., & Tulving, E. (1975). Depth of processing and the retention of words in episodic memory. *Journal of Experimental Psychology: General, 104,* 268–294.

Crane, S. (1895/2004). *The red badge of courage.* New York: Dover.

Crawford, E., & Torgesen, J. K. (2007). *Teaching all students to read: Practices from Reading First schools with strong intervention outcomes.* Tallahassee, FL: Florida Center for Reading Research.

Crystal, D. (2007). *How language works: How babies babble, words change meaning, and languages live or die.* New York: Avery.

Culham, R. (2005). *6 + 1 traits of writing: The complete guide to the primary grades.* Portland, OR: Northwest Regional Education Lab.

Cunningham, A. E. (1990). Explicit versus implicit instruction in phonemic awareness. *Journal of Experimental Child Psychology, 50,* 429–444.

Cunningham, A. E. (2005, June). *The developmental benefits of increasing students' reading volume.* Presentation to the Summer Institute in Reading, University of California, Berkeley.

Cunningham, A. E., & Stanovich, K. E. (1998). What reading does for the mind. *American Educator, 22*(1-2), 8–15.

Cunningham, P. M., & Hall, J. W. (2001). *Four blocks literacy model®.* Greensboro, NC: Carson-Dellosa.

Datrow, A., Park, V., & Wohlstetter, P. (2007). *Achieving with data: How high-performing school systems use data to improve instruction for elementary students.* Los Angeles: University of Southern California, Center on Educational Governance.

Davey, B. (1983). Think-aloud: Modeling the cognitive process of reading comprehension. *Journal of Reading, 26,* 44–47.

Davidson, M. (2000). *Intervention manual in reading: Research based instructional strategies to accompany the Reading Screening Test (RST).* Bellingham, WA: Western Washington University, Applied Research and Development Center.

Delpit, L. (1995). *Other people's children: Cultural conflict in the classroom.* New York: New Press.

Denton, C., Foorman, B. R., & Mathes, P. G. (2003). Schools that 'beat the odds": Implications for reading instruction. *Remedial and Special Education, 24,* 258–261.

Dickinson, D. K., & Tabors, P. O. (Eds.) (2001). *Beginning literacy with language: Young children learning at home and school.* Baltimore: Brookes.

Dickson, S. V., Collins, V. L., Simmons, D. C., & Kame'enui, E. J. (1998). Metacognitive strategies: Instructional and curricular basics and implications. In D. C. Simmons & E. J. Kame'enui (Eds.), *What reading research tells us about children with diverse learning needs* (pp. 361–380). Hillsdale, NJ: Erlbaum.

Dillon, J. T. (1988). *Questioning and teaching: A manual of practice.* New York: Teachers College Press.

Dixon, R., Carnine, D., & Kame'enui, E. (1992). *Curriculum guidelines for diverse learners* (Monograph for National Center to Improve the Tools of Educators). Eugene: University of Oregon.

Dixon, R., & Engelmann, S. (2007). *Spelling mastery.* New York: SRA/McGraw-Hill.

Dobberteen, C. (2000). *Application for Title I Distinguished School.* Unpublished document. La Mesa, CA: La Mesa Dale Elementary School.

Dobberteen, C. (2001). *Second Annual Chase Change Award: Essay.* Unpublished document. La Mesa, CA: La Mesa Dale Elementary School.

Dole, J. (2000). Explicit and implicit instruction in comprehension. In B. M. Taylor, M. F. Graves, & P. van den Broek (Eds.), *Reading for meaning: Fostering comprehension in the middle grades* (pp. 52–69). New York: Teachers College Press.

Donahue, P., Voelkl, K., Campbell, J., & Mazzeo, J. (1999). *NAEP 1998 reading report card for the nation and states.* Washington, DC: U.S. Department of Education, Office of Educational

Research and Improvement. Retrieved April 5, 2000, from http://nces.ed.gov/pubs99/quarterlyapr/4-elementary/4-esq11-a.html.

Dowhower, S. L. (1989). Repeated reading: Research into practice. *The Reading Teacher, 42*(7), 502–506.

Dreher, M. J. (1993). Reading to locate information: Societal and educational perspectives. *Contemporary Educational Psychology, 18,* 129–138.

Duffy, G. G. (2002). The case for direct explanation of strategies. In C. C. Block & M. Pressley (Eds.), *Comprehension instruction: Research-based best practices* (pp. 28–41). New York: Guilford.

Duffy, G. G., & Roehler, L. R. (1987). Teaching reading skills as strategies. *The Reading Teacher, 40,* 414–418.

Duffy, G. G., Roehler, L. R., Sivan, E., Rackliffe, G., Book, C., Meloth, M., Vavrus, L., Weselman, R., Putnam, J., & Basiri, D. (1987). The effects of explaining the reasoning associated with using reading strategies. *Reading Research Quarterly, 16,* 403–411.

Dunn, P. A. (1995). *Learning re-abled: The learning disabilities controversy and composition studies.* Portsmouth, NH: Heinemann-Boynton Cook.

Durkin, D. (1978–1979). What classroom observations reveal about reading comprehension instruction. *Reading Research Quarterly, 14*(4), 481–533.

Eccles, J. S., Wigfield, A., & Schiefele, U. (1998). Motivation to succeed. In N. Eisenberg (Ed.), *Handbook of child psychology: Volume 3—Social, emotional, and personality development* (5th ed.). New York: Wiley.

Edmonds, R. (1981). Making public schools effective. *Social Policy, 12,* 53–60.

Educational Research Service. (1998). *Reading at the middle and high school levels.* Arlington, VA: Author.

Ehri, L.C. (1980). Grapheme-phoneme knowledge is essential for learning to read words in English. In J. Metsala & L. Ehri (Eds.), *Word recognition in beginning reading* (pp. 3–40). Hillsdale, NJ: Erlbaum.

Ehri, L. C. (1983). A critique of five studies related to letter-name knowledge and learning to read words in English. In L. M. Gentile, M. L. Kamil, & J. Blanchard (Eds.), *Reading research: Advances in theory and practice* (Vol. 1, pp. 63–116). New York: Academic.

Ehri, L. C. (1991a). Development of the ability to read words. In R. Barr, J. Kamil, P. Mosenthal, & D. P. Pearson (Eds.), *Handbook of reading research* (Vol. II, pp. 383–417). New York: Longman.

Ehri, L. C. (1991b). Learning to read and spell words. In L. Rieben & C. A. Perfetti (Eds.), *Learning to read: Basic research and its implications* (pp. 57–73). Hillsdale, NJ: Lawrence Erlbaum.

Ehri, L. C. (1995). Teachers need to know how word reading processes develop to teach reading effectively to beginners. In C. N. Hedley, P. Antonacci, & M. Rabinowitz (Eds.), *Thinking and literacy: The mind at work* (pp. 167–188). Hillsdale, NJ: Erlbaum.

Ehri, L. C. (1997). Learning to read and learning to spell are one and the same, almost. In C. A. Perfetti, L. Rieben, & M. Fayoln (Eds.), *Learning to spell: Research, theory, and practice across languages* (pp. 237–269). Mahwah, NJ: Lawrence Erlbaum.

Ehri, L. C. (1998). Grapheme-phoneme knowledge is essential for learning to read words in English. In J. L. Metsala & L. C. Ehri (Eds.), *Word recognition in beginning literacy* (pp. 3–40). Hillsdale, NJ: Lawrence Erlbaum.

Ehri, L. C., Nunes, S. R., Stahl, S. A., & Willow, D. (2001). Systematic phonics instruction helps students learn to read: Evidence from the National Reading Panel's meta-analysis. *Review of Educational Research, 71*(3), 393–447.

Ehri, L. C., & Rosenthal, J. (2007). Spellings of words: A neglected facilitator of vocabulary. *Journal of Literary Research, 39*(4), 389–409.

Ehri, L. C., & Wilce, L. S. (1987). Does learning to spell help beginners learn to read words? *Reading Research Quarterly, 22,* 47–65.

Elley, W. B. (1999). *Raising literacy levels in third world countries: A method that works.* Culver City, CA: Language Education Associates.

Elmore, R. (2003). *Knowing the right thing to do: School improvement and performance-based accountability.* Washington, DC: National Governors Association Center for Best Practices.

Engelmann, S. (1993). *Horizons.* New York: SRA/McGraw-Hill.

Engelmann, S. (various). *Reading mastery.* New York: SRA/McGraw-Hill.

Engelmann, S. (various). *Reasoning and writing.* New York: SRA/McGraw-Hill.

Engelmann, S., Hanner, S., & Johnson, S. (1999). *Corrective reading.* New York: McGraw-Hill.

Engelmann, S., & Osborn, J. (1999a). *Language for learning.* New York: SRA/McGraw-Hill.

Engelmann, S., & Osborn, J. (1999b). *Language for thinking.* New York: SRA/McGraw-Hill.

Engelmann, S., & Osborn, J. (2006). *Language for writing.* New York: SRA/McGraw-Hill.

Engelmann, S., & Silbert, J. (1993). *Expressive writing.* New York: SRA/McGraw-Hill.

Engle, R. W., Cantor, J., & Carullo, J. J. (1992). Individual differences in working memory and comprehension: A test of four hypotheses. *Journal of Experimental Psychology: Learning Memory, and Cognition, 18*(3), 972–992.

Engle, R. W., Kane, M. J., & Tuholski, S. W. (1999). Individual differences in working memory capacity and what they tell us about controlled attention, general fluid intelligence, and functions of the prefrontal cortex. In A. Miyake & P. Shah (Eds.), *Models of working memory: Mechanisms of active maintenance and executive control* (pp. 102–134). Cambridge, UK: Cambridge University Press.

Engle, R. W., Tuholski, S. W., Laughlin, J. E., & Conway, R. A. (1999). Working memory, short-term memory, and general fluid intelligence: A latent-variable approach. *Journal of Experimental Psychology: General, 128*(3), 309–311.

Englert, C. A. (1995). Teaching written language skills. In P. Cigilka & W. Berdine (Eds.), *Effective instruction for students with learning difficulties* (pp. 302–343). Boston: Allyn & Bacon.

English, F. (1992). *Deciding what to teach and test: Developing, aligning, and auditing the curriculum.* Thousand Oaks, CA: Corwin.

Farr, R. (1993). Writing in response to reading: A process approach to literary assessment. In B. E. Cullinan (Ed.), *Pen in hand: Children become writers* (pp. 64–79). Newark, DE: International Reading Association.

Faulkner, H. J., & Levy, B. A. (1999). How text difficulty and reader skill interact to produce differential reliance on word and content overlap in reading transfer. *Journal of Experimental Child Psychology, 58*, 1–24.

Feller, B. (2006, July 3). Mindless reading seen as fundamental. *Seattle Post Intelligence.* Retrieved July 4, 2006, from http://seattlepi.nwsource.com/national/1501AP_Zoning_Out.html.

Ferris, J. (2004). *Once upon a marigold.* Orlando, FL: Harcourt.

Fielding, L., Kerr, N., & Rosier, P. (2004). *Delivering on the promise of the 95% reading and math goals.* Kennewick, WA: New Foundation Press.

Fielding, L., Kerr, N., & Rosier, P. (2007). *Annual growth for all students. Catch-up growth for those who are behind.* Kennewick, WA: New Foundation Press.

Fielding, L., & Pearson, P. D. (1994). Reading comprehension: What works. *Educational Leadership, 51*(5), 62–68.

Fisher, C. W., & Berliner, D. C. (1985). *Perspectives on instructional time.* New York: Longman.

Fitzgerald, J., & Shanahan, T. (2000). Reading and writing relations and their development. *Educational Psychologist, 35*(1), 39–50.

Fletcher, J. M., Foorman, B. R., Boudousquie, A., Barnes, M., Schatschneider, C., & Francis, D. J. (2002). Assessment of reading and learning disabilities: A research-based, treatment-oriented approach. *Journal of School Psychology, 40*, 27–63.

Flood, J., Medearis, A. S., Hasbrouck, J. E., Paris, S., Hoffman, J. V., Stahl, S., Lapp, D., Finajero, J. V., & Wood, K. D. (2001). *Macmillan/McGraw-Hill reading program.* New York: Macmillan/McGraw-Hill.

Florida Center for Reading Research. (2008). *Program reviews.* Retrieved December 4, 2008, from http://www.fcrr.org.

Foorman, B. R. (1995). Research on the great debate: Code-oriented versus whole language approaches to reading instruction. *School Psychology Review, 24*(3), 376–392.

Foorman, B. R. (2007, May). *Text difficulty and assessment: The role of text in comprehending written language.* Presentation at the International Reading Association Meeting, Toronto, Canada.

Foorman, B. R., Fletcher, J. M., Francis, D. J., Schatschneider, C., & Mehta, P. (1998). The role of instruction in learning to read: Preventing reading failure in at-risk children. *Journal of Educational Psychology, 90*(1), 37–55.

Foorman, B. R., Francis, D. J., Davidson, K., Harm, M., & Griffin, J. (2004). Variability in text features in six grade 1 basal reading programs. *Scientific Studies in Reading, 8*(2), 167–197.

Foorman, B. R., & Moats, L. C. (2004). Conditions for sustaining research-based practices in early reading instruction. *Remedial and Special Education, 25*(1), 51–60.

Foorman, B. R., & Nixon, S. M. (2005, Fall). Curriculum integration in a multi-tiered instructional approach. *Perspectives* [Newsletter of The International Dyslexia Association], 27–28.

Forbes, E. H. (1944). *Johnny Tremain.* New York: Houghton Mifflin.

Fountas, I. C., & Pinnell, G. S. (1996). *Guided reading: Good first teaching for all children.* Portsmouth, NH: Heinemann.

Francis, D. J., Shaywitz, S. E., Stuebing, K. K., Shaywitz, B. A., & Fletcher, J. M. (1996). Developmental lag versus deficit models of reading disability: A longitudinal, individual growth curve analysis. *Journal of Educational Psychology, 88*(1), 3–17.

Fuchs, L. S., Fuchs, D., Hops, M. K., & Jenkins, J. R. (2001). Oral reading fluency as an indicator of reading competence: A theoretical, empirical, and historical analysis. *Scientific Studies of Reading, 5*(3), 239–245.

Fuchs, L., Fuchs, L., & Maxwell, L. (1988). The validity of informal reading comprehension measures. *Remedial and Special Education, 9*(2), 20–28.

Gardner, H. (1983). *Frames of mind: The theory of multiple intelligences.* New York: Basic Books.

Gaskins, I. W. (2005). *Success with struggling readers: The Benchmark School approach.* New York: Guilford.

Gaskins, I. W., & Elliot, T. T. (1991). *Implementing cognitive strategy instruction across the school: The Benchmark manual for teachers.* Cambridge, MA: Brookline.

Gaskins, I. W., Satlow, E., Hyson, D., Ostertag, J., & Six, L. (1994). Classroom talk about text: Learning in science class. *Journal of Reading, 3*(7), 558–565.

Gilbar, S. (Ed.). (1990). *The reader's quotation book: A literary companion.* Wainscott, NY: Pushcart.

Glickman, C. D. (1993). *Renewing America's schools: A guide for school-based action.* San Francisco: Jossey-Bass.

Goddard, R. D., Hoy, W. K., & Hoy, A. W. (2004). Collective efficacy beliefs: Theoretical developments, empirical evidence, and future directions. *Educational Researcher, 33*(3), 3–13.

Goldstein, R. (2002, October 14). Stephen Ambrose dies at 66. *The New York Times.* Retrieved April 3, 2003, from http://www.nytimes.com.

Good, R. H., & Kaminski, R. A. (Eds.). (2000). *Dynamic indicators of basic early literacy skills* (6th ed.). Longmont, CO: Sopris West.

Good, R. H., Kaminski, R. A., & Howe, D. (2005, June). *What data tell us about children and how to support their success.* Presentation at the Arizona Reading First Conference, Phoenix, AZ.

Good, R. H., III, Simmons, D. C., & Kame'enui, E. J. (2001). The importance and decision-making utility of a continuum of fluency-based indicators of foundational reading skills for third-grade high-stakes outcomes. *Scientific Studies of Reading, 5*(3), 257–288.

Goodlad, J. (1984). *A place called school: Prospects for the future.* New York: McGraw-Hill.

Goodman, K. (1986). *What's whole in whole language?* Richmond Hill, Ontario, Canada: Scholastic.

Goodman, K. (1996). *On reading.* Portsmouth, NH: Heinemann.

Goodwin, D. K. (1987). *The Fitzgeralds and the Kennedys: An American saga.* New York: Simon & Schuster.

Gough, P. B., Hoover, W. A., & Peterson, C. L. (1996). Some observations on a simple view of reading. In E. Cornoldi & J. Oakhill (Eds.), *Reading comprehension difficulties* (pp. 1–13). Mahwah, NJ: Lawrence Erlbaum.

Graham, S. (2000). Should the natural learning approach replace spelling instruction? *Journal of Educational Psychology, 92*, 235–247.

Graham, S., & Miller, L. (1979). Spelling research and practice: A unified approach. *Focus on Exceptional Children, 12*(2), 75–91.

Graham, S., & Perin, D. (2007). *Writing next: Effective strategies to improve writing of adolescents in middle and high schools.* New York: Alliance for Education.

Graves, M. F., Juel, C., & Graves, B. B. (2004). *Teaching reading in the 21st century* (3rd ed.). Boston: Allyn & Bacon.

Greenleaf, C. L., Jimenez, R. T., & Roller, C. M. (2002). Conversations: Reclaiming secondary reading interventions: From limited to rich conceptions, from narrow to broad conversations. *Reading Research Quarterly, 37,* 484–496.

Greene, J. E. (2004). *Language!® The comprehensive literacy curriculum.* Longmont, CO: Sopris West.

Gregorc, A. F. (1985). *Inside styles: Beyond the basics: Questions and answers on style.* Maynard, MA: Gabriel Systems.

Gunning, T. G. (1998). *Assessing and correcting reading and writing difficulties.* Boston: Allyn & Bacon.

Guthrie, J. T., & Davis, M. H. (2003). Motivating struggling readers in middle school through an engagement model of classroom practice. *Reading and Writing Quarterly, 19*(1), 59–86.

Guthrie, J. T., & Humenick, N. M. (2004). Motivating students to read: Evidence for classroom practices that increase motivation and achievement. In P. McCardle & V. Chhabra (Eds.), *The voice of evidence in reading research* (pp. 329–354). New York: Guilford.

Guthrie, J. T., & Kirsch, I. S. (1987). Distinctions between reading comprehension and locating information in text. *Journal of Educational Psychology, 79*(3), 220–227.

Hague, D. (2008, December). Gering public schools close the achievement gap with direct instruction. *NCSA Today* (pp. 7, 13). Retrieved January 9, 2009, from http://www.ncsa.org.

Haifiz, F., & Tudor, I. (1989). Extensive reading and the development of language skills. *English Language Teaching Journal, 43,* 4–11.

Hall, S. (2008). *Implementing response to intervention: A principal's guide.* Thousand Oaks, CA: Corwin.

Harp, S. F., & Mayer, R. E. (1997). The role of interest in learning from scientific text and illustrations: On the distinction between emotional interest and cognitive interest. *Journal of Educational Psychology, 89*(1), 92–102.

Harris, A. J., & Sipay, E. R. (1985). *How to increase reading ability: A guide to developmental and remedial methods.* New York: Longman.

Harris, T., & Hodges, R. (Eds.). (1995). *The literacy dictionary.* Newark, DE: International Reading Association.

Hart, B., & Risley, T. R. (1995). *Meaningful differences in the everyday experience of young American children.* Baltimore: Brookes.

Hasbrouck, J. E., & Tindal, G. (1992). Curriculum based oral reading fluency for students in grades 2 through 5. *Teaching Exceptional Children, 24*(3), 41–44.

Hatcher, P. J., Hulme, C., & Ellis, A. W. (1994). Ameliorating early reading failure by integrating the teaching of reading and phonological skills: The phonological linkage hypothesis. *Child Development, 65,* 41–57.

Hatcher, P. J., Hulme, C., & Snowling, M. J. (2004). Explicit phoneme training with phonic reading instruction helps youngsters at-risk. *Journal of Child Psychology and Psychiatry, 43,* 338–358.

Heckelman, R. G. (1969). A neurological-impress method of remedial reading instruction. *Academic Therapy, 4*(4), 277–282.

Hefflin, B. R., & Hartman, D. K. (2002). Using writing to improve comprehension: A review of the writing-to-reading research. In C. C. Block, L. B. Gambrell, & M. Pressley (Eds.), *Improving comprehension instruction: Rethinking research, theory, and classroom practice* (pp. 199–228). San Francisco: Jossey-Bass.

Herber, H. L., & Herber, J. N. (1993). *Teaching in content areas with reading, writing, and reasoning.* Boston: Allyn & Bacon.

Heward, W. L., & Dardig, J. C. (2001, Spring). What matters most in special education. *Education Connection,* 41–44.

Heward, W. L., Wood, C. L., & Damer, M. (May, 2004). *Faux fonics: A behavioral and instructional analysis of phonics activities that aren't.* Presentation to the 30th Annual Convention of the Association for Behavior Analysis, Boston, MA.

Hiebert, E. (2003). *QuickReads.* Parsipanny NJ: Pearson Learning Group.

Hiebert, E. (2006a). Becoming fluent: Repeated reading with scaffolded texts. In S. J. Samuels & A. E. Farstrup (Eds.), *What research has to say about fluency instruction* (pp. 204–222). Newark, DE: International Reading Association.

Hiebert, E. (2006b). *What's silent reading got to do with it?* Retrieved April 27, 2009, from http://www.textproject.org.

Hiebert, E. H. (2008a). The (mis)match between texts and students who depend on schools to become literate. In E. H. Hiebert & M. Sailors (Eds.), *Finding the right texts: What works for beginning and struggling readers* (pp. 1–22). New York: Guilford Publications.

Hiebert, E. H. (2008b). *Strategic vocabulary selection: Choosing words from narrative and informational texts.* Presentation to the annual conference of the International Reading Association, Atlanta, GA. Retrieved April 27, 2009, from http://www.textproject.org.

Hiebert, E. H., & Fisher, C. W. (2002, April). *Text matters in developing fluent reading.* Paper presented at the annual meeting of the International Reading Association, San Francisco, CA.

Hiebert, E. H., & Fisher, C. W. (2005). A review of the National Reading Panel's studies on fluency: On the role of text. *The Elementary School Journal, 105,* 443–460.

Hiebert, E. H., & Fisher, C. W. (2006). Fluency from the first: What works with first graders. In T. Rasinski, C. L. Z. Blachowicz, & K. Lems (Eds.), *Fluency instruction: Research-based best practices* (pp. 279–294). New York: Guilford.

Hiebert, E. H., & Martin, L. A. (2002). The texts of beginning reading instruction. In S. B. Neuman & D. K. Dickinson (Eds.), *Handbook of early literacy research* (pp. 361–376). New York: Guilford.

Hiebert, E. H., & Martin, L. A. (2003). *TExT (Text Elements by Task) software* (4th ed.). Santa Cruz, CA: TextProject.

High/Scope. (1992). *The child observation record* (COR). Ypsilanti, MI: Author.

Hillson, M., Jones, J. C., Moore, J. W., & Van Devender, F. (1964). A controlled experiment evaluating the effects of a non-graded organization on pupil achievement. *Journal of Educational Research, 57,* 548–550.

Himmelman, J. (2000). *A Monarch butterfly's life.* New York: Children's Press.

Hirsch, E. D., Jr. (Ed.). (1989). *A first dictionary of cultural literacy.* Boston: Houghton Mifflin.

Hirsch, E. D., Jr. (2003). Reading comprehension requires knowledge—of words and the world. *American Educator, 27*(2), 11–29, 44–45.

Hoffman, J. V., McCarthey, S. J., Abbott, J., Christian, C., Corman, L., Curry, C., Dressman, M., Elliott, B., Matherne, D., & Stahle, D. (1994). So what's new in the new basals? A focus on first grade. *Journal of Reading Behavior, 26,* 47–73.

Honig, B. (1996). *Teaching our children to read: The role of skills in a comprehensive reading program.* Thousand Oaks, CA: Corwin.

Hord, S. M. (1997). *Professional learning communities: Communities of continuous inquiry and improvement.* Austin, TX: Southwest Educational Laboratory.

Howell, K. W., Zucker, S. H., & Morehead, M. K. (1994). *The multilevel academic skills inventory.* Paradise Valley, AZ: H & Z.

Hunt, I. (1964). *Across five Aprils.* New York: Follett.

Ihnot, C. (1995). A plan to attack fluency problems. *Research/Practice, 3*(1). Minneapolis: University of Minnesota Center for Applied Research and Educational Improvement. Retrieved July 14, 2001, from http://carei.coled.umn.edu/Rpractice/Winter95/fluency .htm.

Individuals With Disabilities Education Improvement Act of 2004, P. L. 108-446 (2004).

Institute of Education Sciences. (2007). *Effectiveness of reading and mathematics software products.* Washington, DC: Author. Retrieved September 1, 2008, from http://ies .ed.gov/ncee/pubs/20074005/execsumm_first.asp.

Invernizzi, M., Sullivan, A., Meier, J., & Swank, L. (2004). *Phonological awareness literacy screening PreK (PALS-PreK).* Austin, TX: PRO-ED.

Iversen, S., & Tunmer, W. (1993). Phonological processing skills and the Reading Recovery program. *Journal of Educational Psychology, 8,* 112–126.

Jenkins, J. R., Fuchs, L. S., Espin, C., van den Broek, P., & Deno, S. L. (2000, February). *Effects of task format and performance dimension on word reading measures: Criterion validity, sensitivity to impairment, and context facilitation.* Paper presented at the Pacific Coast Research Conference, San Diego, CA.

Jenkins, J. R., Johnson, E., & Hileman, J. (2004). When is reading also writing: Sources of differences on the new reading performance assessments. *Scientific Studies of Reading, 8*(2), 125–151.

Johnson, D. D., Johnson, B. V. H., & Schlicting, K. (2004). Logology: Word and language play. In J. F. Baumann & E. J. Kame'enui (Eds.), *Vocabulary instruction: Research to practice* (pp. 179–200). New York: Guilford.

Johnson, D. W., & Johnson, R. T. (1989). *Leading the cooperative school.* Edina, MN: Interaction.

Jonassen, D. H. (2000). *Computers in the classroom: Mindtools for critical thinking.* Englewood Cliffs, NJ: Prentice Hall.

Jones, B. F., Pierce, J., & Hunter, B. (1988/1989). Teaching students to construct graphic representations. *Educational Leadership, 46*(4), 20–25.

Jones, J. C., Moore, J. W., & Van Devender, F. (1967). A comparison of pupil achievement after one and one-half and three years in a non-graded program. *Journal of Educational Research, 61,* 75–77.

Joyce, B., & Showers, B. (1995). *Student achievement through staff development.* New York: Longman.

Juel, C., & Minden-Cupp, C. (2000). Learning to read words: Linguistic units and instructional strategies. *Reading Research Quarterly, 35*(4), 458–492.

Juel, C., & Roper-Schneider, D. (1985). The influence of basal readers on first grade reading. *Reading Research Quarterly, 20,* 134–152.

Just, M. A., & Carpenter, P. A. (1987). *The psychology of reading and language comprehension.* Boston: Allyn & Bacon.

Kamberelis, G. (1998). Relations between children's literacy diets and genre development: You write what you read. *Literacy Teaching and Learning, 3,* 7–53.

Kamil, M., & Hiebert, E. H. (2005). The teaching and learning of vocabulary. In E. H. Hiebert & M. H. Kamil (Eds.), *Teaching and learning vocabulary* (pp. 1–23). Mahwah, NJ: Lawrence Erlbaum.

Karlsen, B., & Gardner, E. F. (1995). *Stanford diagnostic reading test* (4th ed.). San Antonio, TX: Psychological Corporation.

Keillor, G. (1985). *Lake Wobegon days.* New York: Viking.

Kelman, M. E., & Apel, K. (2004). Effects of a multiple linguistic and prescriptive approach to spelling instruction: A case study. *Communication Disorders Quarterly, 25*(2), 56–66.

Kibby, M. W. (1993). What reading teachers should know about reading proficiency in the U.S. *Journal of Reading, 27*(1), 48–51.

Kirkpatrick, D. D. (2002, April 9). Pulitzer Prizes and plagiarism. *The New York Times,* p. A22.

Klinger, J. K., Vaughn, S., Hughes, M. T., Schumm, J. S., & Elbaum, B. (1998). Outcomes for students with and without learning disabilities in inclusive classrooms. *Learning Disabilities Research & Practice, 13*(3), 153–161.

Kohl, H. (1998). *The discipline of hope: Learning from a lifetime of teaching.* New York: Harper & Row.

Konigsburg, E. (1996). *A view from Saturday.* New York: Scholastic.

Koskinen, P. S., & Blum, I. H. (1986). Paired repeated reading: A classroom strategy for developing fluent reading. *The Reading Teacher, 40*(1), 70–75.

Krashen, S. (1993). *The power of reading.* Englewood, CO: Libraries Unlimited.

Kroeber, T. (1973). *Ishi: Last of his tribe.* New York: Bantam.

Kuhn, M. R., & Stahl, S. A. (2003). Fluency: A review of developmental and remedial practices. *Journal of Educational Psychology, 95,* 3–21.

Kuhn, T. (1996). *The structure of scientific revolutions.* Chicago: University of Chicago Press. (Original work published in 1962)

Labbo, L. D., & Teale, W. H. (1990). Cross-age reading: A strategy for helping poor readers. *The Reading Teacher, 43,* 362–369.

Laing, E., & Hulme, C. (1999). Phonological and semantic processes influence beginning readers' ability to learn to read words. *Journal of Experimental Psychology, 73,* 183–207.

Learning First Alliance. (2000). *Every child reading: A professional development guide.* Washington, DC: Author.

Lenz, B. K. (2004, March). *Promoting literacy growth in grades 4–12: The content literacy curriculum.* Presentation to the University of Washington-Tacoma Adolescent Literacy Conference, Tacoma, WA.

Leslie, L., & Caldwell, J. (2005). *Qualitative reading inventory-4.* Boston: Pearson Allyn & Bacon.

Leu, D. J., Jr., Kinzer, C. K., Coiro, J., & Cammack, D. (2004). Toward a theory of new literacies emerging from the Internet and other information and communication technologies. In R. B. Ruddell & N. Unrau (Eds.), *Theoretical models and processes of reading* (5th ed., pp. 1568–1611). Newark, DE: International Reading Association.

Levine, M. D., Oberklaid, F., & Meltzer, L. (1981). Developmental output failure: A study of low productivity in school-aged children. *Pediatrics, 67*(1), 18–25.

Levy, B. A. (April, 1999). *Learning to read: Context doesn't matter.* Paper presented at the Society for the Scientific Study of Reading, Montreal, Canada.

Liberman, I.Y., & Shankweiler, D. (1985). Phonology and the problems of learning to read and write. *Remedial and Special Education, 6*(6), 8–17.

Liberman, I. Y., Shankweiler, D., & Liberman, A. M. (1989). The alphabetic principle and learning to read. In D. Shankweiler & I.Y. Liberman (Eds.), *Phonology and reading disability: Solving the reading puzzle* (pp. 1–33). Ann Arbor: University of Michigan Press.

Lie, A. (1991). Effects of a training program for stimulating skills in word analysis for first-grade children. *Reading Research Quarterly, 26*(3), 263–284.

Lightfoot, S. L. (1983). *The good high school.* New York: Basic Books.

Lindamood, C. H., & Lindamood, P. C. (1979). *Lindamood auditory conceptualization test.* Austin: TX: PRO-ED.

Lindamood, P. C., & Lindamood, P. (1998). *Lindamood phoneme sequencing program.* San Luis Obispo, CA: Gander.

Lionni, L. (1971). *Leo, the late bloomer.* New York: Windmill.

Lonigan, C. J., McDowell, K. D., & Phillips, B. M. (2004). *Standardized assessment of children's emergent literacy skills.* In B. Wasik (Ed.), *Handbook on family literacy: Research and services* (pp. 525–550). Mahwah, NJ: Lawrence Erlbaum Associates.

Lovitt, T. C., & Hansen, C. L. (1976). The contingent use of skipping and drilling to improve oral reading and comprehension. *Journal of Learning Disabilities, 9*(8), 486.

Luce, T., & Thompson, L. (2005). *Do what works.* Austin, TX: Ascent.

Lundberg, I., Frost, J., & Peterson, O. (1988). Effects of an extensive program for stimulating phonological awareness in pre-school children. *Reading Research Quarterly, 23,* 263–284.

Lyon, G. R. (1995). Towards a definition of dyslexia. *Annals of Dyslexia, 45,* 3–27.

Lyon, G. R. (1998, March). Why reading is not a natural process. *Educational Leadership, 55*(50), 14–18.

MacArthur, A., Graham, S., Haynes, J., & De La Paz, S. (1996). Spelling checkers and students with learning disabilities: Performance comparisons and impact on spelling. *Journal of Special Education, 30,* 35–57.

MacGinitie, W. H., MacGinitie, R. K., Maria, K., Dreyer, L. G., & Hughes, K. E. (2000). *Gates-MacGinitie reading tests* (GMRT-4). New York: Riverside.

Marshall, K. (2003, July 9). An Orwellian view: Misconceptions on the harsh impact of standards and tests [Letter to the editor]. *Education Week.* Retrieved April 4, 2008, from http://www.educationweek.org.

Martin, B., Jr. (1967). *Brown bear, brown bear, what do you see?* New York: Henry Holt.

Mason, B., & Krashen, S. (1997). Extensive reading in English as a foreign language. *System, 25,* 91–102.

Mason, J., Roehler, L. R., & Duffy, G. G. (1984). A practitioner's model of comprehension instruction. In G. G. Duffy, L. R. Roehler, & J. Mason (Eds.), *Comprehension instruction: Perspectives and suggestions* (pp. 299–314). New York: Longman.

Masterson, J. J., Apel, K., & Wasowicz, J. (2002). *SPELL-2: Spelling performance evaluation for language and literacy®* [Computer software]. Evanston, IL: Learning by Design.

Masterson, J. J., Black, B., Ellman, K., Greig, A., Mooney, R., & Wald, M. (2005, November). *Tailored reading-spelling instruction.* Presentation to the annual American Speech and Hearing Association convention, Atlanta, GA.

Mastropieri, M. A., & Scruggs, T. E. (1997). Best practices in promoting reading comprehension in students with learning disabilities. *Remedial and Special Education, 18,* 197–213.

Mathes, P. G., Denton, C. C., Fletcher, J. M., Anthony, J. L., Francis, D. J., & Schatschneider, C. (2005). The effects of theoretically different instruction and student characteristics on the skills of struggling readers. *Reading Research Quarterly, 40*(2), 148–182.

Mathes, P. G., & Torgesen, J. K. (1997). A call for equity in reading instruction for all students: A response to Allington and Woodside-Jiron. *Educational Researcher, 29*(6), 4–14.

McCarthy, B. (1997). A tale of four learners: 4MAT's learning styles. *Educational Leadership, 54*(6), 46.

McEwan, E. K. (1998). *The principal's guide to raising reading achievement.* Thousand Oaks, CA: Corwin.

McEwan, E. K. (2001). *Raising reading achievement in middle and high schools: Five simple-to-follow strategies for principals.* Thousand Oaks, CA: Corwin.

McEwan, E. K. (2002a). *Teach them ALL to read: Catching kids before they fall through the cracks.* Thousand Oaks, CA: Corwin.

McEwan, E. K. (2002b). *Ten traits of highly effective teachers.* Thousand Oaks, CA: Corwin.

McEwan, E. K. (2003). *Seven steps to effective instructional leadership* (2nd ed.). Thousand Oaks, CA: Corwin.

McEwan, E. K. (2004a). *How to deal with teachers who are angry, troubled, exhausted, or just plain confused.* Thousand Oaks, CA: Corwin.

McEwan, E. K. (2004b). *Teach them ALL to read* [Online seminar]. Oro Valley, AZ: McEwan-Adkins Group.

McEwan, E. K. (2006). *How to survive and thrive in the first three weeks of school.* Thousand Oaks, CA: Corwin.

McEwan, E. K. (2007). *Raising reading achievement in middle and high schools: Five simple-to-follow strategies* (2nd ed.). Thousand Oaks, CA: Corwin.

McEwan, E. K. (2009). *Ten traits of highly effective schools: Raising the achievement bar for all students.* Thousand Oaks, CA: Corwin.

McEwan, E. K., & Bresnahan, V. (2008). *Vocabulary: Grades 4–8.* Thousand Oaks, CA: Corwin.

McEwan, E. K., & Damer, M. (2000). *Managing unmanageable students: Practical solutions for administrators.* Thousand Oaks, CA: Corwin.

McEwan, E. K., & McEwan, P. J. (2003). *Making sense of research: What's good and what's not and how to tell the difference.* Thousand Oaks, CA: Corwin.

McGinley, W. J., & Denner, P. R. (1987). Story impressions: A pre-reading/writing activity. *Journal of Reading, 31,* 248–253.

McGuinness, C., & McGuinness, G. (1998). *Reading reflex.* New York: Simon & Schuster.

McKeown, M. G., Beck, I. L., Omanson, R. C., & Pople, M. T. (1985). Some effects of the nature and frequency of vocabulary instruction on the knowledge and use of words. *Reading Research Quarterly, 20*(5), 522–535.

McLloyd, V. C. (1979). The effects of extrinsic rewards of differential value on high and low intrinsic interest. *Child Development, 50,* 1010–1019.

McMurrer, J. (2008). *Instructional time in elementary schools: A closer look at changes for specific subjects.* Washington, DC: Center on Education Policy. Retrieved April 27, 2009, from http://www.cep-dc.org.

Mehan, H. (1979). *Learning lessons: Social organization in the classroom.* Cambridge, MA: Harvard University Press.

Mehta, P., Foorman, B. R., Branum-Martin, L., & Taylor, P. W. (2005). Literacy as a unidimensional construct: Validation, sources of influence and implications in a longitudinal study in grades 1 to 4. *Scientific Studies of Reading, 9*(2), 85–116.

Menon, S., & Hiebert, E. H. (2005). A comparison of first graders' reading with little books or literature-based basal anthologies. *Reading Research Quarterly, 40*(1), 12–38.

Merton, R. (1968). The Matthew effect in science. *Science, 160,* 56–63.

Metsala, J. L. (1999). Young children's phonological awareness and nonword repetition as a function of vocabulary development. *Journal of Educational Psychology, 91,* 3–19.

Miccinati, J. (1985). Using prosodic cues to teach oral reading fluency. *The Reading Teacher, 39,* 206–212.

Mikulecky, L. (1982). Job literacy: The relationship between school preparation and workplace actuality. *Reading Research Quarterly, 20*(5), 616–628.

Miyake, A., & Shah, P. (1999). Toward unified theories of working memory: Emerging general consensus, unresolved theoretical issues, and future research directions. In A. Miyake & P. Shah (Eds.), *Models of working memory: Mechanisms of active maintenance and executive control* (pp. 442–481). Cambridge, UK: Cambridge University Press.

Moats, L. C. (1995). *Spelling: Development, disability, and instruction.* Baltimore: York.

Moats, L. C. (1998). Teaching decoding. *American Educator, 22*(1–2), 42–49, 95–96.

Moats, L. C. (1999, June). *Teaching reading is rocket science: What expert teachers of reading should know and be able to do.* Washington, DC: American Federation of Teachers. Retrieved April 27, 2009, from http://www.aft.org.

Moats, L. C. (2000). *Speech to print: Language essentials for teachers.* Baltimore: Brookes.

Moats, L. C. (2001). Overcoming the language gap: Invest generously in teacher professional development. *American Educator, 25*(2), 5, 8–9.

Moats, L. C. (2006, September-October). *Implementing research-based reading instruction in high poverty schools: Lessons learned from a five year research program.* Presentation at Pathways to Literacy Achievement for High Poverty Children, Ann Arbor, University of Michigan School of Education, Ready to Read Program.

Moats, L. C., & Sedita, J. (2006). *Language essential for teachers of reading and spelling. Module 11: Writing: A road to reading comprehension.* Longmont, CO: Sopris West.

Morgan, E. F., Jr., & Stucker, G. R. (1960). The Joplin Plan of reading vs. a traditional method. *Journal of Educational Psychology, 51,* 69–73.

Morgan, P. L., Farkas, G., Tufis, P. A., & Sperling, R. A. (2008). Are reading and behavior problems risk factors for each other? *Journal of Learning Disabilities, 41,* 417–436.

Mosteller, F., Light, R., & Sachs, J. (1996). Sustained inquiry in education: Lessons from skill grouping and class size. *Harvard Educational Review, 66*(4), 797–828.

Nagy, W. E. (2005). Why vocabulary instruction needs to be long-term and comprehensive. In E. H. Hiebert & M. L. Kamil (Eds.), *Teaching and learning vocabulary* (pp. 27–44). Mahwah, NJ: Lawrence Erlbaum.

Nagy, W. E., & Anderson, R. C. (1984). How many words are there in printed school English? *Reading Research Quarterly, 19,* 304–330.

Nagy, W. E., Berninger, V. W., & Abbott, R. B. (2006). Contributions of morphology beyond phonology to literacy outcomes of upper elementary and middle school students. *Journal of Educational Psychology, 98*(1), 134–147.

Nagy, W. E., & Scott, J. A. (1990). Word schemas: Expectations about the form and meaning of new words. *Cognition and Instruction, 7,* 105–127.

Nagy, W. E., & Scott, J. A. (2000). Vocabulary processes. In M. L. Kamil, P. Mosenthal, P. D. Pearson, & R. Barr (Eds.). *Handbook of reading research* (Vol. 3, pp. 269–284). Mahwah, NJ: Erlbaum.

National Commission on Writing for America's Families, Schools, and Colleges. (2005). *Writing: A powerful message from state government.* New York: College Board.

National Early Literacy Panel. (2008a). *Developing early literacy: Report of the National Early Literacy Panel.* Washington, DC: National Institute for Literacy.

National Early Literacy Panel. (2008b). *Developing early literacy: Report of the National Early Literacy Panel, executive summary.* Washington, DC: National Institute for Literacy.

National Educational Research and Priorities Board. (2000). *Investing in learning: A policy statement on research in education.* Washington, DC: Author.

National Institute of Child Health and Human Development. (2000). *Report of the National Reading Panel: Teaching children to read: An evidence-based assessment of the scientific research literature on reading and its implications for reading instruction: Report of the subgroups* (NIH Publication No. 00-4769). Washington, DC: U.S. Government Printing Office.

Nelson, N., & Calfee, R. C. (1998). The reading-writing connection viewed historically. In N. Nelson & R. C. Calfee (Eds.), *Ninety-seventh yearbook of the National Society for the Study of Education* (Part II, pp. 1–52). Chicago: National Society for the Study of Education.

Ng, M. M., Guthrie, J. T., Van Meter, P., McCann, A., & Alao, S. (1998). How do classroom characteristics influence intrinsic motivation for literacy? *Reading Psychology, 19*(4), 319–398.

No Child Left Behind Act of 2001, Pub. Law 107-110 115 Stat. 1425 H.R.1. (2002). Retrieved April 27, 2009, from http://www.ed.gov/nclb/landing.jhtml.

Novak, J. D. (1998). *Learning, creating, and using knowledge: Concept maps as facilitative tools in schools and corporations.* Mahwah, NJ: Lawrence Erlbaum Associates.

Oakhill, J., Cain, K., & Yuill, N. (1998). Individual differences in children's comprehension skill: Toward an integrated model. In C. Hulme & R. M. Joshi (Eds.), *Reading and spelling: Development and disorders* (pp. 343–367). London: Erlbaum.

O'Connor, R. E., Bell, K. M., Harty, K. R., Larkin, L. K., Sackor, S. M., & Zigmond, N. (2002). Teaching reading to poor readers in the intermediate grades: A comparison of text difficulty. *Journal of Educational Psychology, 94*(3), 474–485.

O'Connor, R. E., & Jenkins, J. R. (1995). Improving the generalization of sound/symbol knowledge: Teaching spelling to kindergarten children. *Journal of Special Education, 29,* 255–275.

O'Connor, R. E., Jenkins, J. R., & Slocum, T. A. (1993). *Unpacking phonological awareness: Two treatments for low-skilled kindergarten children.* Unpublished manuscript.

Ogle, D. M. (1986a). K-W-L: A teaching model that develops active reading of expository text. *The Reading Teacher, 26,* 564–570.

Ogle, D. M. (1986b). K-W-L group instruction strategy. In A. M. Palincsar, D. M. Ogle, B. F. Jones, & E. G. Carr (Eds.), *Teaching reading as thinking* (pp. 22-31). Alexandria, VA: Association for Supervision and Curriculum Development.

Olson, C. B. (1996). Strategies for interacting with text. In C. B. Olson (Ed.), *Practical ideas for teaching writing as a process at the elementary and middle school levels* (pp. 231–235). Sacramento: California Department of Education.

Opitz, M. F., & Rasinski, T. V. (1998). *Good-bye Round Robin: 25 effective oral reading strategies.* Portsmouth, NH: Heinemann.

Organization for Economic Cooperation and Development. (2002). *Reading for change: Performance and engagement across countries: Results from PISA 2000.* Washington, DC: Author.

Orton Academy. (2008). *Orton-Gillingham approach.* Retrieved April 27, 2009, from http://www.ortonacademy.org/approach.html.

Pacific Resources for Education and Learning. (2003). *NEARStar.* Honolulu, HI: Author.

Pany, D., & McCoy, K. M. (1988). Effects of corrective feedback on word accuracy and reading comprehension of readers with learning disabilities. *Journal of Reading Disabilities, 21,* 546–550.

Pappas, C. C., & Barry, A. (1997). Scaffolding urban students' initiations: Transactions in reading information books in the read-aloud curriculum genre. In N. J. Karolides (Ed.), *Reader response in elementary classrooms: Quest and discovery* (pp. 215–236). Hillsdale, NJ: Erlbaum.

Park, L. S. (2003). *A single shard.* New York: Random House Yearling.

Patterson, K. E., & Coltheart, V. (1987). Phonological processes in reading: A tutorial review. In M. Coltheart (Ed.), *The psychology of reading* (Vol. 12, pp. 421–447). Hillsdale, NJ: Lawrence Erlbaum.

Pearson, P. D. (2006, March 26). Reading, rehashing, 'rithmetic [Letter to the editor]. *New York Times.* Retrieved November 10, 2008, from http://www.nytimes.com.

Pearson, P. D., Cervetti, G., Bravo, M., Hiebert, E. H., & Arya, D. J. (2005, August). *Reading and writing at the service of acquiring scientific knowledge and dispositions: From synergy to identity.* Paper presented at the Edmonton Regional Learning Consortium, Edmonton, Alberta, Canada.

Pearson, P. D., & Fielding, L. (1991). Comprehension instruction. In R. Barr, M. L. Kamil, P. Mosenthal, & P. D. Pearson (Eds.), *Handbook of reading research* (pp. 815–860). White Plains, NY: Longman.

Pearson, P. D., & Gallagher, M. C. (1983). The instruction of reading comprehension. *Contemporary Educational Psychology, 8,* 317–344.

Perfetti, C. A. (1989). There are generalized abilities and one of them is reading. In L. Resnick (Ed.), *Knowing, learning and instruction: Essays in honor of Robert Glaser* (pp. 307–335). Hillsdale, NJ: Lawrence Erlbaum.

Perfetti, C. A., Marron, M. A., & Foltz, P. W. (1996). Sources of comprehension failure: Theoretical perspectives and case studies. In C. Cornoldi & J. Oakhill (Eds.), *Reading comprehension difficulties: Processes and intervention* (pp. 137–165). Mahwah, NJ: Lawrence Erlbaum.

Persky, H. R., Daane, M. C., & Jin, Y. (2003). *The nation's report card: Writing 2002* (NCES2003-529). Washington, DC: Government Printing Office.

Peterson, B. (1991). Selecting books for beginning readers: Children's literature suitable for young readers. In D. E. DeFord, C. A. Lyons, & G. S. Pinnell (Eds.), *Bridges to literacy for young readers: Learning from Reading Recovery* (pp. 119–147). Portsmouth, NH: Heinemann.

Peterson, R., & Eeds, M. (1990). *Grand conversations: Literature groups in action.* New York: Scholastic.

Petty, W., Herold, C., & Stoll, E. (1967). *The state of knowledge about the teaching of vocabulary.* Champaign, IL: National Council of Teachers of English.

Pew Internet & American Life Project. (2006). *Teens and social media.* Washington, DC: Author. Retrieved September 1, 2008, from http://www.pewinternet.org.

Phelps, D. R. (2007). *A tale of two WIRC classrooms: A comparative case study.* Unpublished manuscript. State University of New York, Buffalo.

Pikulski, J. J., & Chard, D. J. (2005). Fluency: Bridge between decoding and reading comprehension. *The Reading Teacher 58*(6), 510–519.

Pilgreen, J., & Krashen, S. (1993). Sustained silent reading with English as a second language high school students: Impact on reading comprehension, reading frequency, and reading enjoyment. *School Library Media Quarterly, 22*(1), 21–23.

Pinnell, G. S., Pikulski, J. J., Wixson, K. K., Campbell, J. R., Gough, P. B., & Beatty, A. S. (1995). *Listening to children read aloud.* Washington, DC: U.S. Department of Education, Office of Educational Research and Improvement.

Pressley, M. (1976). Mental imagery helps eight-year-olds remember what they read. *Journal of Educational Psychology, 68*(3), 355–359.

Pressley, M. (1998). *Reading instruction that works: The case for balanced teaching.* New York: Guilford.

Pressley, M. (2000). Comprehension instruction in elementary school: A quarter-century of reading progress. In B. M. Taylor, M. F. Graves, & P. van den Broek (Eds.), *Reading for meaning: Fostering comprehension in the middle grades* (pp. 32–51). New York: Teachers College Press.

Pressley, M., & Afflerbach, P. (1995). *Verbal protocols of reading: The nature of constructively responsive reading.* Hillsdale, NJ: Erlbaum.

Pressley, M., El-Dinary, P. B., & Brown, R. (1992). Skilled and not-so-skilled reading: Good information processing and not-so-good information processing. In M. Pressley, K. R. Harris, & J. T. Guthrie (Eds.), *Promoting academic competence and literacy in school* (pp. 91–127). San Diego, CA: Academic Press.

Pressley, M., Johnson, C. J., Symons, S., McGoldrick, J. A., & Kurita, J. A. (1989). Strategies that improve children's memory and comprehension of text. *Elementary School Journal, 90*(1), 3–22.

Pressley, M., Rankin, J., & Yokoi, L. (1996). A survey of instructional practices of primary teachers nominated as effective in promoting literacy. *Elementary School Journal, 90*(1), 3–22.

Pressley, M., Wharton-McDonald, R. Allington, R., Block, C. C., Morrow, L., Tracey, D., Baker, K., Brooks, G., Cornin, J., Nelson, E., & Woo, D. (2001). A study of effective first-grade literacy instruction. *Scientific Studies of Reading, 5*(1), 35–58.

Pressley, M., Woloshyn, V., Burkell, J., Carliglia-Bull, T., Lysynchuk, L., McGoldrick, J. A. K., Schneider, B., Snyder, B. L., & Symons, S. (1995). *Cognitive strategy instruction that really improves children's academic performance.* Cambridge, MA: Brookline.

Rack, J. P., Hulme, C., Snowling, J. J., & Wightman, J. (1994). The role of phonology in young children's learning of sight words: The direct-mapping hypothesis. *Journal of Experimental Psychology, 57,* 42–71.

RAND Reading Study Group. (2002). *Reading for understanding: Toward an R & D program in reading comprehension.* Santa Monica, CA: RAND.

Raphael, T., Kirschner, B. W., & Englert, C. S. (1986). *Students' metacognitive knowledge about writing.* Lansing: Michigan State University, Institute for Research on Teaching.

Raphael, T., Kirschner, B. W., & Englert, C. S. (1988). Expository writing program: Making connections between reading and writing. *The Reading Teacher, 41,* 790–795.

Rasinski, T.V., Padak, N., Linke, W., & Sturdevant, E. (1994). The effects of fluency development instruction on urban second graders. *Journal of Education Research, 87,* 158–164.

Raskin, E. (1978). *The westing game.* New York: Dutton.

Rasmussen, D. (1985). *A pig can jig* (Basic Reading Series, Level A, Part I). New York: Science Research Associates.

Rayner, K., & Pollatsek, A. (1989). *The psychology of reading.* Englewood Cliffs, NJ: Prentice Hall.

Rayworth, M. (2008, April 28). Bedtime stories now available on children's iPods. *Associated Press.* Retrieved April 27, 2009, from http://www.seattletimes.com.

Rea, B. (2006). *Monarch! Come play with me.* Union, WV: Bas Relief.

Reading Recovery Council of North America. (2008). *About us.* Retrieved April 27, 2009, from http://www.readingrecovery.org/rrcna/about/index.asp.

Reitsma, P. (1983). Printed word learning in beginning readers. *Journal of Experimental Child Psychology, 75,* 321–339.

Robbins, C., & Ehri, L. C. (1994). Reading storybooks to kindergartners helps them learn new vocabulary words. *Journal of Educational Psychology, 86*(1), 54–64.

Roberts, T. A., & Meiring, A. (2006). Teaching phonics in the context of children's literature or spelling: Influences on first-grade reading, spelling, and writing and fifth-grade comprehension. *Journal of Educational Psychology, 98*(4), 690–713.

Roschewski, P. (2003, March). Nebraska STARS line up. *Phi Delta Kappan,* 517–520.

Rosenshine, B. (1979). Content, time, and direct instruction. In P. Peterson & H. Walberg (Eds.), *Research on teaching: Concepts, findings, and implications* (pp. 28–56). Berkeley, CA: McCutchan.

Rosenshine, B. (1997, March 24–28). *The case for explicit, teacher-led, cognitive strategy instruction.* Paper presented at the annual meeting of the American Educational Research Association, Chicago.

Rosenshine, B., & Meister, C. (1994). Reciprocal teaching: A review of the research. *Review of Educational Research, 64*(4), 479–530.

Rosenthal, J., & Ehri, L. C. (2008). The mnemonic value of orthography for vocabulary learning. *Journal of Educational Psychology, 100*(1), 175–191.

Rosow, B., & Moats, L. (2002). *Spellography.* Longmont, CO: Sopris West.

Routman, R. (1988). *Transitions: From literature to literacy.* Portsmouth, NH: Heinemann.

Ruckman, I. (1986). *Night of the twisters.* New York: HarperTrophy.

Ryan, R. M., & Deci, E. L. (2000). Intrinsic and extrinsic motivations: Classic definitions and new directions. *Contemporary Educational Psychology, 25,* 54–67.

Sadowski, M., & Willson, V. L. (2006). Effects of a theoretically based large-scale reading intervention in a multicultural urban school district. *American Educational Research Journal, 43,* 135–152.

Santoro, L. E., Coyne, M. D., & Simmons, D. C. (2006). The reading-spelling connection: Developing and evaluating a beginning spelling intervention for children at risk of reading disability. *Learning Disabilities Research and Practice, 2*(2), 122–133.

Say, A. (1993). *Grandfather's journey.* New York: Houghton Mifflin.

Scammacca, N., Vaughn, S., Roberts, G., Wanzek, J., & Torgesen, J. K. (2007). *Extensive reading interventions in grades K–3: Research to practice.* Portsmouth, NH: RMC Research Corporation, Center on Instruction.

Scardamalia, M. (1981). How children cope with cognitive demands of writing. In C. H. Frederiksen, M. G. Whiteman, & J. F. Dominic (Eds.), *Writing: The nature, development, and teaching of written communication* (Vol. 2). Hillsdale, NJ: Erlbaum.

Schank, R. (1999). *Dynamic memory revisited.* Cambridge, UK: Cambridge University Press.

Schlechty, P. C. (1990). *Schools for the 21st century.* San Francisco: Jossey-Bass.

Schlechty, P. C. (2005). *Creating the capacity to support innovations. Occasional paper #2.* Louisville, KY: Schlechty Center for Leadership in School Reform.

Schmoker, M. (1999). *Results: The key to continuous school improvement* (2nd ed.). Alexandria, VA: Association for Supervision and Curriculum Development.

Schmoker, M. (2001, October 24). The "Crayola curriculum." *Education Week, 42,* 44.

Schoenbach, R., Greenleaf, C., Cziko, C., & Hurwitz, L. (1999). *Reading for understanding: A guide to improving reading in middle and high school classrooms.* San Francisco: Jossey-Bass.

Schooler, J. W., Reichle, E. D., & Halpern, D. V. (2004). Zoning out while reading: Evidence for dissociations between experience and metaconsciousness. In D. T. Levin (Ed.), *Thinking and seeing: Visual metacognition in adults and children* (pp. 203–226). Cambridge: MIT Press.

Scott, J. A., Jamieson-Noel, D., & Asselin, M. (2003). Vocabulary instruction throughout the day in 23 Canadian upper-elementary classrooms. *Elementary School Journal, 103*(3), 269–286.

Scott, J. A., Skobel, B. J., & Wells, J. (2008). *The word-conscious classroom.* New York: Scholastic.

Searfoss, L. (1975). Radio reading. *The Reading Teacher, 29,* 295–296.

Secretary's Commission on Achieving Necessary Skills. (1992). *What work requires of schools: a SCANS report for America 2000.* Washington, DC: U.S. Department of Labor.

Seuss, Dr. (1990). *Oh, the places you'll go!* New York: Random House.

Shanahan, T. (1998). On the effectiveness and limitations of tutoring. In P. D. Pearson & P. A. Iran-Nejad (Eds.), *Review of research in education* (Vol. 23, pp. 217–234). Washington, DC: American Educational Research Association.

Share, D. L. (1999). Phonological recoding and orthographic learning: A direct test of the self-teaching hypothesis. *Journal of Experimental Child Psychology, 72,* 95–129.

Share, D. L., & Stanovich, K. E. (1995). Cognitive processes in early reading development: Accommodating individual differences into a model of acquisition. *Issues in Education: Contributions from Educational Psychology, 1,* 1–57.

Shefelbine, J. (1999). Reading voluminously and voluntarily. In *Scholastic reading counts research.* New York: Scholastic. Retrieved June 12, 1999, from http://apps.scholsatic.com/readingcounts/research/voluminouslky/Voluntarily.

Shostak, J. (2005). *Vocabulary workshop (Levels A–G).* New York: Sadlier-Oxford.

Sitton, R. (1996). *Sitton spelling.* Cambridge, MA: Educators Publishing Service.

Slavin, R. E., & Madden, N. (1983) *Cooperative integrated reading and composition (CIRC).* Baltimore: Johns Hopkins University, Center for Social Organization of Schools.

Smith, F. (1971). *Understanding reading: A psycholinguistic analysis of reading and learning to read.* New York: Holt, Rinehart & Winston.

Smith, F. (1994). *Understanding reading: A psycholinguistic analysis of reading and learning to read* (2nd ed.). New York: Holt, Rinehart & Winston.

Smolkin, L. B., & Donovan, C. A. (2000). *The contexts of comprehension: Information book read alouds and comprehension acquisition.* Ann Arbor: University of Michigan School of Education, Center for the Improvement of Early Reading Achievement.

Snicket, L., & Helquist, B. (various). *Various titles.* New York: HarperCollins.

Snow, C. E., Burns, M. S., & Griffin, P. (Eds.). (1998). *Preventing reading difficulties in young children.* Washington, DC: National Academy Press, Committee on the Prevention of Reading Difficulties in Young Children, Commission on Behavioral and Social Sciences and Education, National Research Council.

Spalding, R. B., & Spalding, W. T. (1990). *The writing road to reading: The Spalding Method of phonics for teaching speech, writing, and reading.* (4th rev. ed.). New York: William Morrow. (Original work published in 1957)

Speare, E. G. (1958). *The witch of blackbird pond.* New York: Houghton Mifflin.

Spear-Swerling, L. (2000). *Straw men and very misleading reading: A review of Misreading Reading.* Retrieved March 25, 2000, from http://www.ldonline.org/ld_store/reviews/swerling_coles.html.

Sprenger, M. (1999). *Learning and memory: The brain in action.* Alexandria, VA: Association for Supervision and Curriculum Development.

Squire, L. R., & Kandel, E. R. (1999). *Memory: From mind to molecules.* New York: Scientific American Library.

Stahl, S. A. (1999). *Vocabulary development.* Cambridge, MA: Brookline.

Stahl, S. (2000). *Fluency-oriented reading instruction.* Ann Arbor: University of Michigan Schools of Education, Center for the Improvement of Early Reading Achievement.

Stahl, S. (2005). Four problems with teaching word meanings and what to do to make vocabulary an integral part of instruction. In E. H. Hiebert & M. L. Kamil (Eds.), *Teaching and learning vocabulary* (pp. 95–114). Mahwah, NJ: Lawrence Erlbaum.

Stahl, S. A., & Fairbanks, M. M. (1986). The effects of vocabulary instruction: A model-based meta-analysis. *Review of Educational Research, 56*(1), 72–110.

Stahl, S. A., & Heubach, K. M. (2005). Fluency-oriented reading instruction. *Journal of Literacy Research, 37,* 25–60.

Stanovich, K. E. (1986). Matthew effects in reading: Some consequences of individual differences in the acquisition of literacy. *Reading Research Quarterly, 21,* 360–407.

Stanovich, K. E. (1994). Romance and reality. *The Reading Teacher, 47,* 280–291.

Stanovich, K. E., & Cunningham, A. E. (1993). Where does knowledge come from? Specific associations between print exposure and information acquisition. *Journal of Educational Psychology, 85,* 211–229.

Sternberg, R. (1996). *Successful intelligence: How practical and creative intelligence determine success in life.* New York: Simon & Schuster.

Stotsky, S. (2001). Writing: The royal road to reading comprehension. In S. Brody (Ed.), *Teaching reading: Language, letters and thought* (pp. 276–296). Milford, NH: LARC.

Swanson, H. L., Hoskyn, M., & Lee, C. (1999). *Interventions for students with learning disabilities: A meta-analysis of treatment outcomes.* New York: Guilford.

Swope, S. (2000). *Gotta go! Gotta go!* New York: Sunburst Books.

Taguchi, E., Takayasu-Maass, M., & Gorsuch, G. J. (2004). Developing reading fluency in EFL: How assisted repeated and extensive reading affect fluency development. *Reading in a Foreign Language, 16*(2), 70–96.

Taylor, B. M., & Beach, R. W. (1984). The effects of text structure on middle grade students' comprehension and production of expository text. *Reading Research Quarterly, 19*(2), 134–146.

Taylor, B. M., Pearson, P. D., Clark, K. F., & Walpole, S. (1999). Effective schools/accomplished teachers. *Reading Teacher, 53*(2), 156–159.

Taylor, M. (1976). *Roll of thunder, hear my cry.* New York: Puffin.

Teachers Pet Publications. (2008). *LitPlans.* Ocean City, MD: Author. Retrieved January 12, 2009, from http://www.tpet.com.

Templeton, S. (2004). Spelling: Best ideas = best practices. *Voices from the Middle, (10)*4, 48–49.

Texas Education Agency. (1998). *Texas primary reading inventory.* Austin, TX: Author.

Texas Reading Initiative. (2002). *Beginning reading instruction: Components and features of a research-based program.* Austin, TX: Texas Education Agency.

Tompkins, G. (1998). *Fifty literacy strategies step by step.* Upper Saddle River, NJ: Merrill.

Topping, K. (1987). Paired reading: A powerful technique for parent use. *The Reading Teacher, 40,* 608–614.

Torgesen, J. K. (2002). Lessons learned from intervention research in reading: A way to go before we rest. In R. Stainthorpe (Ed.), *Literacy: Learning and teaching* (pp. 89–104; BJEP Monograph Series II, Vol. 11, No. 1). London: British Psychological Association.

Torgesen, J. K. (2006). *Intensive reading interventions for struggling readers in early elementary school: A principal's guide.* Portsmouth, NH: RMC Research Corporation, Center on Instruction.

Torgesen, J. K. (2007, June). *Using an RTI model to guide early reading instruction: Effects on identification rates for students with learning disabilities.* Tallahassee: Florida State University, Florida Center for Reading Research.

Torgesen, J. K., Alexander, A. W., Wagner, R. K., Rashotte, C. A., Voeller, K., Conway, T., & Rose, E. (2001). Intensive remedial instruction for children with severe reading disabilities: Immediate and long-term outcomes from two instructional approaches. *Journal of Learning Disabilities, 34,* 33–58.

Torgesen, J. K., & Hayes, L. (2003, Fall). Diagnosis of reading difficulties following inadequate performance on state level reading outcome measures. *CORE Reading Expert* [Newsletter for the Consortium on Reading Excellence, Emeryville, CA].

Torgesen, J. K., & Hudson, R. F. (2006). Reading fluency: Critical issues for struggling readers. In S. J. Samuels & A. E. Farstrup (Eds.), *What research has to say about fluency instruction* (pp. 130–158). Newark, DE: International Reading Association.

Torgesen, J. K., & Mathes, P. G. (2000). *A basic guide to understanding, assessing, and teaching phonological awareness.* Austin, TX: PRO-ED.

Torgesen, J. K., Rashotte, C. A., & Alexander, A. W. (2001). Principles of fluency instruction in reading: Relationships with established empirical outcomes. In M. Wolf (Ed.), *Dyslexia, fluency, and the brain* (pp. 333–355). Timonium, MD: York.

Torgesen, J. K., Wagner, R. K., & Rashotte, C. A. (1997). The prevention and remediation of severe reading disabilities: Keeping the end in mind. *Scientific Studies of Reading, 1,* 217–234.

Torgesen, J. K., Wagner, R. K., & Rashotte, C. A. (1999). *TOWRE: Test of word reading efficiency.* Austin, TX: PRO-ED.

Torgesen, J. K., Wagner, R. K., Rashotte, C. A., & Herron, J. (2003). *Summary of outcomes from first grade study with Read, Write, and Type, and Auditory Discrimination in Depth instruction and software with at-risk children* (FCRR Technical Report 2). Gainesville: Florida State University, Florida Center for Reading Research.

Torgesen, J. K., Wagner, R. K., Rashotte, C. A., Rose, E., Lindamood, P., Conway, T., & Garvin, C. (1999). Preventing reading failure in young children with phonological processing disabilities: Group and individual responses to instruction. *Journal of Educational Psychology, 91,* 579–593.

Tovani, C. (2000). *I read it, but I don't get it: Comprehension strategies for adolescent readers.* Portland, ME: Stenhouse.

Towse, J. N., & Houston-Price, C. M. T. (1999). Reflections on the concept of the central executive. In J. Andrade (Ed.), *Working memory in perspective* (pp. 240–260). New York: Taylor & Francis.

Trabasso, T., & Bouchard, E. (2000). *Text comprehension: Report of the National Reading Panel, report of the subgroups* (Ch. 4, Pt. 2, pp. 39–69). Washington, DC: NICHD Clearinghouse.

Trabasso, T., & Bouchard, E. (2002). Teaching readers how to comprehend text strategically. In C. C. Block & M. Pressley (Eds.), *Comprehension instruction: Research-based best practices* (pp. 176–200). New York: Guilford.

Treiman, R. (1993). *Beginning to spell.* Oxford, UK: Oxford University Press.

Treiman, R. (1998). Why spelling? The benefits of incorporating spelling into beginning reading instruction. In J. L. Metsala & L. C. Ehri (Eds.), *Word recognition in literacy* (pp. 289–313). Mahwah, NJ: Erlbaum.

Treiman, R., & Bourassa, D. C. (2000a). Children's written and oral spelling. *Applied Psycholinguistics, 21,* 183–204.

Treiman, R., & Bourassa, D. C. (2000b). The development of spelling skills. *Topics in Language Disorders, 20*(3), 1–18.

Tsang, W. K. (1996). Comparing the effects of reading and writing on writing performance. *Applied Linguistics, 17*(2), 210–233.

Tunley, R. (1957, October). Johnny can read in Joplin. *Saturday Evening Post, 230*(17), 23, 108–110.

Turner, J. C. (1995). The influence of classroom contexts on young children's motivation for literacy. *Reading Research Quarterly, 30*(3), 410–441.

van den Broek, P. (1994). Comprehension and memory of narrative texts: Inference and coherence. In M. A. Gernsbacher (Ed.), *Handbook of psycholinguistics* (pp. 539–588). San Diego, CA: Academic Press.

van den Broek, P., Young, M., Tzeng, Y., & Linderholm, T. (1999). The landscape model of reading: Inferences and the online construction of a memory representation. In H. van Oostendorp & S. R. Goldman (Eds.), *The construction of mental representations during reading* (pp. 71–98). Mahwah, NJ: Lawrence Erlbaum.

Vandervelden, M. C., & Siegel, L. S. (1997). Teaching phonological processing skills in early literacy: A developmental approach. *Learning Disability Quarterly, 20*(2), 63–81.

van Someren, M. W., Barnard, Y. F., & Sandberg, J. (1994). *The think-aloud method: a practical guide to modeling cognitive processes.* San Diego, CA: Academic Press.

Vaughn, S. (2005). *Interpretation of the 3-tier framework.* Retrieved July 23, 2008, from http://texasreading.org/uctcrla/materias/3tier_letter.asp.

Vaughn, S., Moody, S. W., & Schumm, J. S. (1998). Broken promises: Reading instruction in the resource room. *Exceptional Children, 64,* 211–225.

Vellutino, F., & Scanlon, P. (1987). Phonological coding, phonological awareness, and reading ability: Evidence from a longitudinal and experimental study. *Merrill-Palmer Quarterly, 33,* 321–363.

Venezky, R. L. (2000). The origins of the present chasm between adult literacy needs and school literacy instruction. *Scientific Studies of Reading, 4,* 19–39.

Vygotsky, L. S. (1986). *Thought and language* (A. Kozulin, Ed. & Trans.). Cambridge: MIT Press. (Original work published in 1934)

Wagner, R. K., & Torgesen, J. K. (1987). The nature of phonological processing and its causal role in the acquisition of reading skills. *Psychological Bulletin, 101*(2), 192–212.

Wagner, R. K., Torgesen, J. K., & Rashotte, C. A. (1999). *Comprehensive test of phonological processes.* Austin, TX: PRO-ED.

Waits, M. J., Campbell, H. E., Gau, R., Jacobs, E., Rex, T., & Hess, R. K. (2006). *Why some schools with Latino children beat the odds . . . and others don't.* Phoenix, AZ: Center for the Future of Arizona and Morrison Institute for Public Policy.

Walberg, H. J., & Tsai, S. L. (1983, Fall). Matthew effects in education. *Educational Research Quarterly, 20,* 359–373.

Walker, M. H. (1996). What research really says. *Principal, 73*(4), 41.

Wallace, B. (2005). *Pick of the litter.* New York: Simon & Schuster.

Walpole, S., & McKenna, M. C. (2007). *Differentiated reading instruction.* New York: Guilford.

Walsh, K. (2003). Basal readers: The lost opportunity to build knowledge that propels comprehension. *American Educator, 27,* 24–27.

Wasik, B. A., & Slavin, R. E. (1993). Preventing early reading failure with one-to-one tutoring: A review of five programs. *Reading Research Quarterly, 28*(2), 178–200.

Wasowicz, J. (2007) *What do spelling errors tell us about language knowledge?* Evanston, IL: Learning by Design.

Wasowicz, J., Apel, K., Masterson, J., & Whitney, A. (2004). *SPELL-Links to reading & writing: A word-study curriculum.* Evanston, IL: Learning By Design.

Weaver, C. (1994). *Reading process and practice: From socio-linguistics to whole language* (2nd ed.). Portsmouth, NH: Heinemann.

Weiderhold, J. L., & Bryant, B. R. (2001). *Gray oral reading tests: GORT-4.* Austin, TX: PRO-ED.

Weinstein, C. E., & Hume, L. M. (1998). *Study strategies for lifelong learning.* Washington, DC: American Psychological Association.

Weinstein, C. E., & Mayer, R. E. (1986). The teaching of learning strategies. In M. C. Wittrock (Ed.), *Handbook of research on teaching* (pp. 315–327). New York: Macmillan.

Wells, C. G. (1985). *Language development in the preschool years.* New York: Cambridge University Press.

Whipple, P. (2008, July 1). *Professional learning communities: Teacher leaders leading the way.* Presentation to the New York State Reading First Conference, Brooklyn, NY.

White, B. L., & Watts, J. C. (1973). *Experience and environment.* Englewood Cliffs, NJ: Prentice Hall.

White, E. B. (1980). *Charlotte's web.* New York: Harper & Row.

White, T. G., Sowell, J., & Yangihara, W. (1989). Teaching elementary students to use word-part clues. *The Reading Teacher, 42*(4), 302–308.

Wilder, L. I. (1953). *Little house on the prairie.* New York: HarperCollins.

Williams, C., & Hufnagel, K. (2005). The impact of word study instruction on kindergarten children's journal writing. *Research in the Teaching of English, 39*(3), 233–270.

Willingham, D. (2004, Spring). Practice makes perfect: But only if you practice beyond the point of perfection. *American Educator.* Retrieved August 17, 2008, from http://www.aft.org/pubs-reports/american_educator/spring2004/cogsci.html.

Wilson, B. (1988). *Wilson reading system.* Millbury, MA: Wilson Language Training.

Wilson, K., Erickson, J., & Trainin, G. (April, 2007). *Teaching fluency: Can technology based feedback help?* Paper presented at the annual meeting of the American Educational Research Association, Chicago.

Wise, B. W., Ring, J., & Olson, R. K. (1999). Training phonological awareness with and without explicit attention to articulation. *Journal of Experimental Child Psychology, 72,* 271–304.

Wood, K. D. (1984). Probable passages: A writing strategy. *Reading Teacher, 37,* 496–499.

Wooden, J. (with Jamison, S.). (1997). *Wooden: A lifetime of observations and reflections on and off the court.* Chicago: Contemporary Books.

Zigmond, N., & Baker, J. M. (1996). Full inclusion for students with learning disabilities: Too much of a good thing. *Theory Into Practice, 35*(1), 26–34.

Index

CORWIN

A SAGE Company

The Corwin logo—a raven striding across an open book—represents the union of courage and learning. Corwin is committed to improving education for all learners by publishing books and other professional development resources for those serving the field of PreK–12 education. By providing practical, hands-on materials, Corwin continues to carry out the promise of its motto: **"Helping Educators Do Their Work Better."**